Child Prodigies
and Exceptional Early Achievers

Child Prodigies
and Exceptional Early Achievers

John Radford

THE FREE PRESS
A Division of Macmillan, Inc.
New York

The Free Press
A Division of Macmillan, Inc.
866 Third Avenue, New York, N.Y. 10022

Collier Macmillan Canada, Inc.

First American Edition 1990

Printed in Great Britain

printing number

1 2 3 4 5 6 7 8 9 10

Library of Congress Cataloging-in-Publication Data
Radford, John.
    Child prodigies and exceptional early achievers / John Radford.—
1st American ed.
        p.   cm.
    Includes bibliographical references.
    ISBN 0–02–925635–6
    1. Gifted children.   2. Exceptional children.   I. Title.
BF723.G5R33   1990
155.45'5—dc20   89–77993
                                                                              CIP

Contents

Preface

It happens that on the day I write this preface, 22 April 1989, *The Times* announces the West End production, on the following Sunday, of a first play by one Ned Ramsay. The author is 5 years old. It seems he won a young playwrights competition, inspired to enter when his sister aged 8 did so. His father also writes plays and has done so for twelve years. On the same day there is to be seen on television the film *Lost Angel* of 1943, in which an infant girl abandoned by her mother is reared by the professors of the Pickering Institute of Child Psychology on 'entirely scientific principles', with a view to producing a genius. They do so, but like most film scientists neglect the human aspect, in this case the need of the child (Margaret O'Brien) for magic and fantasy and above all love. Fortunately at 6 she melts the heart of a hard-bitten newsman, and all ends happily. Next day Shirley Temple is performing a similar office in *The Little Colonel* (1935), while on the 24th I can add Tom McLaughlan, an extremely youthful (age not stated) heavy metal guitarist ('Box Office' Channel Four).

Notable achievements at remarkably young ages are featured regularly in the mass media, and the word 'prodigy' is frequently used. There are books on individual prodigies, but I have not come across one on the phenomenon as a whole, though there is an extensive literature on the wider group of gifted children. Prodigies are by definition rare, and there has been a great deal less research carried out on the upper ends of ranges of ability than on the average and lower. Gifted children receive only a fraction of the attention and resources that go to the handicapped (who themselves, of course, come fairly low in terms of national expenditure).

I have tried to draw together what I could find that seemed to be relevant. My criteria for relevance will not be everyone's. To some there may seem to be too much on intelligence or giftedness; to others perhaps too little on cognitive theory. Some may think that, in places, there are too many examples of exceptional achievements about which little more is said, and would prefer to have fewer cases in more detail. The plan I have followed is partly dictated by what is available, but also by the wish to show, within the space of 80,000 words, a fairly wide range of behaviour. There are certainly prodigies I have not mentioned at all, such as Oliver Madox Brown (1855–1874), a precocious poet and painter (Ingram, 1883); and no doubt many others of whom I am ignorant. I do not offer a new theory of prodigies, which may be what some look for to answer the natural question 'But how do they do it?' when some particularly exceptional case occurs. This is at least partly because I incline to the view that the exceptional can be accommodated within more general principles. The reader may be able to make up her or his own mind on this.

There is certainly considerable interest in the general question of exceptionality. Even since finishing the main text several relevant books have come to hand. Donald Treffert's study of 'idiots savants' is perhaps the first book-length work on the subject. *Optimal Experience* by Csikszentmihalyi and Csikszentmihalyi seems to offer something new on intense motivation and intellectual excitement. Bereiter and Scardamalia discuss the psychology of written composition. Jean Lave's book on mind, mathematics and culture in everyday life is clearly of interest, as are Jean-Michel Hoc's on the cognitive psychology of planning and Dennis Holding's on human skills. So one could go on.

It has often been remarked that psychology is prone to changes of fashion, yet more than just fashion is involved here. The 'idiot savant' syndrome was studied by Binet, who died in 1911, but for years seemed mainly a curiosity. Only recently has it seemed possible to embrace it within a wider view of human abilities, often termed a modular view: 'roughly, the view that many different kinds of psychological mechanism must be postulated in order to explain the facts of mental life' (Fodor, 1987). So quickly do such changes occur that newspapers refer to 'savants' without explanation. There almost seems to be a readiness to cast ideas in a particular form which is widely acceptable at a given moment; something less than a scientific paradigm shift yet more than a fashion. Currently the interest is not just in a modular view of the mind, but in the detailed interaction of the developing mind with particular aspects of culture; partly as a result of (or is it the other way round?) renewed attention being given to the ideas of the Soviet genius L.S. Vygotsky and those he inspired (Madsen, 1988; Wertsch, 1985).

Such general speculations would lead us too far. I should like to record my thanks for help received from the following, with apologies to any I have omitted: Robert Bairamian, Headmaster, and boys of Claremont School, Sussex; Dr John Beloff; Dr Colin Berry; Professor Peter Bryant; Professor George Butterworth; Dr John Dunstan; Dr Joan Freeman; Dr Leba Goldstein; Dr Mike Howe; Dr Keith Phillips; Stewart Reuben; Steve Rowley; Dr John Willats; Officers of the Royal Humane Society; the Sports Council; members of British *Mensa*.

John Radford
London, April 1989

1 Forbidden Experiments

Children of the wild, and others

Among the other books were a primer, some child's readers, numerous
picture books, and a great dictionary. All of these he examined, but the
pictures caught his fancy most, though the strange little bugs which covered
the pages where there were no pictures excited his wonder and his deepest
thought. . . . In his hands was a primer opened at a picture of a little ape
similar to himself, but covered, except for face and hands, with strange,
coloured fur. . . . Beneath the picture were three little bugs –

B O Y

. . . Slowly he turned the pages, scanning the pictures and the text for a
repetition of the combination b-o-y. . . . And so he progressed very, very,
slowly, for it was a hard and laborious task which he had set himself without
knowing it – a task which might seem to you or me impossible – learning to
read without having the slightest knowledge of letters or written language, or
the faintest idea that such things existed.

Tarzan's achievement in learning to read – 'with the help of the
great dictionary and the active intelligence of a healthy mind
endowed by inheritance with more than ordinary reasoning
powers' (Edgar Rice Burroughs, *Tarzan of the Apes, 1912*) –
would qualify him as a child prodigy. Burroughs' skill in
narration makes us suspend disbelief, at least momentarily, in
what on reflection must seem practically, and perhaps logically,
impossible. Curiously enough his creator did not himself think
that Tarzan could have existed, let alone have become king of
the jungle through his superior intelligence. He believed that a
child could never survive in the wild, but since that would not

make much of a story he decided to ignore it and carry on (Porges, 1975). In fact there are well-authenticated accounts of feral (wild) children who have lived apart from human contact for considerable periods. Even infants can survive for a time. Lucia Rojas was 1 day old when she was buried in the earthquake of August 1985 in Mexico City; she was found alive a week later. Altogether some twenty babies survived for up to 9 days, and seem so far to be developing normally (*The Times*, 31 August 1986). Eric Taylor, aged 2, wandered off into the Australian bush and was found after five days, twelve miles from home, dehydrated but alive, having apparently survived by eating insects and sucking wet leaves; and this despite storms, the cold, wild pigs, snakes and crocodiles (*The Times*, 19 July 1988).

Burroughs was rather sensitive to the accusation that Tarzan was merely an imitation of Kipling's Mowgli (1907); it seems that he had not read *The Jungle Book*. The story of children reared by animals, Romulus and Remus for example, is, however, perhaps as old as men themselves. The wodehouse or wild man is widely spread in Celtic and other folklore (Jarman, 1976), and might very well originate in feral children. Maclean (1977) reviews a number of cases. The most famous, perhaps, is the unfortunate Victor, the Wild Boy of Aveyron, who was found – captured, perhaps one should say – in 1800 at the apparent age of 12 or 13, and who died, marginally civilized by his almost equally unusual tutor J.M.G. Itard, in 1828 (Lane, 1977). It is difficult to know whether to call his pathetic hard-won accomplishments prodigious, since one cannot really assess his starting-point. A comparable modern case would seem to be that of an 'ape boy' of 4 found in Uganda. He was described after nine months as being unable to speak or to walk other than in an ape-like crouch, and as rejecting clothes and social contacts (*The Times*, 24 June 1986).

The fact of such survivals demonstrates the remarkable adaptability of the human infant, and they must, in themselves, count as exceptional achievements. They also seem to show that the adaptability is far from infinite. If it were, such children would become as adept and successful as the animals they live among, or, given their human genetic endowment, even more so, like Tarzan. This is not the case, although there are occasional reports of extraordinary development, such as that of the 'gazelle boy' described by Armen (1971). This child was said to run with the swiftness of the herd he lived among, but there seems to be no corroborating evidence to support the story and one is inclined to discount it. All such cases present the difficulty that it is almost never possible to know what was the child's original condition. Some may well have been abandoned because they were deficient in some way, perhaps mentally. Assuming that some at least have been of normal endowment, the cases clearly show that, however remarkable their feat in surviving, they can never reach normal levels of human accomplishment without a human environment. The same can be said of those sad cases where a child has been deliberately deprived of virtually all human contact. One such – 'Genie' – is described by Curtiss (1977, 1988). This wretched child was for twelve years, from the age of 20 months onwards, kept confined in a small back bedroom, harnessed to a potty seat, fed only infant food and deprived of virtually all normal stimulation including speech. When discovered she could barely walk, could not chew or bite, understood only a few words and did not speak. Although she made remarkable progress, Genie never attained anything like normal language use, especially in any spontaneous, socially interactive way. The supposedly similar famous case of Kaspar Hauser is described in Chapter 11.

Conversely, the children whose early intellectual feats stand out have enjoyed at least adequate cultural resources, from which they have been able to construct their own rich environment. The great-uncle of Jeremy Bentham (1748–1832) was a bookseller, whose unsold wares were readily available to the boy. At 3 he picked on a long adult history of England (by Rapin) and read it with enjoyment; he began Latin at the same age and at 4 was writing both that and Greek. At 10 he obtained admission to Oxford University, but was so undersized and sensitive that this was delayed for two years. He graduated at 15. The father of Thomas Macaulay (1800–59) was a distinguished administrator and Fellow of the Royal Society, with an ample library, in which his son from the age of 3 read incessantly and with a phenomenal memory. At 6 he wrote a compendium of universal history running to a quire of paper (twenty-four sheets). The father of Leibniz (1646–1717), a university professor, died when he was 6, but the boy had access to his prized library. Goethe (1749–1832) was carefully taught by his father, as was Pascal (1623–62), whose father was a mathematician. Both as children were mainly in the company of adults (compare Norbert Wiener, Chapter 3). Grotius (1583–1645) was likewise close to his father, a highly cultured scholar, and in addition had a private tutor. These are, with J.S. Mill, at the top of the list of exceptional children compiled by Cox (1926) and studied further by McCurdy (1957); see Chapters 3 and 9.

In the next group below, Cox gives Chatterton, Leopardi, Voltaire, Coleridge, Von Haller, and Schelling. With the possible exception of the rather odd case of Chatterton, described in Chapter 6, all enjoyed favourable, even exceptional early educational environments. Again this is true of the next lowest group, except perhaps for Wolsey, the future Cardinal, about whose background less is known. It is not suggested that having access to books and adult conversation will by themselves lead to exceptional development; merely that such resources, on the face of it, seem to be necessary both for general intellectual stimulation and for specific knowledge.

R.S. Peters (1953) remarks that the twentieth century has been marked by a tendency to humanize animals and brutalize men. This has been true in fiction, in science, and in many ways in society generally. H.G. Wells's Dr Moreau (*The Island of Dr Moreau*, 1896) sought to make men out of beasts by surgery followed by the teaching of cultural rules; Freud puzzled over the same problem. The wholly fictitious 'apes' who reared Tarzan were far closer to us than any real species, using language and tools and killing each other in quite a human way. Experiments in teaching non-humans, especially chimpanzees, to use language, albeit in an extremely limited way, have become familiar, as have the complex social patterns of many species. Conversely men, since Freud, have been less rational animals. Works such as Desmond Morris's *The Naked Ape* (1967) and E.O. Wilson's *Sociobiology: The new synthesis* (1975) have carried on the theme, which seems only too profoundly true in an age of mass murder and destruction almost beyond belief – brutish though not animal-like. For most of the first half of the century a version of Behaviourism which saw humans as nonhuman dominated psychology, and its fictional expression appeared in, for example, Orwell's *1984* (1949) and Huxley's *Brave New World* (1932). These also reflected an urge to uniformity that seems almost pathological.

Because such views seem to diminish human freedom and dignity there may be a tendency to deny that man has any animal nature, being purely a creation of culture. But as Mary Midgley (1978) points out, it is only because we possess a nature that we can avoid being socialized into automatons. Rousseau's assertion that 'Man is born free' is to be taken literally; and it 'makes sense only as a description of our innate constitution, as something positive, already determined, and conflicting with what society does to us'. This constitution is an animal one, but that of a particular species, which has the capacity, in favourable circumstances, to develop what we like to think of as characteristically human features. Among these are the achievements we regard as exceptional. The circumstances must include, as a minimum, human culture and language.

Language and culture

At least four monarchs are reputed to have performed the experiment of isolating infants in order to see what language, if any, they would develop: Psamtik I of Egypt, Frederick II of Sicily, James IV of Scotland and Akbar the Great of India. The last of these is the most likely actually to have carried out the experiment, albeit with equivocal results (Campbell and Grieve, 1982). If such an experiment did succeed, the children would indeed have been prodigies. Modern studies of hearing children of deaf parents who lack speech suggest that they develop normally given some experience of language from other sources. There would appear to be a potential for language, requiring suitable, even if only minimal, conditions for development.

The relation between language and thought is complex, but all theorists would agree that language is an essential component of the highest levels of thinking. Similarly it is the most powerful medium for the transmission of culture, within which human potential develops. Thus the course of language acquisition is of interest in the present context. Typical figures reported for rate of language acquisition are shown in Table 1.01. Wide variations are found. For example, Howe (forthcoming) quotes a report of a boy speaking at 5 months, and having a vocabulary of fifty words a month later. By 2 years and 3 months he knew five languages and could read in three of them. Feldman (1986b) describes 'Adam', who apparently spoke in complete sentences at 3 months; and Barlow (1952) mentions a child, Kenneth Wolfe, of Cleveland, Ohio, as speaking at 4 months (see Chapter 3 for his later career). By these standards, prodigies of the past such as Thomas Macaulay, reading widely at 3, and John Stuart Mill, learning Greek at the same age, seem quite laggardly. None past or present matches Christian Friedrich Heinecken, born 1721, 'the Infant of Lubeck', who is said to have talked within a few hours of birth, to have known at the age of 1 all the principal events of the Pentateuch, at 2 the historical events of the whole Bible and at 3 history, geography, Latin and French. Sadly, at 4 he died. Scarcely more fortunate was Jean Louis Cardiac (1719–26), who repeated the alphabet at 3 months, at 3 years read Latin and at 4 translated it into either English or French.

It is obviously impossible to be sure of such cases, reports of which are probably distorted over time. Nevertheless it seems clear that exceptional variations in language acquisition do occur. Whitehurst and others (1988) have reported quite significant acceleration of language development by means of short sessions in which parents read to their children, but deliberately encourage them to speak more often by asking questions, repeating and expanding the child's speech, and praising and correcting it.

The development of language is immensely complex (see, for example, Horowitz and Samuels, 1987; Coltheart, Sartori and Job, 1987), but broadly it parallels, indeed is part of, general cognitive growth. Cases occur in which language outstrips other cognitive functions, but the language ability does not appear before the child reaches the cognitive level equivalent to a normal 2 to 4 year-old. In other words these children are

Table 1.01: Typical figures showing the rate of language acquisition (Morris, 1983)

Years	Months	Words
1	0	3
1	3	19
1	6	22
1	9	118
2	0	272
2	6	446
3	0	896
4	0	1540
5	0	2072
6	0	2562

generally retarded, but one specific ability has developed exceptionally (Bates, Bretherton and Snyder, 1988).

Individual differences exist not only in rate of language development but in the style of acquisition (Nelson, 1981: Bates *et al.*, 1988). Some children have been found to emphasize single words, simple productive rules for combining words, nouns and noun phrases, and referential functions; others use whole phrases and formulas, pronouns, compressed sentences and expressive or social functions. Differences of this kind cast doubt on the assumptions that were in vogue following the work of Noam Chomsky some twenty years ago, which implied that the properties of grammar were in some sense innate, so that language would develop in essentially the same way in all individuals, differing only in rate. What causes the differences is still unclear. There might be variations in subjects themselves, in the brain or in cognitive style; the function of language and the nature of the language learning task might differ; or environmental factors may vary. Nelson (1981) quotes an experiment by Lieven (1978) in which Beth, a second-born child, showed mainly expressive speech, Kate, a first-born, referential. Both mothers adjusted their speech to the child, but Kate's mother responded to her utterances 81 per cent of the time, Beth's only 46 per cent. Kate's mother responded more often with questions and took turns in a conversation; Beth's mother replied with ready-made phrases or corrections, or comments that ignored the child's remarks. These two children appeared to be using language for different ends. Kate talked slowly and coherently about things happening around her and objects in her environment, while Beth devoted more time to using her speech to try and engage her mother's attention.' This sort of approach has suggested the possibility, at least, of significantly influencing language development.

The next fundamental change in language after the emergence of speech is that of writing. Some have argued that it is this, indeed, that makes possible scientific thought in both the culture (Havelock, 1963) and the individual (Olson, 1986). Olson suggests that only the existence of an objective, stable text makes possible the distinction between fact and interpretation which is fundamental to scientific thinking. We must leave to fiction what cognitive changes might follow from new methods of transmitting information, but already it is clear that now-commonplace technology such as electric typewriters, or even better word processors, transforms the actual task of writing – though as yet no child seems to have typed a work as commercially or artistically successful as that Daisy Ashford wrote in pencil in a twopenny notebook (see Chapter 6).

Lebrun, Van Endert and Szliwowski (1988) report the case of Isabelle, a severely retarded girl who nevertheless was able to read aloud in three languages – Dutch, French and English – at a level far above her overall mental development. This is an example of hyperlexia, apparently comparable to other cases of exceptional development of one limited ability by otherwise retarded individuals. Aram and Healy (1988), reviewing the evidence, conclude that some neurological dysfunction is involved, though it is less clear just what. Nearly all cases, despite Isabelle, are male; and there seems to be a family history of language, especially reading, difficulty. Hyperlexia refers to reading without understanding. Jackson, Donaldson and Cleland (1988) report an analysis of precocious true reading ability. The pattern of skills appears to be similar to those found in poor and average readers, though very early readers seem to be diverse in their specific skill patterns or reading styles.

Hothouse children

A story which became well-known for a time is that of *The Children on the Hill* described by Michael Deakin (1972). The children were Christian, who at 12 had GCE A levels in science and mathematics, Adam (9) was a brilliant pianist and Ruth (7), a painter, while Paul (5) was adept in the computer language Fortran; their parents, Martin and Maria (all pseudonyms), were even more unusual. They had evolved, it seems, partly on spiritual and partly on psychological grounds, a system of upbringing based on love, expressed as acceptance and giving. It involved creating an environment secure from outside influence but full of intellectual stimulation; the absence of any pressure to achieve; a non-authoritative, reciprocal approach; and complete dedication by the parents. The children were never forced, but always encouraged, to make the most of each impulse of curiosity, from speaking to writing to number to any other activity. Some of this came from the Montessori method which Maria had studied, but much was her own invention. The result, so it seems, was a prodigy in the classic fields of music and mathematics and, less certainly, in art and computing. What one now desires is a follow-up report, but this has not come to hand. It is interesting to contrast other cases of complete parental involvement which took a demanding, authoritarian, even harsh attitude, such as those of John Stuart Mill and William James Sidis, which will be discussed later. Martin is described as a person of 'stillness, repose, and inner certainty'. It might seem that intense involvement and stimulation relate to intellectual development, while emotional adjustment and even happiness are not necessarily linked but depend on other factors. However, while much can be learned from such cases there is always the possibility (the opposite of that with the feral children) that the children were highly gifted to start with, and would have done well with or without their parents' efforts.

More recently, there has been a spate of interest in the encouragement of intellectual development. A television series, 'Hot House People' (and book of the same title by Walmsley and Margolis, 1978) showed many examples of precocious children, and it was claimed that most children could develop to an extent that is at present exceptional. Glenn Doman's books, such as *Teach Your Baby to Read* (1964), are well known though they have been heavily criticized. David Lewis's book *You Can Teach Your Child Intelligence* (1981) seeks to identify 'key aspects of behaviour which can unlock the intellect or imprison it for ever'. They are attitudes, self-image, motivation and problem-handling skills. Undoubtedly all these are of importance, but precisely how and why they function is still far from fully understood. A significant feature of Lewis's methods, and of 'hothouses' generally, is their intensive nature and the correspondingly great demands they make on adults, generally parents. This seems to be a feature of the upbringing of many exceptional children of both past and present. It may be one reason for the generally negative attitude taken by the media to such programmes. Reviews of another of Lewis's books, *Mind Skills* (1987), for example in *The Times* (13 April) and *The Guardian* (20 April), make much of the fact that the author is unmarried and childless. The general line is that a good deal of what he says is 'common sense' – i.e. that with which the reviewer agrees – and the rest is either impossible or danger-ous; the whole being more or less an exploitation of parents' natural anxieties. (It is not uncommon to find that psychology is at one and the same time regarded as common sense, ineffective, and dangerous; see Radford, 1985.)

Michael Howe (1988b, 1988c) points out that it is indeed 'most important that such claims should be properly investigated'. If, in fact, parents (and teachers) can do little to alter a child's natural abilities, then the effort to do so will not only be wasted but will lead to frustration and disappointment for both. On the other hand, if intellectual powers can really be increased, it may seem wrong not to maximize them – although some may consider this incompatible with other attributes such as happiness or spirituality. Ken Adams, the father of John Adams who passed 'O' levels at 8 and 'A' levels at 9, has published *Your Child Can Be A Genius – And Happy!* (1988), and so far as newspaper reports go this seems to be true enough in John's case: 'But most important, his father maintains, he is a happy-go-lucky, sports-mad schoolboy with loads of friends, and would much rather be out playing with them or watching children's television programmes with his brothers than debat-ing the theory of relativity' (*The Times*, 25 July 1988). A far cry from James Mill, who deliberately isolated his John from other children lest they interfere with his education. And it is not really clear why happiness cannot be found in discussing the theory of relativity.

Howe considers that several fallacious beliefs are widely held concerning ability and its development. One is that artistic and scientific achievements, at any rate for some people, come as a flash of inspiration, with little conscious effort. In fact this is seldom if ever true; even if there is a sudden thought, it has always followed a great deal of previous work. Similarly it is thought that geniuses can cut short the long periods of training usually necessary and produce great works at very early ages. Again it is not true. Even the early works of Mozart, probably the most extraordinary of musical child prodigies, while indeed remarkable for a child were not exceptional by adult standards – although of course far exceeding what most people could do. A third belief is that some individuals may emerge, as exceptionally gifted children and later as outstanding adults, from backgrounds that are not particularly stimulating or even disadvantageous; in other words that genius will always find its proper level. This too is not supported by the facts. When biographies are studied closely, it is found that even in apparently deprived homes from which an exceptional person has emerged, there was in fact more intellectual stimulation and support than might be thought. A fourth fallacy, Howe thinks, stems from some early research by Arnold Gesell, an American developmentalist who seemed to show that training produced little effect. The famous case was that of two twins, one of whom was taught to climb stairs; when the other was given the same opportunity it rapidly caught up with the first in level of skill. This sort of experiment is far too limited to allow general conclusions, and it is quite unjustified to make inferences about cognitive development.

One might perhaps add that there may also be a belief that at any rate some abilities, at least, such as music and mathematics and perhaps sport, are the preserve of the fortunate few, and if we don't have them there is little we can do about it. It is customarily implied in the mass media, for example, that all Welsh people can sing, with the corollary that the rest of the population cannot. In fact there is no reason at all to think the popularity of choirs in Wales other than a cultural phenome-non; as far as one can tell, all human groups possess musical potential, though individuals vary as they do in almost every respect. Those with near zero musical capacity are extremely rare, as are those with the greatest endowment. How many individuals develop their potential, to what degree and in what form are determined by society. A century, even half a century, ago many people certainly habitually sang, at work or in social gatherings, as they had done throughout recorded history, in a way that has now vanished probably for ever, replaced by television and personal stereo.

On the question of the effectiveness of training Howe has no doubt. While it is going too far to say that every child can be a genius, the evidence shows that:

it is indeed true that the babies of parents who make conscientious efforts to promote the early acquisition of basic skills will show accelerated develop-ment. Moreover, providing that the parental support and encouragement is not abruptly terminated after early childhood, the effects of accelerated development will be cumulative and long-lasting. (Howe, 1988b)

One might properly regard such children not as hothouse plants but robust outdoor specimens naturally fulfilling their potential for growth. What total good accrues in the long run is more difficult to say. There are two rather likely advantages: one is that natural fulfilment of potential is in general benefi-cial and its frustration the opposite; the other is that an early start gives some advantage over those whose development is more slow, simply by giving more time for later achievement. It is by no means clear, however, whether more races are won by front-runners or by those who come from behind; anecdote and biography supply numerous examples of success after a relatively slow start, though this does not necessarily mean that ability was absent, merely that it did not show in a way that attracted attention.

In Western society, with its emphasis on individuality and the nuclear family, children's upbringing is regarded as largely a matter for parents, and this applies to the fostering of talent of all kinds. Formal education is seen more as a kind of background resource; perhaps more so in the UK than the USA, where the gifted children movement has taken stronger hold. State or institutional control has an almost nightmarish quality about it which Huxley and Orwell made the most of, although the concept, of course, goes back at least to Plato (*The Republic, c.* 380 BC). Anna Hughes and Joseph Drew (1984) challenge the emphasis on individuality in creativity, examining it instead from the point of view of a single large collective, the State. Reviewing a wide literature, they identify three main categories of critical conditions – physical/biological, political/ social, and cultural – conducive to creative behaviour: that is both by the state itself, and to its stimulation in the population. They cite as examples the foreign policy of Romania and Japan's emphasis on education-based science and technology (discussed further in Chapter 11). Their aim seems to be not so much to advocate state control as to develop a theory embracing the individual, the physical and social environment, and the political system.

Paul Lees-Haley (1980) gives an account of Akademgorodok (the city of the gifted), which is located near Novosibirsk in the USSR. It is the home of the Siberian headquarters of the Soviet Academy of Sciences, where some thousands of scientists and gifted students live and work; and of one of the special boarding-schools for mathematics and physics, described by Dunstan (1978, 1988), where students are taught research skills by the finest senior research scientists, following a nation-wide selection process. Presumably the results are satisfactory enough for the State to continue its massive support (but see Chapter 11). Certainly there is nothing comparable in the West.

Eugenics

Eugenics is the science of producing the finest offspring, especially human. There are two ways of doing this, by selective breeding and by genetic manipulation. The former was a prominent idea around 1900, deriving partly from the centuries -old experience of breeding of livestock and partly from Darwinian evolutionary theory, to which Francis Galton added a mainly hereditarian explanation of differences in the human species. In 1869, Galton sought to show how the superiority of the classical Greeks over present-day English, and of the latter over other races, was largely a matter of racial inheritance. In 1903 he wrote:

There is no question that the pick of the British race are as capable human animals as the world can at present produce. Their defects lie chiefly in the graceful and sympathetic sides of their nature, but they are strong in mind and body, truthful and purposive, excellent leaders of the lower races.

At the time when Great Britain ruled a quarter of the world's population this view would have seemed less idiosyncratic than it does now. Galton rapidly comes up to date:

The lower middle classes of Britons are quite as efficient by nature . . . but they are of coarser fibre than the Latins. Our average holiday-maker and cheap-excursion tourist is proverbially unprepossessing.

To investiate the causes of these deficiencies and if possible remedy them, Galton tirelessly urged, and financially supported at University College, London, a programme of National Eugenics, 'The study of the agencies under social control that may improve or impair the racial qualities of future generations either physically or mentally'. One of the most important of such agencies is marriage, and an effective eugenics programme would encourage the better-endowed to marry each other, perhaps by financial incentives, and discourage the less fortunate from doing so. As Galton pointed out, marriage had never in any society been a matter of free choice; there are always rules against related persons marrying, and usually many more restrictions. And his aim was not to produce uniformity:

Society would be very dull if every man resembled the highly estimable Marcus Aurelius or Adam Bede. The aim of Eugenics is to represent each class or sect by its best specimens; that done, to leave them to work out their common civilisation in their own way.
    A considerable list of qualities can be easily compiled that nearly every-one except 'cranks' would take into account when picking out the best specimens of his class. It would include health, energy, ability, manliness and courteous disposition.

It seemed to Galton, and to many others, such as H.G. Wells and Bernard Shaw, foolish not to take measures to increase the national stock of such desirable qualities (Forrest, 1974), although Shaw famously pointed out to a lady who wished him to father her child, thus endowing it with her beauty and his brains, that the result might be just the opposite. But the programme made little headway. There was disagreement over selection of qualities. For example, Galton wanted to prevent criminals breeding, whereas Wells thought they might be among the most energetic and intelligent. It is difficult in a democracy to persuade the mass of voters of the merits of favouring a few, and eugenics has not been adopted by a major political party. Thirty years later, National Socialism in Germany embarked on a monstrous policy of not only breeding a pure, so-called Aryan race – there has in reality never been any such thing – but of eliminating what it saw as less desirable groups such as Jews and gypsies, and eugenics became associated with these vile concepts.

More recently the idea has revived, in the form (for example) of the Repository for Germinal Choice in California, a scheme by which intending mothers can have themselves artificially inseminated with sperm from a panel of Nobel prize winners, the first announced donor being William Shockley, the inventor of the transistor, in 1980. A favourable environment is readily available in prosperous California and the Repository, according to its Director Robert Graham, ascertains that:

the wife is in prime condition for motherhood, that the child will have parents to love and nurture him or her and that the family can afford adequate housing and appropriate education. . . . We do not expect the offspring to be geniuses but the mother does have the opportunity to bear the best offspring possible for her (*Mensa: The British Mensa Magazine*, August/September 1986).

With this we approach the second eugenic method, that of directly altering genetic material. This is on the threshold of being practical. Work has already begun on producing a complete analysis of human genetic make-up, a project estimated by the American National Research Council to require 30,000 man-years of effort, more than £2,000 million and more than fifteen years (*The Times*, 5 September 1988). Even such vast expenditure is relatively small by military standards, and there seems no reason why the enterprise should not be completed. It would certainly lead to control over many inherited illnesses such as haemophilia, muscular dystrophy and sickle cell anaemia. Further, according to Sir Walter Bodmer, President of the British Association for the Advancement of Science, at that body's annual meeting, 1988:

We know now that the inherited tendencies underlying more complex patterns of inheritance, such as susceptibility to breast cancer, or perhaps the ability to compose music like the Bach family, depend essentially on these same laws of inheritance.

The last item is more questionable. Even if it is true, it is only one half of the equation. It is obvious that even if one were to produce an exact genetic replica of Johann Sebastian Bach, a sort of posthumous twin, and then place it among wild animals like Tarzan, or deprive it of language, or let it be reared among Australian aboriginals, it is impossible that it should eventually compose like a Bach. It is not impossible, it may even be likely, that given some musical experience such as exists in all known human societies, some musical talent would show itself. More than that is at present guesswork.

Eugenics is not concerned with the production of exceptional children as such, but quite clearly the prospect does now really exist of at least exerting considerable control over children of the future. While the details of the other, environmental, side of the equation are by no means worked out, and perhaps in principle cannot be, let alone the interaction between them, it is perfectly possible to control social behaviour in broad outline, as was seen during the Chinese cultural revolution. More recent events have shocked the world; but suppose it were possible to increase an inherited tendency towards conformity. Before quite recent times Chinese society, despite political upheavals, was largely stable for many centuries (Needham, 1969). It is neither wild nor alarmist to suggest that the possibility does begin to emerge of a society in which control should pass a point of no return, and in which the human potential for change, which has never quite vanished in the most adverse circumstances, should be effectively extinguished. (Woodlice, unaltered, pre-date the dinosaurs.)

Albert Jacquard (1985) has discussed the 'eugenic temptation' which has fascinated scientists and philosophers for so long. Now that the means are at last within our grasp, what eugenics should strive for is not the development of better genes, for it is not possible to say what these are, but the development of human beings' capacity to develop themselves. The British Medical Association is currently drawing up guidelines on genetic engineering to avert the creation of 'designer children' and 'supermen' (*The Times*, 6 July 1988). Dr Ian Jessiman, a GP from Bromley, Kent, is reported as saying: 'We have no right to interfere with the genetic library of the human race when this might be irremediable.' Of course this is already being done on a large scale with the effective extirpation of native races in South America, Australia and many other places, but certainly we should not add to the destruction. Dr John Dawson, BMA Under-secretary, adds that doctors must have genetic information restricted to ensure it is used 'only for the good of the patient and only, if ever, for the most exceptional claims that society might make – for instance in the case of a mass murderer'. A press quotation may well be unfair, but this raises more problems than it solves. Apart from the fact that it is hardly a medical, but a scientific and general problem, what is the good of the patient, and what is the distinction of the mass murderer: is this, but not other crimes, inherited?

I am normal, you are eccentric, he is mad

The concept of 'designer children' verges on the notion, virtually a myth, of the mad scientist after the model of Mary Shelley's Frankenstein (1818) (thus; neither Doctor nor Baron as he is so often). His creature was not intended as a monster, but as a superman, the prodigious 'child' of his creator (see Tropp, 1977). Fictional 'superchildren' today are often malevolent in the style of John Wyndham's *The Midwich Cuckoos* (1957). Even when the opposite, like Olaf Stapledon's *Odd John* (1935), they find it difficult to avoid conflict with society, for which exceptional behaviour is always likely to be a problem. Kroll and Bachrach (1984) compared the symptoms of psychiatric patients with the reported experiences of religious visionaries of the period AD 500–1500. There was sufficient overlap, for example in the hearing of the voices of angels or devils, for them to conclude that today's patients would not then have been counted insane. The notion that 'genius is next to madness', apart from being rather reassuring to the average majority, could mean either that the behaviour of both is unusual, or that extreme ability in the individual is associated with mental instability. The latter theory was seriously held by, among other, Cesare Lombroso, who in *The Man of Genius* (1891) stated that 'genius is a true degenerative psychosis' and 'a symptom of hereditary degeneration of the epileptoid variety', and is 'allied to moral insanity'. Hollywood owes much to Lombroso. The notion persists in various forms: for example, Eysenck and Eysenck (1976, quoted by Kline and Cooper, 1986) reported positive correlations between the personality dimension of psychoticism and measures of creativity; but Kline and Cooper, using different measures, found no such relationship. Aylward, Walker and Bettes (1984), reviewing research, concluded that there was strong evidence that diagnosed schizophrenic patients scored lower on standard tests of intelligence than would be predicted from family and environmental variables. Unfortunately for all research using 'schizophrenia' as an independent variable, Mary Boyle (in press) has shown conclusively that ever since the term was invented by Eugene Bleuler in 1911, it has been used arbitrarily and inconsistently as a diagnosis of all sorts of conditions, many of them probably quite unrelated.

Becker (1978) argues that the 'mad genius' image stems largely from artists and writers of the early nineteenth-century Romantic period who, lacking a recognised position in society such as had existed previously, revived the classical notion of 'divine madness' or 'inspiration' as a defining mark of the extraordinary individual. Even if they did not do so deliberately, a number of them, for whatever reason, certainly fitted and contributed to a stereotype – William Blake (1757–1828), for example, or Lord Byron (1788–1824).

On the other hand it is plausible to see some relationship between creative achievement and unusual, even eccentric behaviour. First, any outstanding individual in any field is by definition unusual. Further, by virtue of this, they tend, especially now, to be under constant public scrutiny and subjected to all sorts of pressures and temptations, the more so if young. Pop stars, for example, are typically young people with one particular talent (large or small) who almost overnight pass into a world where fame and money remove all the rules of their usually very average childhood. The wonder is not that some like Janis Joplin or the pathetic Sid Vicious, succumb, but that so many survive. DeLong and Aldershof (1988) suggest that there is an association between special ability and juvenile manic-depressive illness. The ability may be manifest in a broad area of knowledge, pursued with creativity and imagination, or it may be a very limited, although remarkable, accomplishment such as mental calculation. Rather typically there is often an obsessive aspect to the ability (see Chapters 5 and 10).

Certainly some of the famous child prodigies of the past have had parents that can only be described as eccentric – often obsessive – at least as regards education. This seems to apply, for example, at any rate in a mild form, to the father of Martha, a child studied by Lewis Terman (1918) and referred to by Glenn Doman in support of his early reading programme. Martha's father decided, when she was 14 months old, to teach her to read, as an experiment to see if it could be done. She soon came to know a few letters, but for various reasons the experiment was then halted for five months. At 19 months her development in walking and talking was reported as average. The experiment was then resumed systematically and intensively. Although Martha's father had no knowledge of educational theory, for the most part his methods were in line with modern approaches to learning, in particular that of operant conditioning. Essentially he devised numerous small simple reading tasks – recognizing letters, recognizing words, and so on – and rewarded each correct response with anything that seemed to work: praise, toys, candy. When Terman saw Martha at 26 months she 'read from any primer fluently and with better expression than most first grade children' (one assumes with understanding also). Two weeks later he assessed her reading vocabulary at more than 700 words, and her spoken vocabulary at more than 2,000.

There seems to be only one psychological study of eccentrics as such, by Weeks and Ward (1988). Their subjects were self-selected and may not be wholly typical, but their unselfconscious and sometimes brilliant single-mindedness is reminiscent of the fathers of John Stuart Mill, Norbert Wiener, the inventor of cybernetics, and William Sidis the so-called 'world's greatest child prodigy', to name just three. Maria and Martin, the parents of the 'children on the hill', would surely qualify as eccentric, as, in a totally different way, would the remarkable Sir George Sitwell, father of three outstandingly gifted children, Osbert, Sacheverell and Edith. The last not only later produced the delightful *English Eccentrics* (1933) but was one herself throughout life. Edith, when asked patronisingly at the age of 4 what she was going to be when she grew up, replied coldly: 'A genius!' (Sitwell, 1966).

The current fashion seems to be held that exceptional, or at any rate famous, individuals are 'really' very ordinary, a quality convincingly demonstrated in incessant chat shows. At the same time, at least in Britain, anything intellectual or artistic is by definition peculiar and requires justification in terms of popular standards of normality. Normality is a notoriously slippery concept. Social norms certainly supply one meaning, but, as in the Kroll and Bachrach example, vary widely with the particular culture. The same problem besets an apparently more objective statistical approach – regarding normal as equivalent to average or not too far from it. This works fairly well for some characteristics, such as physical measurements. Thus a man of five feet would probably be regarded as within the normal range, but one of four feet outside it. Pygmies would not be happy with this, and when it comes to behaviour we are back with the problems of social definition. One alternative is some concept of 'natural' development, which again is satisfactory for physical growth; given adequate nutrition humans will grow to within certain limits, and not indefinitely. But we do not know what is the range of behavioural and social conditions within which humans might flourish and produce prodigies. To say, as some do, that exceptional development of a particular talent is normal for the individual, however unusual it may be, is only true within a particular cultural context. It might seem to imply that a potential chess prodigy, for example, born into a non-chess-playing culture, must necessarily develop abnormally. Yet a third approach tries to define some kind of ideal development, sometimes in spiritual terms, sometimes in accordance with belief or dogma. The dangers here are obvious.

While perhaps insoluble, the problem cannot be ignored, for the rules we adopt, consciously or not, define not only what counts as exceptional but how far it is legitimate to go in either encouraging or suppressing it. Child prodigies, whatever else they are, must by definition be exceptional; but in comparison to some group.

2 The Marvellous Child

Younger and younger

Rubik's Cube is famous as an extremely difficult puzzle – 150 million sold. In July 1988 Professor Erno Rubik launched his clock puzzle, reputedly even more difficult and unsolved even by himself. On 27 July the London *Evening Standard* reported that Alexander Scrivenor, aged 15, had solved the clock in just under an hour and a half. His stepfather Mr Christian Tyler remarked: 'Perhaps youngsters have brains which are better able to cope with these sort of problems than ours'. At any rate, it does not appear from the report that Alexander is either a puzzle addict or exceptional at school. The record for the cube, 22.95 seconds, is held (1988) by a teenage Vietnamese refugee, Minh Thai.

In March 1988 Tony Aliengena, aged 9, became the youngest solo pilot, taking off and landing an ultra-light plane in California (*Early Times*, 27 December 1988). (In July 1989 he piloted a plane around the world.) On 15 July *The Times* reported the youngest pilot to fly the Atlantic, Christopher Marshall, a veteran of 11. *The Times* for 29 June 1988 carried a picture of Mrs Margaret Thatcher checking the press credentials of a journalist at the meeting of European leaders in Hanover: Alexander Blume, aged 12, reporting for his school newspaper *The Mole*. On 17 August the story was of James Harris, aged 10, inviting Mrs Thatcher to the opening of his antiques shop in Cardiff. The Prime Minister's response to this photocall opportunity is not reported, but James did get a few seconds of national TV time the following February.

Each summer brings another record performance in GCE examinations, generally in mathematics – Ruth Lawrence, John

Adams, and the 1988 champion, Ganesh Sittampalam, with a grade A pass at A level at 9 years and 4 months. We shall return to all of these. Child internationals in gymnastics have become commonplace. In the 1987 French tennis championships, the eventual winner Steffi Graf was, at 19, the *oldest* semi-finalist. In January 1989 she won her fifth consecutive grand slam title. Possibly the most remarkable tennis feat of our time, in terms of age, has been that of Boris Becker, winner of the men's singles at Wimbledon in 1985 at the age of 17 and again the following year.

In other ways too attention is drawn to remarkable activities of the young. A boy of 14 was cleared of a charge of rape after he had persuaded a woman of 48 to have intercourse with him by posing as her doctor's assistant (dressed in his school uniform) and persuading her that it was necessary in order to diagnose whether she had cancer. As Prosecuting Counsel Michael Pratt told the jury, 'Doubtless your immediate reaction would be that this was incredible', but both parties confirmed it (*The Times*, 24 June 1988). A boy of 13 from Southwark in South London, wanted in connection with twenty burglaries, was said to be the youngest British fugitive from justice to flee to what has become known as the Costa del Crime in Spain. He was first arrested at the age of 9, and frequently thereafter, but because there is no secure accommodation for those under 14 he is always remanded on bail. His mother claimed 'police harassment' had driven him abroad, and added: 'I am not giving my son up to anybody. He is just a boy trying to go straight'. (*The Times*, 14 June 1988).

There is nothing really new about such cases, which in spite of their real seriousness assume a slightly comic aspect. Cyril Burt's classic *The Young Delinquent* (1925) is full of them, while further back the reporting of Charles Mayhew and the fiction inspired by fact of such writers as Horatio Alger and Charles Dickens show a youthful Victorian underworld now almost forgotten in 'advanced' societies. It is the remarkable and recent increase in general respectability that makes delinquency and hooliganism seem out of the ordinary. In the case of outstanding achievements, intellectual, sporting or what not, there is perhaps an increased interest, certainly by the mass media, in anything exceptional; although at the same time there are more objective criteria – the GCE, for example, is a very thoroughly standardized examination. In sport, there are vastly increased financial rewards, and better training methods. The likelihood is that while potential may or may not be much the same, actual achievement is indeed getting younger, at least in some fields. John Evelyn (1620–1706), the diarist, however, having started Latin at 5, in adult life considered his education deficient because he had begun so late, and set his own children to it at four (Baker, 1983).

There is some suggestion that children are currently more sophisticated than say fifty or a hundred years ago. One must always beware of the immemorial habit of bemoaning the shortcomings of the present generation. But it is a simple fact that the mass media, in particular, provide an intellectual environment quite different to any that has existed before. Rather like the vanishing rain forests, vast tracts of ancient culture have disappeared for ever before modern technology. To give just one example, Iona and Peter Opie compiled a famous and massive account of *The Lore and Language of Schoolchildren* (1959), parts of it certainly hundreds, possibly thousands of years old in origin; a repertoire which might now seem extraordinary. Observation suggests that at any rate where I happen to live in East London, all this has gone without trace in the last ten years. Boys play football, girls gossip, and that is all.

Sue Keane, a psychologist, conducted a survey, on behalf of the confectionery firm Nestlé, of the habits and preferences of children now as compared to fifty years ago, to mark the fiftieth anniversary of Milky Bar chocolate. A child of 10 in 1937 was 'innocent, naive, and had a real child's life'. The favourite activity of children today is sitting alone in their room playing with their computer, watching television or working out their bank balance (*The Times*, 31 August 1987). While this is no doubt true, one wonders how much the 'real child's life' was a product of a particular time and place. In most cultures, children have contributed to the adult economy at a rather early age, except for those who obtained full-time education.

Expectations of children undoubtedly change. Murphy, Jenkins-Friedman and Tollefson (1984), for example, found that teachers saw the ideal child as one who is independent, courageous, sincere, affectionate, humorous and healthy. They contrast this with teachers' views collected in 1965 (Torrance), 1974 (Buchtold) and 1978 (Kaltsounis), which emphasized traits that were conformist and socially acceptable. Longer-term changes are discussed by, for example, Aries (1960) and Kessel and Siegel (1983); though Illick (1985) warns against the too simplistic view that the very concept of childhood has only emerged in modern times.

There have certainly been physical changes since systematic records began to be kept. Figures from Scandinavia, the UK and the USA show that the average age of the onset of menstruation in girls dropped from 16–17, in the 1860s, to 13 in the 1960s. Over the same period the average height of 12-year-olds increased by an average 1.5 cm per decade. That of adults increased by 0.4 cm. These changes are attributed to better health and living conditions. The last twenty years have seen no further changes, but of course this may not mean that limits have been reached (Smith and Cowie, 1988).

Prodigies and portents

Perhaps nowhere have attitudes changed more than in relation to those children who are bizarrely different from others. For many centuries physical oddities were regarded as either portents or commercial exhibits. They were generally either what are commonly called Siamese twins or those born with vestigial or supernumerary limbs or other deformities. The original 'Siamese' pair Chang and Eng, born in 1811, were at first considered a portent of evil by the King of Siam, who it seems proposed to have them killed but was eventually persuaded that they were harmless. Happily their later lives were more fortunate; they settled in America, married two sisters, had twenty-two non-handicapped children and lived until 1874.

Thompson (1968) quotes astrological documents from the library of Assurbanipal, King of Assyria, who lived from 668 to 626 BC. These include detailed prognostications from all sorts of possible malformed infants:

When a woman gives birth to an infant that has the ears of a lion – there will be a powerful King in the country; whose right ear is small – the house of the man (in whose house the birth took place) will be destroyed; that has two ears on the right side and none on the left – the gods will bring about a stable reign, the country will flourish and it will be a land of repose; and so on.

Before the development of modern medical methods and understanding, malformed individuals were both more obvious and more mysterious than now; and in most societies, if they survived physically, were likely to subsist by means of exhibiting themselves (or be exploited by others for the same purpose). Medieval accounts tend to be fabulous; in the modern period, say the last three centuries, we come to recognize physical syndromes that are known to science today. Although understanding of the causes and treatment of such conditions is now vastly greater, attitudes do seem to show some similarities. Alongside an urge to conformity, there is a tendency to make the unusual, once it is classified as such, seem even more marvellous than it is; in other words to exaggerate. When freaks were commonly shown to the public there was a financial incentive to do so which now pertains to any celebrity. Secondly, there is curiosity, voyeurism even, as regards the odd and unusual. Fairly typical of his time, Samuel Pepys, for example, expressed his 'entire satisfaction' with such a show. Multiple births which attract media attention today are quite a close parallel. Thirdly, there is an inclination to attribute to nature a kind of compensatory action, so that, for example, the handicapped are nevertheless exceptionally skilful; again there is a parallel in the 'idiot savants' discussed later. Of course, all these are related: exhibiting and media coverage would not exist without public interest, and it is far better for a showman to have a performer than a mere freak. An early but well-documented case is that of the 'Scottish brothers': Siamese twins, born around 1490 near Glasgow, having two trunks and heads and four arms, but apparently joined above the hip and having two legs. They were taken to the court of James IV, who had them brought up and educated. The Scottish historian Lindsay says that 'they learned to sing and to play instruments of music, singing two parts, treble and tenor. They knew Latin, French, Italian, Spanish, Dutch, Danish and Irish.' The attribution of linguistic ability is particularly common. Perhaps it is not so difficult to pick up and use a few phrases when one is constantly being shown to a succession of strangers and (in many cases) travelling widely.

Thompson quotes an account by J. Bulwer (1653) of one John Simons, born without arms or legs:

He is about 20 years of age, he writeth with his mouth, he threads a needle with his mouth, he tyeth a knot upon thread or hair though it be never so small, with his mouth. He feedeth himself with spoon meat, he shuffles, cuts and deals a pack of cards with his mouth. . . . Nature upon such occasions is, that her unsearchable industry as it with great wittinesse appeareth everywhere, yet more eminently in those bodies wherein as t'were unmindful of her charge or business she hath frustrated of this or that member, which errour, as it were, with some shamefacedness she abundantly recompenceth by a munificent liberality.

Perhaps it is not too fanciful to suggest that we feel in our time that as we have supplanted nature in so many respects, so it is right to compensate not only for physical handicaps by advanced prostheses, but for every kind of disadvantage in every possible way. Some notion of compensation possibly informs a feature film released at the time of writing, *Rain Man*, starring Dustin Hoffman as an autistic with a special talent. Such cases are discussed later. Contrariwise, attitudes to the especially gifted are at least ambiguous, and despite the evidence to the contrary such gifts are often felt to be accompanied by deficiencies in other respects or to be the prelude to misfortune.

Zigler and Farber (1985), comparing attitudes toward the gifted and the retarded, argue that the explanations for both have in the past involved mystical or extrahuman forces:

In some societies retarded people were thought to be possessed by divine spirits. . . . Luther felt that they were possessed by the devil and that exorcism and drowning were the only effective solutions. The abilities of gifted people . . . were also thought to come from supernatural intervention. As Ashby and Walker (1968) explain, the term *gifted* implies that one has received a gift and, because it is bestowed at birth, it must come from God. Similarly, it is not uncommon to hear parents of a retarded child ascribe their plight to God's will as His way of testing their faith and religious commitment.

David Feldman (1986b) in the only recent book-length

study of child prodigies as such – he concentrates on six particular cases – starts by describing how the term 'prodigy' has become restricted, at least in American usage, to refer to exceptional intellectual gifts. Part of his aim is to restore some of the earlier meaning: 'for I believe that the child who performs extraordinarily well in a highly demanding field is a distinctive, significant, and revealing phenomenon and cannot be explained by invoking the "high IQ" argument or any other relatively simple explanation'. This argument risks circularity, since if there is a presumption of inexplicability then attempted explanations will probably be written off as simplistic. And it is by no means clear, in any case, what is to count as an explanation. Feldman makes a good deal, in the case at least of one of the six children he studied in detail, Adam (a pseudonym), of what he terms the boy's 'other side'. This was shown by a tendency to have vivid and frightening fantasies which seemed to be of real historical events, such as Nazi atrocities, of which he could not otherwise have known. He seemed also to have memories of experiences immediately after, or even before, birth. There were family accounts of him being somehow perceived as of great spiritual importance, even by those who hardly knew him. The notion that children might have some form of supernatural power or ability has persisted for centuries and still continues (Inglis, 1986; Peterson, 1987); see also the next section of this chapter.

Feldman asks not just how exceptional children develop but why. His answer reverts almost to the notion of prodigies as portents, but in a scientific, evolutionary context: 'I believe that the prodigy has something special to tell us about the psychological purposes of human development – in effect, how potential is fulfilled. Again: 'The prodigy. . . gives us a hint about why we are here and what we are trying to make of ourselves'.

Beliefs and myths

There is something more to be said about how exceptional children have been regarded. Young heroes are universal in legend, from Alexander through George Washington to Robin,

Batman's Boy Wonder. The mother of Alexander (b.356 BC) reputedly dreamed of a thunderbolt falling on her and flames coming out of her; his father, that his son should be as strong as a lion. Other omens predicted a victorious career, while in medieval legend the child grew miraculously fast – as did Cuchulinn, Ögmundr and many others. Hercules strangled two snakes in his cradle. Often precocity foreshadows revenge against an oppressor, as in the ballad of *Jellon Grame* (Child 90): 'he grew as big in ae year as some boys woud in three'. Early speaking often has the same function, for example in *Johnnie Armstrong* (Child 169), or it serves to save life, vindicate innocence, etc. (Child, 1884–94). Some of the multiple strands of the legend of Merlin tell how he was begotten by a devil on a virgin yet, inheriting only her virtue, he spoke as soon as he was born and soon defended her chastity at a public trial (Jarman, 1976). Precocious speaking may well have seemed magical and helped to strengthen legend. Other inexplicable behaviour might be attributed to the child being a changeling, a fairy infant substituted for the real one. The Grimm Brothers collected several examples.

Where a child is royal there is all the more reason to expect marvels. When much hung upon the succession children were often formally advanced to office at very early ages; for example, the future Henry VIII became Lieutenant of Ireland, Duke of York and Knight of the Garter at the age of 3. Something of this remains in the British monarchy. Today's frantic mass media hubbub over the birth and naming of royal infants possibly has roots in a lingering sense of the divinity of kingship and the importance of omens whether for good or ill. Ethelred II the 'Unready' (actually 'ill-advised') was said to have urinated in his baptismal font, thus presaging his unfortunate reign.

Miraculous infants feature in a number of religions. It is said that 108 Brahmins attended the name-giving ceremony of the future Buddha when he was 5 days old, eight of whom were experts in interpreting bodily marks. Seven predicted that if he remained at home he would become a universal monarch, but that if he left home he would become a buddha; the eighth predicted the latter outcome in any case. Portents surrounding the birth of Jesus, some in the Gospels and some accumulated subsequently are too well known to describe. Fifty years after Jesus' death, Luke added, perhaps from oral tradition, the account of the 12-year-old Jesus debating with elders in the Temple. As with most religions, Christian mythology has incorporated elements from numerous sources. Many scholars see the doctrine of the virgin birth as originating in pagan stories of divinely begotten heroes. The House of Bishops of the Church of England published in 1986 a response to those, such as the Bishop of Durham, who find problems in a simplistic belief in that doctrine. They acknowledge differences between Christian scholars as to whether the Virginal conception is to be regarded as historical fact as well as imagery symbolic of divine truth:

But all of us accept first that the belief that Our Lord was conceived in the womb of Mary by the creative power of God the Holy Spirit without the intervention of a human father can be held with full intellectual integrity; secondly, that only this belief, enshrined in the Creeds, can claim to be the teaching of the universal Church. (*The Nature of Christian Belief*, published for the General Synod of the Church of England.)

Unless one is of the minority of the human race that actually holds these particular beliefs, the fact that they have generated so much passion for so long suggests that they do correspond to something in the human psyche. This is the approach adopted by C.G. Jung. Jung is not in general highly regarded by mainstream psychologists, but he was at least not afraid to tackle such intangible yet important mysteries. His repetitious and somewhat mystical language helped to obscure his ideas, one of which was that human beings have tendencies to respond in typical ways to basic situations which have recurred in every generation. Such situations arise from their mutual experiences of each other by male and female, mother, child. These tendencies have some similarities to instincts, as Jung himself points out. The word 'instinct' has long been out of favour, particularly with regard to human behaviour, yet it seems undeniable that we have what might be called 'propensities', to use an almost forgotten term of William McDougall: tendencies to act towards certain ends and respond to certain stimulus situations. All infants have propensities, which develop more or less normally depending on their particular nature and the environment. Thus breathing and (initial) feeding generally function in a relatively autonomous and standard way, whereas language is more modifiable and relationships with others still more so. Human 'instincts' differ in another way from those of other species, so far as we know, in having significant cognitive aspects. Jung used the term 'archetype' or 'psychic apprehension of the object'. An archetype is 'a symbolical formula, which always begins to function when there are no conscious ideas present' (Jung, 1923). There is for most people an almost automatic reaction to infancy; it is difficult to see a small child without some benign feelings, smiling, and so on. Most couples desire children, and even originally 'unwanted' babies are often beloved by their mothers once they are born. Children arouse passion. Women in rare cases go so far as to steal infants, and legal battles over children are sadly common. Of course this behaviour is shaped by individual and social factors, but it does not seem unreasonable to speak of a parental propensity. More modern work on what used to be called 'instinct' has made us familiar with such concepts as sign stimuli and innate releasing mechanisms; automatic responses to standard situations: and if these exist in human beings a cognitive aspect is just what we should expect.

In the case of the child who is to become a redeemer or saviour, according to Jung, a particular archetype is involved: 'The symbol always says: In some such form as this will a new manifestation of life, a deliverance from the bondage and weariness of life, be found. . . . Love and joy is the message of the "wonder-child", the new symbol.' When a specific case as it were 'fits' the archetype, it becomes invested with great emotional power. It is not at all easy to see how to test a concept such as that of archetypes, and yet undoubtedly many millions of people have put their faith in a miraculous redeemer who will one day appear, often in the form of a child. And some individual children have been cast in that role, either during their youth or retrospectively when it is felt that an adult, now seen as the saviour, ought to have had a marvellous childhood. It may be that remarkable children are still vaguely felt to be inexplicable.

However this may be, the science of behaviour has tended to

discount the notion of the unique individual. Individuals are notoriously tricky to bring within the bounds of general laws. As that great student of behaviour Sherlock Holmes put it: 'While the individual man is an insoluble puzzle, in the aggregate he becomes a mathematical certainty.' Certainly the study of individual differences and their measurement – psychometrics – from Francis Galton to the present has sought such mathematical certainty by establishing the distribution of characteristics in large populations. The individual is then defined by his position on a number of dimensions, few or many according to theory. It has generally been assumed that such dimensions, like so many in the natural world (for example height or weight, Quetelet's measurements of which offered Galton one of his starting-points), will tend to follow the 'normal' or Gaussian curve of error. This assumption has been attacked: for example by Walberg (e.g. Walberg, Strykowski, Rovai and Hung, 1984) on the basis that many distributions of natural phenomena are in fact skewed; and by Waterhouse (1988), who argues that special talents are not the extreme ends of normal distributions but are uniquely determined. Both arguments will be discussed later, but if accepted would seem to give support to the age-old belief in the unique outstanding individual.

The question arises as to whether there are any abilities peculiarly associated with childhood, just as there have been thought to be mystical or spiritual powers. There are two possibilities: there might be 'critical periods' for the development of certain capacities, or there might be capacities that manifest themselves at certain times and then diminish. The accounts of children deprived of experience of speech suggest that language is an example of the first, and this is supported by the difficulty of second-language learning in later years. It is extremely rare to attain 'native' fluency; but cases do occur. The publisher Robert Maxwell, whose English appears to be perfect, has stated in interviews that he knew none before the age of twenty. Novoa, Fein and Obler (1988) describe the case of CJ, an exceptionally gifted linguist who retained virtually native-like learning abilities. Numerous psychological tests revealed little but that, as would be expected, he had an exceptional verbal memory. There was some suggestion of bilateral cerebral organization, which has been thought to be associated with verbal skills; and there were hints that CJ's personality was such as to make him more ready than most people to take the risks of venturing into a new language. (It has been remarked anecdotally that while the English have notoriously been bad at European languages, they have produced many outstanding scholars of oriental and 'third world' tongues, the suggestion being that these present no threat.)

One of the very few ways in which it has been seriously suggested that children possess special abilities concerns visual imagery. Haber and Haber (1988) have studied the phenomenon of eidetic imagery for over twenty-five years. Subjects, almost always children, appear under certain circumstances to see images not as normally 'in the mind's eye' but as if existing on a suitable blank screen in front of them; in other words they see them more or less as a picture would appear. Haber and Haber consider that this trait is a peculiar characteristic, distinct both from normal perception and from other forms of imagery, possessed by a few children and a rare adult. What significance it may have remains unclear.

The study of prodigies

There are at least half a dozen strands in the development of the scientific study of individual differences. Quetelet's work of 1837–46 was one aspect of one of these, the statistical approach. Another aspect was the development of probability theory, leading to Gauss's formulation of the distribution that tends to result from 'chance' factors. One can imagine throwing darts at the centre point of a line: hits will tend to pile up near the centre, and become rarer and rarer with distance from it. Similarly it is as if nature were aiming to produce human beings of a standard height. Sir Francis Galton (1832–1911), in many ways the pioneer of the study of individual differences, assumed that whatever underlay human abilities (for instance brain capacity) would be distributed similarly to other physical characteristics; thus the abilities themselves would be so also. This was the origin of a fundamental change in the way we think about ourselves; even Galton's cousin Charles Darwin had until then assumed that there were a few geniuses and a few idiots, with between them a vast mass of equal ability. Galton, it is customary to note, was himself a very forward child who read at 2½ years.

Abilities, however, are not physical but behavioural. It follows from Galton's concept that human abilities can be measured, but also that these measurements are, for the most part, relative rather than absolute. It is possible to assess intelligence (say) but only by reference to others, a selection from the totality of human beings. Genius shows itself as the capacity to do something much better than most other people; thus it is defined by what human beings can do. This in turn is not fixed but constantly changes as we continually create our own environment. It is for this reason that one can never answer those fascinating questions of sport such as whether Bradman was really greater than Hobbs, or Muhammed Ali than Mike Tyson, or John McEnroe than Rod Laver. This is so even where objective measurement is possible as in athletics. In 1893 C.B. Fry equalled the world long jump record, with 23 feet 6½ inches. If he jumped that today he would hardly be in the international class. But would he, especially if he had today's training, diet, and so forth? The question is impossible to answer, not just in practice but in principle.

A second strand in the study of individual differences emerged when in 1796 the Astronomer Royal, Maskelyne, dismissed his assistant Kinnebrook for carelessly making incorrect observations. Accuracy was becoming increasingly important. What Maskelyne did not realize was that the unfortunate assistant simply had different reaction times from himself. This eventually led to the systematic study of this particular human variation, and then of others, which is still going on. Then there was the age-old attempt to classify individuals, going back to the search by the earliest philosophers of classical Greece for the ultimate constituents of matter. The theory that these were earth, air, fire and water, and that there were derivatively four components of the human constitution and four types of personality, persists to our own time and is indeed not inconsistent with some modern theory. Fourthly we may mention the interest in heredity, brought sharply into focus with Darwin's *Origin of Species* in 1859. Fifthly there was a movement toward the systematic assessment of individuals: Esquirol in 1838 proposed a system of grading levels of mental deficiency, and Galton devised many ingenious techniques of measurement, the forerunners of a multitude of psychological tests. Finally there was, especially in the nineteenth century, a growing interest in comparative studies: of different species, of cultures and races, of adults and children.

The last two lines overlap with a parallel development, that of the study of children. Educational theorists such as Jean-Jacques Rousseau (1712–38), J.H. Pestalozzi (1746–1827) and F. Froebel (1782–1852) brought to prominence the idea of children as something other than miniature adults. Darwin himself made a start on detailed observation of children with his *Biographical Sketch of an Infant* (1877). A more extensive work is *The Mind of the Child* by Wilhelm Preyer (1881), while in the USA G. Stanley Hall, who returned from what was then an almost obligatory period of study in Germany in 1880, lectured on educational problems and undertook a questionnaire study of what Boston primary school children knew. (Eighty per cent knew that milk comes from cows, but only 6 per cent where leather originates.) His *Pedagogical Seminary*, 1891, was the first journal to be devoted to the subject: James Sully founded the British Association for Child Study in 1895. Child psychology rapidly became a proliferating discipline and profession, as it remains. The complexity of its successes and failures cannot be traced here. We should note that, overall, the greatest concentration has been firstly on diagnosis and treatment of deficiencies and problems, and secondly on psychological assessment of the whole range of ability for purposes of guidance and selection. Exceptional children at the upper end of scales of ability of any sort have received relatively far less attention.

The same is true, of course, of psychology as a whole. This is so despite the fact that one of Galton's principal aims was to understand exceptional individuals. Indeed, his first epoch-making work in 1869 was entitled *Hereditary Genius: An inquiry into its laws and consequences*. Galton begins by explaining what he is to count as genius, and the book (like all his writings) is original and fascinating. Galton was entranced by measurement, and it occurred to him to:

look upon social and professional life as a continuous examination. All are candidates for the good opinions of others, and for success in their several professions, and they achieve success in proportion as the general estimate is large of their aggregate marks. . . . The world . . . almost unconsciously allots marks to men. It gives them for originality of conception, for enterprise, for activity and energy, for administrative skill, for various acquirements, for power of literary expression, for oratory and much besides of general value, as well as for more specially professional merits. . . . Those who have gained most of these tacit marks are ranked, by the common judgment of the leaders of opinion, as the foremost men of their day.

This may seem to reflect Galton's stable Victorian world, in which merit will, in general, rise (although he noted it might often not be recognized until past the age of 50), so that reputation is a reasonable index of ability. It is also a Darwinian world of the survival of the fittest – actually Herbert Spencer's phrase. What is fundamentally new is the notion that merit can be assigned a numerical value. Once that is done behaviour can be analysed mathematically: what had until then been the preserve of opinion and tradition is for the first time brought within the bounds of science. This was ten years before the conventional date for the beginnings of scientific psychology with the establishment of Wundt's laboratory at Leipzig. It should also be noted that Galton is concerned with what can be observed, and with a wide range of it, rather than with an abstracted entity such as intelligence.

Galton started by calculating the numbers of persons achieving different levels of reputation. Most of his attention was focused on those of 'extraordinary genius' so great as for them to total not more than 400 throughout history. The history of the western world, one assumes, but the argument is not affected. The argument was, after establishing the range of differences, that most of this can be attributed to heredity, and consequently that it lies within the power of the human race to improve itself from generation to generation by systematic eugenics. As we have seen, this idea has revived in recent times.

Galton, working with established reputations, was less interested in ability in childhood, although in *Inquiries into Human Faculty* (1883) he noted among other things that children's imagery was often stronger than that of adults and their hearing more acute. *A Study of British Genius*, by Havelock Ellis (1904), takes a somewhat similar starting-point, a selection of 975 men and 55 women from the *Dictionary of National Biography*. Ellis, a contemporary and almost a counterpart of Freud, whose largest work was the multi-volume *Studies in the Psychology of Sex*, here analysed, among other things, the childhoods of his subjects. He noted, for example, a frequency of constitutional delicacy in infancy and early life – at least 213 cases – though later they were often robust. But the chief feature of his data was precocity, which took one of three forms: exceptional ability at the general run of studies; engrossment in a particular speciality; or extreme physical activity, even brutality. The first occurred both in those who were, and were not, later outstanding (although all were good enough to reach the Dictionary of National Biography). This suggested to Ellis the existence of two sorts of ability. In general, the biographies showed 292 of the 1,030 as being in some sense precocious, and only 44 as definitely not precocious. Precocity was most marked in musicians and artists (40 of 64). There was a suggestion that the physically precocious do not achieve later intellectual eminence. Precocity was not the same as achievement:

> It scarcely appears that any actual achievements of note date from early youth. It is only in mathematics, and to some extent in poetry, that originality may be attained at an early age, but even then it is very rare (Newton and Kant are examples), and it is not notable until adolescence is completed.

Ellis's work is, in general, descriptive rather than theoretical. Theory in the twentieth century took the route of testing and analysing general cognitive ability – intelligence. One very major investigation, that of Lewis Terman, was made of the upper end of the spectrum (see Chapter 3). Leta S. Hollingworth studied twelve *Children Above 180 IQ* (1942). F.D. Mitchell (1907) published on mathematical prodigies, and G. Révész (1925) made a detailed study of one musical prodigy. F. Baumgarten's *Wunderkinder Psychologische Untersuchungen* (1930) is perhaps the only other major work of this period on child prodigies. Baumgarten studied nine outstanding children: two pianists, two violinists, one orchestral leader, one artist, one geographer and one chess wonder. She stressed their normal though very distinct personalities; personalities containing an unusual mixture of child and adult (summary from Feldman, 1980). F. Barlow's *Mental Prodigies* (1952) is a collection of material about various mental feats including calculating, chess, music and memory, as well as stage magic.

However the study of intelligence began to appear inadequate; it did not seem to account for many achievements, especially those that required new or original thinking. With an echo of Galton, creativity came into fashion from about 1950. Wallach (1985), among others, tells the story. But the testing and analysis of creativity, which often seemed to reduce to relatively trivial tasks such as thinking of novel uses for a brick, was far less theoretically sophisticated, less valid and reliable, and hence less useful, than that of the somewhat despised intelligence. More recently intelligence has resumed centre stage, with a number of new approaches such as those of Gardner, Sternberg and (quite differently) Eysenck.

Another sort of reaction to conventional psychology was the so-called 'third force' of humanistic psychology. Ill-named and somewhat ill-defined, it nevertheless helped to redress the balance of behaviourism and psychometrics by focusing once more on the human individual. Gowan (1977) sees in it the origins of what is currently, in the 1980s, a thriving interest in gifted children. Humanistic psychology, the legacy according to Gowan of William James, embraces first a broad humanism; second, the measurement of individual differences; third, intelligence and gifted children; fourth, creativity; fifth, development; and last, possibly parapsychology. These areas are connected by a sense of the dignity of man, by measurement and by a concern for the individual. While this is a somewhat idiosyncratic view of the nature and role of humanistic psychology, there is no doubt that all these elements have come together.

Definitions

It is in this context that studies of gifted and talented children are appearing. Sometimes those terms are used, occasionally 'genius' (e.g. Adams, 1988) and 'prodigy' (e.g. Feldman, 1986b).

Attempts have been made to define all these. Albert (1975) for example offers a behavioural definition of genius which is quite Galtonian: a genius is one who '. . . produces, over a long period of time, a large body of work that has a significant influence on many persons for many years'. Giftedness, the term of the moment, is sometimes defined as ability measured in standard ways, either by intelligence tests or a wider range of tests (Baldwin, 1985; Humphreys, 1985). Sternberg and Davidson (1985) argue that this wider range should include intellectual, artistic, physical, and what they term niche-fitting skills, the last seeming to mean general social competence. Tannenbaum (1986) thinks that giftedness (in children) should refer to potential, rather than achievement, since the latter does not appear before adulthood.

A prodigy, according to the *Concise Oxford Dictionary*, is a 'marvellous thing, esp. one out of the course of nature; wonderful example of (some quality); person endowed with surprising qualities, esp. precocious child'. My title glosses the term 'child prodigies' with 'exceptional early achievers' in an attempt to cast the net wide enough for phenomena that it seems interesting to discuss together, or that a reader might expect to find. 'Achievers' means that interest is focused on what children actually do, rather than on possibilities that may show themselves later; but not on physical qualities such as unusual height. 'Early' normally means under 21, but generally much younger depending on the particular activity. And 'exceptional' means, as Humpty Dumpty said, what you want it to mean. Or rather, it depends on the context. Playing a musical instrument, even in simple fashion, would be exceptional at the age of 2 or 3; as it is for a child of any age who is otherwise mentally retarded, or autistic. Indeed it is not very common among normal adults, though it might well be possible to make it so. Speaking even a few words before 12 months is exceptional, as is winning at Wimbledon at 17. It is perhaps less helpful to attempt anything more definite. In particular, it does not seem satisfactory to restrict the word 'prodigy' to performances of children that are equivalent to those of adults, as some writers suggest. For one thing, standards change: less than a hundred years ago public school boys commonly wrote Greek verse, which very few adults could match now. Even if the comparison is restricted to the same time, the question arises as to which adults are to be the standard. Even the most remarkable prodigies such as Mozart did not, at least until their teens, produce work of lasting merit in adult terms, though what Mozart did produce would be an extraordinary accomplishment for most of us. Indeed, if the work of children is always to be measured against the highest adult standards, there would probably be none who could be called prodigies at all. Not too many of the population could pass GCE mathematics 'A' level. No-one, however, would wish to call this prodigious at the normal age of 18, or even 17, but it certainly is at 9. There seems little point in trying to establish a cut-off point.

3 Top of the Class

Lewis N. Terman's studies of genius

True democracy demands that every child, whether superior, average, or
inferior in ability, be given the fullest opportunity to develop to the limit of
his mental capacity. (Terman, 1929, cited Seagoe, 1975)

This sentiment led Lewis N. Terman to initiate what remains
the largest and longest, and perhaps the most influential, study
of gifted children ever undertaken. Terman (1877–1956), a man
of vast energy and scholarly thoroughness, devoted his long life
to the promotion and use of psychometrics – measurement of
individual differences. In the tradition stemming directly from
Galton (whose childhood he studied exhaustively, as an example of genius), Terman concentrated on mental capacity
assessed by standardized tests. While this covered the whole
spectrum – his Ph.D. at Clark University was published as
Genius and Stupidity (1906) – it was the upper end that
occupied him most.

Early in his career Terman began to study individually highly
gifted children, some of whom could read by the age of 2. The
most remarkable of these prodigies was probably Henry
Cowell, a boy of great musical gifts who, coming from a poor
and broken home, was largely self-taught. At the age of 12 he
was supporting himself and his mother by working as a school
caretaker, playing the piano when he could get access to one
and teaching himself botany. Terman believed that talent in the
arts was highly specialized, but that high intelligence was also
needed for achievement. This Henry had, and Terman considered his the most original mind among his various protégés.

41

Cowell later married a rich girl and wrote novel, if not particularly influential music (Seagoe, 1975). Other factors are also needed for success, it seems.

In 1921 Terman obtained the first of several then very large research grants – some $200,000 in all, to which he added substantial sums of his own – to undertake an extensive study of gifted children. Terman at first used the word 'genius' but felt it implied something peculiar, whereas 'gifted' referred only to the upper end of the normal curve of ability. Terman spent his academic career at Stanford University in California, and his gifted children, aged between 2 and 13 but mostly around 10, came from schools in that state. Terman's method was to have teachers nominate their brightest children, who were then assessed first by a group and then by an individual test of intelligence. The IQ range was 130–190, with a mode (most frequent score) around 140.

It is worth pausing to explain what is not always known even after it has been in common use for seventy years – that the Intelligence Quotient or IQ is an index derived from performance on a specified test, for which scores have been obtained from a specified population. These scores form a distribution with a midpoint given the value of 100. An IQ of 100 means that an individual has scored on a particular test at a level equivalent to those coming at the centre of the distribution. To put it loosely, that individual is of average intelligence. But this has to be taken with two qualifications: intelligence as assessed by a particular test, and as manifested by a particular set of people. Some of the complexities of this are explored in Chapter 9. Furthermore, the midpoint of 100 is the only one that is common to all tests. As with the scales on thermometers, an IQ of any other value has to be interpreted (to say the temperature today will be 30 degrees means nothing without the addition of 'Fahrenheit' or 'Celsius'). Of course one can see at once that an IQ is above or below average, and in general about 120 would mark the beginning of (say) a population of university students, 150 would be around the top of the class, and 200 would mark the few most able persons in history. Here though are further qualifications, one being the extent to which performance in general corresponds to test performance, which in turn depends both on how alike are the test and the real life activity and on the host of factors that determine what an individual actually does as compared to what they are capable of.

It turned out for Terman's subjects that the best predictor of high test scores was not teachers' ratings but age – the youngest child in a class was usually the brightest. The criterion for selection was the highest ½ per cent in the population as a whole. Terman identified in this way a total of 1,528 children whose parents agreed to their taking part, of whom 661 were studied more intensively. Records were made of racial and social origin, physical measurements, health and physical history, medical examinations, educational history, school accomplishments, specialized abilities, interests, character and personality.

The overall results showed that the highly intelligent were generally also superior according to every other standard by which they were assessed. They exceeded the average most markedly in intellectual and motivational traits; next in emotional and moral qualities; and least in physical and social characteristics, though they were still superior here.

Every sociocultural group present in California was represented, with Jews the most numerous minority. Boys exceeded girls in the ratio of 116 to 100. The homes of the gifted children were somewhat above average in socioeconomic status, and two-thirds of the fathers were in professional, semi-professional or higher business occupations. Divorce and separation rates among the parents were below average. A greater proportion of both parents and grandparents had completed high school than average. Parents showed little sign of pushing their children into early achievement: for example they did not teach reading early; but they responded with interest to children's curiosity and supplied words and books when asked for them.

School achievement was in general nearly as far above average as intelligence, as might be expected. On tests of personality and character, the gifted were as mature at the age of 9 as most children at 14. They were more than normally generous, honest, persistent, goal-oriented, conscientious and socially concerned. They were less than normally conceited, nervous and emotionally unstable. In social behaviour, the gifted group were near the norm, though they spent fewer hours playing, played alone more and preferred older playmates. They read omnivorously and had many hobbies.

At birth, the group were taller and heavier than average. They walked and talked early, and were more often breast-fed. They were normal or above normal on all medical tests except for there being a slightly higher proportion of eye difficulty (Terman, 1925).

These were essentially group investigations, but Terman does give case studies, for example of the highest scorers in each age group. One HMJ had an IQ of 192 at 6 years 9 months. She scored exceptionally high on arithmetic, but low on music and art. She learned to read at 3, when she could also count to 100. Before she was 6, to while away a Sunday afternoon she mentally carried the powers of two to twenty (1,048,576), when her father stopped her for fear of tiring her.

These results were influential in many ways. They tended to confirm a notion of giftedness as being primarily intellectual and specifically involving tested intelligence, with other traits less central. They seemed conclusively to disprove traditional notions of the bright child as being below average in other ways – the weakly, introverted swot. They strengthened the view that very high ability is best seen as the upper end of a continuum, rather than as a unique special quality possessed by a few. And they led, eventually, to current interest in and provision for gifted children.

A further special feature of Terman's programme is that it has been systematically carried on ever since: the group has been followed up at intervals, though it is now, in the 1980s, declining in numbers. What the follow-ups (e.g. Terman and Oden, 1947, 1959; Oden, 1968; Janos, 1987) have shown is that the group remains, on average, superior: the central trait measured, intelligence, tends to remain the most stable, but the others diversify more. This has the effect that as the group gets older, individuals vary more widely in 'success' considered as 'the extent to which a subject made use of his intellectual ability'. This was assessed by such criteria as listing in *Who's Who* or *American Men of Science*, literary or scholarly publications, responsible managerial positions, achievement in professions, and so on. Many of these increase with age and thus the initially successful individual draws further away from the less successful. The more successful differ from the less relatively little on intellectual tests – after all, the whole group was initially very high indeed – but more on social and mental adjustment, on family background, and on perseverance, self-confidence and integration towards goals.

It is also noticeable that despite achievements which are in general well above average, and in many cases markedly so, the group does not seem to have produced any individuals of the very highest calibre – say Nobel prize level. This might be chance: such persons are so very rare that even this large sample might well not include one; or it might be that they do not show up as very gifted children.

Finally the study does not of itself explain why the gifted are gifted: clearly in this group both inherited and environmental factors are likely to have played a part.

Exceptional promise

In his major programme Terman was not concerned with individual prodigies as such. Taking her lead largely from his research, however, Leta S. Hollingworth (1942) gave an account of twelve *Children Above 180 IQ*. She took family and individual histories and many psychometric measures, but the quality of these children comes out more in a qualitative way. (Pseudonyms were used because such children are perfectly capable of reading published research reports about themselves and possibly being embarrassed by them, though one may doubt that.) Thus Child A: before the age of 3 A

objected to stories containing gross absurdities. For example he rejected the story of the gingham dog and the calico cat who 'ate each other up'. A pointed out that this could not be, 'because one of their mouths would have to get eaten up before the other mouth, and no mouth would be left to eat that mouth'. He was irritated by this obvious lapse from logic and requested that the story be read to him no more.

Several of these exceptional children for a time had imaginary companions or imaginary worlds. For example Child D. 'From the age of about 4 years to about the age of 7, D was greatly interested in an imaginary land which he called "Born-ingtown". He spent many hours peopling Borningtown, laying out roads, drawing maps of its terrain, composing and record-ing its language (Bornish), and writing its history and liter-ature. He composed a lengthy dictionary – scores of pages – of the Bornish language.' Such fantasies are not peculiar to children of high ability, but one is struck by the almost adult complexity; it is quite reminiscent of the elaborate pseudo-scholarship underlying Tolkien's *Lord of the Rings*. D was also extremely talented in music, art and science, in which he graduated at 16 years and 2 months, only to die prematurely at 28.

Again, Child H, a girl, was a prolific writer of verse, for example:

If I had Aladdin's lamp, you see,
I'd give one wish to you and me
And then we'd wish for every toy
That every child should have some joy. (age 5½)

On the clover fields he roams
In the mountains
At the homes
Makes the trees and flowers grow
And manufactures pure, white snow.
– God – (age 8½)

Admittedly hardly great poetry, but more than most adults could easily produce. The second example is almost like an Anglo-Saxon riddle.

Hollingworth drew some general conclusions from her case studies and from research generally. One was just how exten-sive the range of ability is: 'The child at the top of this group exceeds the child who barely reaches the group by much more than the latter exceeds the average child'. In accordance with the findings of Terman, Hollingworth's subjects were generally physically well developed, but she adds a finding that in an experiment, the faces of highly intelligent adolescents were judged to be more beautiful than those of average ability. This does not seem to have been followed up (Liggett, 1974). Hollingworth points out that, in contrast to those of low ability, children of very superior intelligence are not 'socially annoying'. They may have problems of personality adjustment, but these arise from the difficulty of fitting in with an average society. This may be one reason for the prevalence of fantasy – it is difficult to find real companions of comparable size, mentality and interests. One of her children, an early and avid reader, on starting school, was greatly distressed because the other children not only rejected the books he wanted to share with them but laughed at him and indeed bullied him for his peculiar tastes. Hollingworth notes similar accounts from an early study of the boyhood of eminent men by Yuder (1894).

Hollingworth's general conclusion is worth quoting:

As far as observations go at present, intellectually gifted children between 130 and 150 IQ seem to find the world suited to their development. As a group, they enjoy the advantages of superior size, strength, health, and beauty; they are emotionally well-balanced and controlled; they are of good character; and they tend to win the confidence of their contemporaries, which gives them leadership. This is the 'optimum' range of intelligence, if personal happiness is being considered. . . . Above this limit, however – surely above IQ 160 – the deviation is so great that it leads to special problems of development which are correlated with personal isolation. As one boy with an IQ of 190 has said: 'It isn't good to be in a college so awfully young (12). It produces a feeling of alienation'.

Clearly much depends on the particular circumstances of the individual, and, currently, less weight would probably be put on IQ, but there is at least a potential problem.

The other side of this problem is the extra attention that unusual ability may attract. In the 1940s and early 1950s a group of children became famous in the USA as the Quiz Kids, taking part in game shows and knowledge contests on radio and TV. Terman said at the time: 'I predict for (them) life success far beyond the average'. They all had very high IQs, but were also selected on grounds of personality. One of them, Ruth Duskin Feldman, later published an account of their subsequent careers (1982). It turned out that, on the whole, they did better than Terman's top half of one per cent in terms of academic distinction and successful careers. One of them was James D. Watson, joint Nobel prize winner in 1962 for the discovery of the structure of DNA. Even so, it seems that they did not as a group reach the supereminence that their early achievements might suggest. Feldman points out that these were based on certain traits – knowing the right answers, while at the same time being cute and modest and waiting to be called on – which may not necessarily be the most effective in adult life. She also suggests that exceptionally creative individuals may well not be found on quiz shows, being too occupied in pursuing their own special interests.

An investigation that is in some ways a British counterpart to that of Terman, although much less extensive, was reported by E.M. Hitchfield in 1973. A sample of 238 gifted children born between 3 and 9 March 1958, were studied between the ages of 7 and 11. They were selected on the basis of the Goodenough Draw-A-Man Test (effectively, intelligence), high attainment in reading and number, and parental recommendation. Hitchfield warns against oversimplifying the concept of giftedness. There is no well-established map of abilities, and of the 'subjects' to which they are related:

individual children may stand out from their peers by reason of their advanced skill in a sport, or their advanced ability in mathematics, or music, or language, and though each one is alike in terms of the 'standing out from' or 'advancement over' his peers, they may have no other defining attributes in common. Yet all studies focussed on 'giftedness' search for common attributes.

If such attributes are found in a sample, the danger is that they may be used as a kind of definition. So, for example, because any group of gifted children will tend to have high intelligence, this becomes the defining characteristic of giftedness. It is also the case that some sorts of ability stand out early much more clearly than others. Hitchfield mentions music, and one might add mathematics and chess. For this reason tests of intelligence or reasoning, which at least enter into many different capabilities, are probably the best means of distinguishing those who are likely to do well. But it must be remembered that high test scores do not necessarily mean that children will stand out in any particular school subject. School subjects are only a sample of what it is possible to be good at, and are affected by amount and quality of teaching, educational opportunities and social conditions; as well as such individual variables as interest and motivation.

The broken twig

All the research so far quoted, and indeed all that is available, shows that early promise in general carries through into later achievement, though not necessarily consistently or evenly, nor in every individual case. Yet it sometimes seems that the opposite view is held, that prodigies will 'burn out' or otherwise come to nothing. There may be in this a lingering element of the 'genius next to madness' notion. Kathleen Montour (1977) thinks that much is due to one particular case, that of William James Sidis (1898–1944), sometimes called 'the world's greatest child prodigy' (Wallace, 1986), and probably more famous in the USA than elsewhere. He was the son of an unusual father. Boris Sidis was a Russian Jewish emigré who, knowing no English on arrival in America, graduated from Harvard University, took Ph.D. and M.D. degrees, and became well known as a medical psychologist, although often regarded as a crank for his ideas on education. He taught his wife Sarah, also an immigrant, English, and she too qualified in medicine. Their son was named after the philosopher and psychologist William James, some of whose ideas Dr Sidis passionately espoused. One of these was that living organisms possess stores of normally unused energy which can be tapped and put to use if the organism is forced, or forces itself, past an initial layer of fatigue. In pursuance of this, he educated his son largely at home. In fact his methods now appear quite Montessori-like, and little more unusual than those of the parents of the 'children on the hill'. The significant differences were, first, that Dr Sidis did not, like them, avoid publicity but positively courted it, boasting of his son's achievements and future success, which were due in his view not to the latter's ability but to the method; and second, his failure to provide emotional security.

Certainly the early achievements were sufficiently remarkable. William's training in reasoning and logic began before the age of 2; one of his father's beliefs was that education was generally started too late. By 3 he read fluently, by 4 he used a typewriter, by 5 he read in Russian, French and German as well as English. At 6 he entered a grammar school and in the six months he was there passed easily through all seven grades. Before he was 8 he had passed the entrance examination for Massachusetts Institute of Technology and the Harvard Medical School anatomy examination (anatomy was one of his enthusiasms). At the same age he devised a table of logarithms using the base twelve instead of ten. Although eligible academically he was refused admission to Harvard at 9 as being too young, and was eventually admitted at 11. Shortly after his arrival he gave a lecture to the Harvard Mathematical Club on the subject of the fourth dimension. A contemporary of his was another remarkable prodigy, Norbert Wiener, the pioneer of cybernetics. Wiener later wrote: 'The talk would have done credit to a first or second year graduate student of any age. . . . Sidis had no access to existing sources' – thus the content was his own.

Both the lecture, which in retrospect can be seen as his academic high point, and his early entry brought increased publicity, and this was to dog Sidis throughout his life. He graduated at the age of 16 but shortly after was arrested for taking part in a radical protest march. This would mean little now, but at that time and for that person it was a shock, and one the press exploited to the full. Sidis started on graduate work but failed to complete it. He obtained a college teaching post but lacked the personal maturity to make a success of it. He dropped out of academic life and public view, taking a series of low-paid clerical jobs, apparently seeking a less demanding life. The press now found his failures as good a story as his early successes. On a later occasion in 1937 when once again he was pilloried as an inadequate eccentric Sidis sued, taking the case up to the highest level but ultimately failing. Sidis did publish two books, one a serious work on the philosophy of science, but never achieved any recognition. He died destitute and unemployed, though he did not, as some rumours had it, commit suicide.

This sad and unfulfilled life appeared to exemplify proverbial wisdom such as 'early ripe, early rot'; but it is, in fact, as we have seen, quite untypical. Montour points out some of the reasons for what happened, particularly in contrast to the successful career of Wiener. He too had an ambitious and demanding father, also a self-made Russian Jew who used his son to illustrate his educational theories. Whereas Boris Sidis kept his son mainly at home, however, Leo Wiener sent his to public schools (in the American sense), although only for a short time. Where Sidis insisted on Harvard as the most prestigious institution available, Wiener chose the more modest Tuft's College, where Norbert graduated at 14 before going on to Harvard. When his son came under attack, Wiener defended him stoutly in public; Boris Sidis, on the other hand, disowned his son when he failed to live up to expectations. Leo Wiener sought to avoid undue attention to his son's achievements and stressed his ordinariness, in contrast to the publicity-seeking Sidis. Despite this, Norbert Wiener had, like William Sidis, a difficult adolescence, and only made the transition from a father-dominated, socially inept prodigy to adult at around thirty. This was due at least partly to the support of his wife; Sidis never succeeded in forming a comparable stable relationship. This in turn probably reflects the inability of either of his parents to supply the emotional security a child, particularly such an odd and isolated one, must have needed. A combination of emotional starvation and parental exploitation, exacerbated by continual hostile publicity, and not his original talents or even his education as such, produced the unhappy life of William James Sidis.

Fortunately, as Montour (1976) points out, such a set of circumstances is rare if not unique. She quotes several examples of early college entrants who were later successful, from Paul Dudley who was at 10 actually the youngest person to enter Harvard – not Sidis, as is sometimes said. Admittedly this was in the late seventeenth century, when colleges fulfilled more the role of high schools. But A.A. Berle entered at 14, and later became Secretary of State under Franklin D. Roosevelt. Verill Kenneth Wolfe (he who had spoken so precociously) graduated from Yale at 14 and became a professor of neuroanatomy at the University of Massachusetts. Robert B. Woodward graduated from Massachusetts Institute of Technology at 19 and later won the Nobel prize for chemistry.

Montour also gives the life-histories of three anonymous

children, one of whom, named as E, had been one of Hollingworth's subjects. E was born in 1908, and when first studied at the age of 8 was assessed as having an IQ of 187. His verbal ability was particularly high. For example, on a test of definitions he gave for 'harpy' 'a kind of half-bird, half-woman, referred to in Virgil', and for 'mosaic' 'a picture made of many small pieces of marble'. Oddly, perhaps, he did not speak until he was 2, but could read by 3. In addition to his school work he was studying geometry and algebra (as far as equations), and to varying degrees, Latin, Greek, German, Spanish, Portuguese, Hebrew and Anglo-Saxon. He was also greatly interested in astronomy (Garrison, Burke and Hollingworth, 1917).

E enrolled at Columbia University at 12 and graduated at 14 (in 1923). He took a doctorate in 1931, but meanwhile had turned to religion, taking several degrees in theology and becoming a minister of the Episcopal church; from 1972 he was Dean of Chapel of Jesus College, Cambridge, a fact which rather invalidates the anonymity. (Presumably he has now, 1989, retired.)

Another of these children, M, entered Harvard at 15 and took a first degree at 18, followed by an MA at 19 and a Ph.D. at 21. He joined the staff of the University of California, but published little and failed to gain rapid promotion, not being created full professor until 65. His main interest had become music. Finally L, who passed the Harvard entrance examination at 12 and was admitted at 14. At 3 he had been fluent in, and could read, both English and German, a fact not realized when he went to school at 5 until his teacher found him reading a newspaper. His ambition always was to become a professor of classics, to which end he taught himself Latin and Greek. His family however wanted him to follow his father into medicine. He graduated with high honours from Harvard at 18 and went to Oxford where he took another first degree and an MA, but left before completing a doctorate. Unable to find a permanent academic post he qualified in medicine, served in the Army Medical Corps in the Second World War, and after it took on his father's old practice. He retained an academic interest by lecturing occasionally on the religion he had adopted, that of witchcraft.

Although Montour presents these histories as examples of

success following early achievement, in contrast to William Sidis, it is rather obvious that in each case the later years, while very far from representing failure, do not equal the exceptional performances of childhood and youth. Nevertheless Montour is probably right to regard Sidis as a particularly unfortunate exception. In similar vein, Lenneberg (1980) describes the 'myth of the unappreciated (musical) genius'. He presents evidence that several composers popularly supposed to have been unappreciated, either critically or financially or both, were in fact well received and/or paid; in particular Schumann, Schubert, Berlioz, Beethoven and Mozart. Lenneberg thinks the myth a Romantic notion which is related to Freud's concept of creativity as compensation, and which is not true of other artistic periods.

Parents and teachers

An historical parallel to Sidis and to Wiener is the case of John Stuart Mill (1806–1873), whose name generally figures in any short list of child prodigies – in that of Cox (1926) at the very top. His father James Mill, son of a Scottish shoemaker, was Examiner of India Correspondence, that is effectively chief executive, of the East India Company, which then governed large parts of India; a post into which his son eventually followed him. Apart from this demanding occupation his energies were devoted to philosophy and political science, and for some years to educating his son with a view to carrying forward his work in those areas. John Stuart Mill's *Autobiography* shows us a most unusual childhood. James Mill formed and carried out a systematic plan of education, which depended in the first instance on what now might be called 'milieu control':

he . . . carefully kept me from having any great amount of intercourse with other boys. He was earnestly bent upon my escaping not only the corrupting influence which boys exercise over boys, but the contagion of vulgar modes of thought and feeling . . . no holidays were allowed, lest the habit of work should be broken, and a taste for idleness acquired.

On the other hand 'I had ample leisure each day to amuse

myself', but this was mainly alone. In his plan of education James Mill spared neither himself nor his son, teaching him at the same time as he was actually writing his own massive works. 'My father, in all his teaching, demanded of me not only the utmost that I could do, but much that I could by no possibility have done.' This began with Greek at the age of 3, and in the next few years Mill read substantial parts of the classics as well as a great deal in English, especially history. Everything he read he made notes on, and the next day gave an account of it to his father as they took a morning walk in what were then the green fields of Stoke Newington. Evenings were devoted to mathematics, which he disliked.

Whether from natural inclination or training, Mill seems to have enjoyed most of this extraordinary regime. At 7 his father gave him Pope's translation of Homer, a work now read only by scholars but which quickly became a favourite. Mill says he would not have mentioned 'a taste so natural to boyhood' had he not noticed that 'the keen enjoyment of this brilliant specimen of narrative and versification is not so universal with boys, as I should have expected both *a priori* and from my individual experience'. (Jeremy Bentham had read it at the age of 6 'with extreme satisfaction' – Cox, 1926). Mill in fact did not regard himself as unusual; he had no one to compare himself with, and later held that anyone could do what he had done if only taught correctly. In some ways at least James Mill's methods have a modern ring. For example, having introduced Greek, he spent little time on grammar but went on as soon as possible to translation. And, says Mill:

There was one cardinal point in this training . . . which, more than anything else, was the cause of whatever good it effected . . . My father never permitted anything which I learnt to degenerate into a mere exercise of memory. He strove to make the understanding not only go along with every step of the teaching, but, if possible, precede it. Anything which could be found out by thinking I never was told, until I had exhausted my efforts to find it out for myself.

John Stuart Mill's reputation stands higher than that of his father, who in that sense could be said to have succeeded in his aims. It is clear, however, that it cost the son considerable effort, and almost a complete breakdown, to develop away from his father's tutelage, and to produce original work of his own. At 20 it suddenly seemed to him that all he had done was pointless: '. . . the whole foundation on which my life was constructed fell down. . . . I seemed to have nothing left to live for.' Isolated as he still was Mill had no one to turn to, and realized that his father would probably have been unable either to understand or to help. Eventually it seems his own natural resilience carried him through. Shaw (1982) and Kelly (1985) describe how he at least partially resolved the conflict between his father's influence and the need for autonomy, at the same time achieving a sense of self and of sexual maturity; the one romance of his life was with a married woman whom he met in 1830 but who was not free to marry him until 1851.

Ambitious and demanding parents are perhaps not such a rare phenomenon; certainly they are more frequent than prodigies, and they are not always male. Montour (1977) quotes Winifred Stoner who, rather like Boris Sidis, reared her daughter to be a genius. The girl obediently produced poems at 3 and plays at 7, but after her mother's death in 1928 did nothing more. A parent is likely to be the most motivated and readily available adult to devote themselves to a child's education, but, as is suggested by the famous cases just described, emotional factors are likely to complicate things. Other individuals besides parents can certainly play the most significant role. There has been considerable interest in what have come to be called 'mentors'. The concept has ancient and aristocratic roots: the original Mentor was chosen by Ulysses to guard, guide and teach his son Telemachus.

Torrance (1983) repeats an observation he had made in 1962 of the frequency – 'almost always', he claims – with which creative, independent achievement is associated with some other person who takes the part of a sponsor or patron: someone

who is not a member of the peer group, but who possesses prestige and power in the same social system. This person does several things. He/she encourages and supports the other in expressing and testing his/her ideas and in thinking through things. He/she protects the individual from the reactions of peers and superiors long enough for the person to try out ideas and modify them. He can keep the structure of the system open enough for originality to occur and persist, if found valid.

As part of a long-term twenty-two-year study of 212 young adults, Torrance found that having a mentor was significantly correlated with various criteria of adult creativity, and with completed years in higher education. Ninety-seven of the sample reported having had a mentor, and although this hardly justifies the claim of 'almost always', it is clearly consistent with the biographical evidence of extra attention from (usually) one adult so often found in outstanding individuals. None of this conclusively shows a causal relationship; it might be that potential mentors tend to seek out, or to stick with, the more able protégés.

Here we approach the formal role of a teacher, some of whom act in just such a role. An example among many is the remarkable 'master of novices' at Eton and King's College, Cambridge, Oscar Browning (1837–1923), a man of that eccentricity that so often marks notable teachers (Wortham, 1927). Jere Brophy (1986), reviewing research on teacher influences on student achievement, concludes that students achieve more when their teachers emphasize academic objectives in establishing expectations and allocating time, use effective management strategies to ensure that academic learning time is maximized, pace students through the curriculum briskly but in small steps that allow high rates of success and adopt curriculum materials based on their knowledge of students' characteristics. None of this would probably surprise a good teacher, nor even Leo Wiener, Boris Sidis or James Mill.

Nor Dr Thomas Arnold, possibly the most famous of professional teachers. 'Arnold of Rugby' (1795–1842) is popularly credited with having virtually created the British public school in its nineteenth-century form. In fact his main interests were in religious and social reform, and his fame rests largely on the effect he had on a small number of particularly gifted pupils to whom he was an inspired teacher (Bamford, 1960). He would have added to Brophy's list another important item, the need for the teacher to be also an enthusiast for learning: 'If the mind once becomes stagnant, it can give no fresh draught to another mind; it is drinking out of a pond instead of from a stream'. Arnold's influence depended largely on personal and emotional relationships, which may have been the stronger for his own personal conflicts and erratic temper.

Six more prodigies

D.H. Feldman (1986b) quotes an (anonymous) parent who wrote to him that her son, at about 22 months, became interested in languages, and in the next couple of years studied Hebrew, classical Greek, French, Italian, Russian, Spanish, Yiddish, German, Egyptian hieroglyphics and Sanskrit. He then appeared to lose interest, and on being asked why this was so explained that he had found the answer to the question he had had. 'I've figured out', he said, 'that there was a parent language for these languages [he listed the Indo-European ones] but not for these. It had eleven cases.'

Feldman considers that children such as this reveal talents and abilities 'out of the usual course of nature', which cannot be explained by possession of high intelligence 'or any other relatively simple explanation'. He describes, in greater or lesser detail, six children who can hardly be called anything other than prodigies. All the names are fictitious. Nils Kirkendahl already wanted to learn music just before his third birthday, and started Suzuki classes just after. He was developing into a potential concert artist. Franklin Montana started playing chess at 4. This was a passion for a time but later he turned to sport and business. 'He liked to get very good at something and then leave it.' Ricky Velasquez also took up chess at 4 but was a good all-rounder, later mainly interested in sport but also gifted academically. Billy Devlin was outstandingly precocious in reading and mathematics, entered high school at 9 and graduated from it at 14, then turned to physics and engineering at state university. Adam Konantowitch by the age of 3½ read and wrote, spoke several languages, was studying mathematics and composing for the guitar. At 10 his interest was mainly in composing. Finally, Randy McDaniel at 3 taught himself to type using one finger. This enabled him to write and to turn out a flood of stories, plays and essays. At 14 he was producing mainly lyrics for rock music.

Feldman presents his findings largely in qualitative and descriptive terms. What is it, he asks, that makes these children so different from others?

The answer lies in the fact that these children are special-purpose organisms, designed and geared to perform in a specific field of endeavour. The prodigy seems to be unique in having an extremely specialised gift that is expressed only under very specific, culturally evolved environmental conditions. In contrast, the high-IQ individual possesses generalised intellectual abilities that seem to permit high levels of functioning in a wide range of environments.

It is worth spending a moment on this since it seems to be virtually the only recent attempt to say something specific about prodigies, rather than the gifted in general. What is said, though, is not entirely clear. First of all Feldman begins his book by objecting to the modern tendency to restrict the meaning of 'prodigy'. But in order to restore some of the old 'out of the usual course of nature' meaning, he in effect restricts it still further by ruling out the merely very highly intelligent. This makes his account circular, for he first defines prodigies as those with an extremely specialized gift, and then concludes that this is what they 'seem to be'. Then, it is clear from his own accounts that even his selected six prodigies are not in fact restricted to one specialized talent. Franklin Montana is specifically described as liking to get very good at something and then leave it. Billy Devlin was precocious at both reading and mathematics; most theories of intellectual development regard verbal and numerical ability as relatively independent. Adam Konantowitch was outstanding at both languages and music. Finally, if one adopted Feldman's view rigidly it would appear to rule out calling John Stuart Mill a prodigy, to give just one historical example.

It seems also to rule out Stephen Baccus who, at least according to *The London Standard* for 21 May 1986, was at 17 the youngest person ever to qualify as a lawyer (in the USA), too young in fact to practice. He 'graduated from college at 14, had a vaudeville act at 7, possesses an encyclopaedic memory and crunches numbers like a computer', and has an IQ of 190. At the time of writing he had a difficult career choice to make between law, science, or show business – or, it seems, anything else that took his fancy. According to the report Stephen was the product of a mother who 'believes virtually any child can be a genius if taught to use more brain capacity early enough'. A not unfamiliar notion, though in this case hardly consistent with the observation that Stephen 'taught himself to read with the aid of *Sesame Street* before the age of 2'.

In fact, the research mentioned so far suggests that exceptional ability, whether general or more specialized, is, like any pattern of ability, the product of both potential and upbringing, heredity and environment. To restrict the word 'prodigy' to only one sort of pattern seems unnecessary. What is true is that a very odd impression can be created by some children who happen to excel at something very specific. This is probably true whether their own general ability is good, average or low. As we have seen it has often been the case in the past that any sort of rarity seemed uncanny. It is not clear that extraordinary ability at a very young age in chess or music or mathematics requires a unique sort of explanation, any more than do unfortunate freaks of times past.

4 Sports and Games

Record breakers and young talent

Youthful achievements in sport proliferate, and here are some of them as of 1988. The youngest Olympic athletics gold medallist was Bob Mathias aged 17, in the 1948 decathlon; he won again in 1952. In baseball, the youngest major league player was Henry Nuxhall, who was 15 when he played one game for Cincinnati in 1944. He did not play in the National League (one of the two major leagues) again until 1952. Mike Tyson at 20 was the youngest world heavyweight boxing champion, in 1986. The youngest at any weight was Wilfred Benitez, who won the World Boxing Association version of the light welterweight championship in 1976, at 17. The youngest Test (i.e. international) captain at cricket was the Nawab of Pataudi who was 21 when he led India against the West Indies at Bridgetown in 1962. The youngest Test player was Mushtaq Mohammed, who at 15 played for Pakistan against the West Indies at Lahore in 1959. Cricket records tend to swamp all others in number and complexity, but: Quasim Feroze is reputed to have been the youngest ever first-class player, at two days short of 13, in 1971 for Bahawalpur against Karachi Whites. The youngest English first-class player was Charles Robertson Young, at 15, for Hampshire against Kent in 1867. And of course the highest score ever recorded in any class of cricket stands to a schoolboy, A.E.J. Collins, who made 628 not out in 1899 playing for Charles House against North Town at Clifton Preparatory School. He was 13. An army career prevented him devoting himself to cricket, and he was killed in action in 1914. Another schoolboy, aged 15, Sachin Tendulkar, contributed 329 not out to the highest ever partnership in any

60

cricket, 664 in a schools championship match in Bombay in 1988.

The 1988 British croquet champion was Mark Saurian, aged 17. Andrew Awford at 15 was the youngest player in the Football Association Cup, coming on as substitute for Worcester City in 1987. Tom Morris Jr was the youngest British Open Champion at golf when he won in 1868 at 17. Coby Orr was only 5 when he hit a 94-metre hole in one at San Antonio in 1975. Some of the most consistently youthful achievements are in gymnastics. Pasakevi Kouna was the youngest international winner, at 9 in the Balkan Games of 1981, and Olga Bicherova the youngest world champion, at 15 in the same year. The youngest male world champion was Dmitry Belozerchev, at 16 in 1983. In motor cycle racing Alberto Cecotto of Venezuela was 19 when he became world 350cc champion in 1973. On the other hand the two youngest motor (car) racing champions have both been 22. Rodeo boasts an amateur world champion of 11, Metha Brorsen in 1975, and a professional world champion of 13, Jackie Jo Perrin in 1977. Sonja Henie was Norwegian figure skating champion at 11 and Olympic gold medallist four years later in 1928, winning again in the next two Games, as well as being ten times world champion, from 1927 to 1936. Stephen Hendry at 18 is the youngest winner of a major snooker title. Thomas Gregory in 1988 swam the English Channel at 11 years 11 months, taking the record from his friend Marcus Hooper who did it at 12 in 1979. The youngest girl to have swum the Channel is Samantha Bruce, also 12, in 1983. Gertrude Ederle is said to have been the youngest ever world record breaker in organized sport; she set a time of 13 minutes 19 seconds for the 880-yard women's freestyle swimming event in 1919 at the age of 12.

The youngest Wimbledon champion remains Charlotte 'Lottie' Dod, who won at 15 in 1887. Boris Becker is the youngest male winner, at 17 in 1985. (He has also displayed consistency, retaining his title in 1986, and winning again in 1989.) Mita Klima at 13 is thought to have been the youngest actually to play at Wimbledon, and the youngest to win a match is Kathy Rinaldi, who was 14 in 1967. In the USA the youngest singles winner was Tracy Austin, 16 in 1979. The youngest title winner was Vincent Richards, who won the doubles in 1918 at

15. However, he was partnered by the player soon to be the best in the world, 'Big Bill' Tilden. Richards was one of the many young male protégés with whom Tilden was emotionally, though not physically, involved throughout his career (Deford, 1975). In 1983 Naim Suleimanov of Bulgaria set a 56 kg world record in weightlifting at the age of 15. Zhou Lunmei of China set three records in the 67.5 kg category at the same age in 1988.

Such records in themselves prove little, but do raise several questions. One is that of all sporting records, namely whether record breaking can go on indefinitely, as at present it seems set to do. Some points are fairly clear. First, there are some records which are mainly accumulations, albeit at the highest level. Thus Ian Botham has passed S.F. Barnes's total for taking five wickets in an innings in Test matches; but it took him about three times as many matches. The last half-century has seen an unprecedented growth in sport, and this alone makes records likely to fall. But the nature of sport has also changed from being a somewhat specialist interest to being mass entertainment, especially because of television. This in turn has meant immense financial rewards for both performers and entrepreneurs; Boris Becker's earnings up to mid-1988 are reckoned at around $25 million. In socialist countries where this trend has been less marked there are corresponding incentives of prestige and privilege. This is all common knowledge, but the effects are still working themselves out. There is perhaps more pressure in sport than in any other area for young talent to be identified, developed, and indeed exploited. As a result, it is likely that exceptional performances will appear at younger and younger ages, and it would be rash to set limits to this, just as it would be to say that any particular record will never be broken, except of course where this is made impossible by the rules of the sport. At the same time the process is likely to be asymptotic, that is to say record breaking must get less and less probable as one goes on. In some instances this can probably be seen already, for example in the short races in athletics.

In the case of young games players or athletes, it would be impossible to put a theoretical lower limit on achievement. In 1988 at Wimbledon Michael Chang at 16 lost in a memorable match to Henri Leconte; there seems no reason in principle why another 16 year-old could not beat even Boris Becker's record. Yet at the same time there must be a limit; surely a 5 year-old could not do it, nor a 10 year-old, nor even perhaps a 15 year-old. (The next year, Michael Chang became, at seventeen years and three months, the youngest winner of a Grand Slam male singles title, that of the French Open). But given that there are exceptional youthful performances, the same question arises as in other fields, namely whether such early promise is fulfilled. Systematic research does not seem to have been done, at least not on these very highest levels. Cursory sampling suggests what one would expect, that is a positive but not consistent relationship. Tracy Austin, Kathy Rinaldi, Mita Klima did not reach the very top. Lottie Dod, admittedly under very different conditions, retained her title the following year, did not compete for two years, and then returned to win three more times. Finding this too easy she gave up tennis and became a champion golfer, a hockey international, a fine skater and the best woman archer in England. In 1894 she was one of the first women to attempt the Cresta Run at St Moritz, where she also played in a cricket match on ice skates, taking five wickets for four runs. Known from the age of 12 as 'the little wonder', she seems to have succeeded in tennis partly through exceptional anticipation and partly through developing a modern game, volleying and smashing like a man. Boris Becker, although he won again at Wimbledon in 1986 and 1989, has otherwise had a more chequered career, even on grass which suits his game best; certainly he has not to date reached number one in the world.

Another remarkable young tennis player, Maureen Connolly (the product of a famous coach, 'Teach' Tennant), won the USA singles title at 16 in 1951, and in the remaining three years of her career lost only four matches. She retired after breaking a leg in a riding accident. Such chance factors clearly cannot be predicted, and must prevent some prodigious young athletes reaching their theoretical maximum. Success itself may in some reduce rather than sustain motivation; having attained what was aimed at there is less incentive to go on. In the case of mainly amateur sport there may be the need to seek financial rewards elsewhere; conversely, where these are great from the sport itself there may be less need to go on striving to the utmost, on the principle of the best fighter being a hungry fighter. In many sports now a very handsome living can be made by remaining in the top class; to reach the absolute top of that class and stay there requires extraordinary dedication as well as talent. At the same time the financial rewards probably make the kind of change of interest shown by Lottie Dod less likely. Another outstanding example both of an athlete of outstanding promise, and of an athlete changing her interests, is provided by Mildred 'Babe' Didrikson, who broke the world javelin record at 16 and at 18 won Olympic gold medals in that and in the 80-metres hurdles. In the same Games (1932) she equalled the world high-jump record but was placed second because the judges did not approve of her head-first style. She then abandoned athletics for golf, winning the US Open three times. Golf was already much more lucrative.

Tom MacNab (1981), British Olympic athletics coach in 1972 and 1976, gives the names of the winners in the 1972 National Championships for boys (thirteen events) and girls (nine events), for ages 13–15 and 15–17. Of the forty-four winners only two can be said to have reached the top level of competition and become nationally known: Steve Ovett in the 800 metres and Tessa Sanderson in the javelin.

The making of a champion

The converse approach is to examine the early histories of champions to see whether their talent was prodigious from the start. I have not come across any systematic study, but biography and anecdote would suggest that, as in other areas, on the whole potential appears early, but is often not sufficiently remarkable to allow prediction of the future career. Cricket provides a good case study, being not only intrinsically more interesting but also probably better documented than other sports. To take The Champion first, W.G. Grace (1848–1915) made his first fifty just before his twelfth birthday, remarking long afterwards that his greatest subsequent efforts had not given him more pleasure. Probably more has been written about the Great Cricketer than about any other single sports personality, and the temptation to expatiate must be resisted. It is the fact, though, that he provides almost a classic case of the emergence, development and triumph of supreme sporting talent. His father's enthusiasm for the expanding game, his mother's shrewd guidance, Uncle Pocock's coaching, the nearly equal skills of brothers E.M. and G.F., local rivalry, inspiration from the mighty All England Eleven trouncing twenty-two of Bristol, all in the context of society ready for the growth of spectator sport, combined with great athleticism, intensive practice and an immense (and life-long) boyish zest for competitive games, seem to provide an almost complete recipe. Yet other boys of 12 have scored fifty in club games, and not until he was nearly 16 did even W.G. play, successfully, against first-class sides. Even then, John Lillywhite's *Companion* remarked cautiously at the end of the season: 'Mr W.G. Grace promises to be a good bat: bowls very fairly' (Grace, 1899; Thomson, 1957).

Cricket's classic periods, above all the 'golden age' of 1890–1914, can be examined historically with a unique wealth of detail. Cricket is now but one sport among many competing for a public and for sponsorship. Then, it was in a position no other game has ever enjoyed: a craft raised to an art; a philosophy or religion, almost, for some. It was also a mass entertainment, and it was virtually a full-time occupation for wealthy players and a good living for poor ones. Grace himself, though technically an amateur, got money through expenses and testimonials quite unparalleled until modern times. The prestige and the monetary rewards of cricket meant that wherever talent might show itself, in great public schools or back streets, it was likely to be spotted and encouraged. Possibly the three most remarkable English batsmen of the period, C.B. Fry (1872–1956), Gilbert Jessop (1874–1955) and K.S. Ranjitsinhji (1872–1933), all had exceptional physical gifts in different ways, all showed early talent, yet were respectively 20, 20 and 21 on their first-class débuts, and took some time longer to reach their full potential. All owed their apparently effortless play at least in part to unremitting practice. On Jessop's début for Gloucestershire Grace famously remarked: 'Well, we've found something this time!', but it is not known how often he said the same of others less subsequently outstanding (Brodribb, 1974; Ellis, 1984; Ross, 1983).

The making of a champion is now a major business and professional enterprise. An unusually detailed account is that by Breskvar (1987). Boris Breskvar was Boris Becker's first tennis coach, at the age of 6, and for nine years taught him almost every day until he signed with Ion Tiriac in the spring of 1984. He also coached Steffi Graf. Breskvar throughout emphasizes general principles which are adapted to the individual player. One of the first things he noticed in Becker – at 6 – was his determination to reach every ball, as a last resort throwing himself to the ground like a goalkeeper. Accordingly one of the first things he taught him, which he had not done with any other pupil, was how to fall and roll without injury, thus capitalizing on the natural inclination. Again, an important part of the Baden Tennis Association's programme, within which Becker's training took place, was a detailed series of physiological measurements to allow, among other things, accurate prediction of ultimate growth. Boris Becker was expected to grow to 1.90 metres; his adult height is 1.91 metres. This made it worthwhile for training to concentrate on the serve-and-volley game, while for a shorter player a baseline game would be better.

Breskvar's selection methods show how intuition must combine with system in successful coaching. The same could be said of all teaching. First children are asked to play against each other. Then coaches give them awkward balls to return, with a view to judging co-ordination, dexterity and fighting spirit. Then comes throwing the tennis ball, for co-ordination and muscular power in the shoulder; hitting lobs and drop shots for ball sense; and finally other games, such as football, hockey and, especially, basketball. But finally it is a matter of personal judgement. Boris Becker clearly had outstanding potential from the start, especially in ball sense and determination, and he was certainly a prodigy; at 13 by far the youngest competitor in the German Youth Championships. But to go from demonstrating potential to winning Wimbledon was a matter of systematic training. Becker had certain advantages: he lived almost next door to the Baden training centre at Leimen; his family co-operated with him and supported him; he had one coach consistently. This last meant not only that methods and philosophy remained the same, but that the whole regime was a steady progression, with increasing demands at each stage. At the same time a key element in Breskvar's approach with children is variety: the aim is first to maintain interest and motivation, and second to develop imagination and flexibility. Variety may be achieved through different activities and different games or merely through careful scheduling of training sessions: the sort of principles of spaced and massed learning familiar to psychologists.

There could be said to be three intermingled aspects to Breskvar's training programme (and others, of course): tennis technique, physical development and mental development. The first involves strokes, tactics, and so on, and has its specific counterpart in whatever is being learned. The other two are more general, though geared to the particular game and the particular player. Thus the physical programme has three components: co-ordination, speed and muscular power, and endurance. Among the specific additional training techniques for Becker were some for endurance, such as carefully planned sequences of slow and fast running, running in deep sand, and so on. Breskvar notes that Becker himself would add additional sessions on 'free' weekends, and increase the difficulty of exercises. Such commitment is nearly always found in the greatest champions though it does not by itself ensure success. Other specialized exercises stressed agility, an outstanding characteristic of the adult Becker, large man as he became. Training the mind is in Breskvar's system equally important, using such techniques as relaxation exercises, mental rehearsal of skills, concentration training and competitive situations to improve controlled aggression. Throughout, Breskvar is skilfully making the most of whatever the athlete already has, while at the same time building up the weaker aspects, within a programme wholly directed to the one end of success. This does not quite mean a life of nothing but tennis, but it does seem to mean virtually total dedication; for several years every decision, every activity, is judged by its relevance to the game.

The basis of sporting excellence

Kane and Fisher (1979), in a report to the (British) Sports Council, see sporting talent as one aspect of giftedness as a whole, pointing out that human abilities overlap, both within the individual and conceptually. As Terman showed, talents tend to go together; and different areas of activity share components of ability: an obvious example would be the skills of dancers, gymnasts and skaters. Kane and Fisher review the still relatively sparse research under three headings. First, it is clear that heredity has some importance, at least in determining morphological (bodily) characteristics. They quote results from the USA showing that fathers and sons at the same age correlated 0.49 on the 100 yards and 0.80 on the standing long jump. Grebe (1956) found that 50 per cent of outstanding German athletes had sporting ability in the family. Gedda (1960) reported that in 351 sets of twins, 94 per cent of monozygotic (identical) twins agreed in their degree of participation in sport, whereas only 15 per cent of dyzygotes did so. One would expect twins, whether identical or not, to have very similar opportunities for sport. One could suggest that modern athletics results, as more and more nations compete, have the same implication of a genetic influence. Broadly, negroid athletes seem to dominate speed events, which require heavily muscled physiques and explosive power; North Africans, Kenyans and Europeans still seem to do better at endurance events. In many sports there is still inequality of opportunity between racial and cultural groups, but this can hardly be so for different lengths of race.

In respect of cognitive abilities Mahlo (1975) distinguished what was termed 'game intelligence', based on three components: perception, that is the analysis and comprehension of situations; problem solving by quick and decisive thinking; and reaction times. 'Game intelligence' correlated positively with actual performance in games, but neither of these did so with conventional IQ tests. Rodionov (1973), basing his findings on several studies of sportsmen and others on various factors, concluded that the main advantage of the better sportsman lay in his speed of perceiving and effecting a solution, and that this ability was noticeable as a differentiating factor at an early age of specialization. The notion of 'game intelligence' looks forward to some recent ideas on intelligence generally (see Chapter nine), and it does seem to relate to common experience in that the superior player seems to 'know what to do' more quickly and effectively than the lesser. (References in the preceding two paragraphs are cited by Kane and Fisher (1979).)

There is perhaps even less research on the personalities of young athletes. Kane and Fisher quote a study of 600 athletes aged 10–29 by Gaitzarska, Siris and Gorozhanin, who concluded that speed and endurance performers were differentiated by the 'strength' or 'weakness' of the nervous system. This is nothing to do with strength of character, but is a concept deriving from Pavlov and concerned with the capacity of the nervous system to handle stimulation. Beyond this, Kane and Fisher fall back on general findings about the gifted, such as their tendency to be well-adjusted, mature, and so on.

A recent and substantial, although rather unsystematic, study has been done by David Hemery (1986), 400-metres hurdles Olympic gold medallist in 1968, and world record holder. Hemery's method was to interview sixty-three top performers in twenty-two different sports and a dozen countries. While all showed early talent, the most remarkable at a young age was Shane Innes (née Gould), who started breaking records at 13, and who shortly after her fifteenth birthday held every freestyle world swimming record: 100, 200, 400, 800 and 1,500 metres.

Such people are quite difficult to get hold of, and the interviews were extensive, making the study worth while; but of course the sample is still a relatively small one for statistical conclusions, as well as being rather haphazard. Nevertheless some of Hemery's results are of considerable interest. For example, the average age of specialization in the sports in which his sample achieved fame was 16, which might seem rather late. Two-thirds considered they had been late physical developers, and just over half thought they were also late in emotional development. One of the drawbacks of Hemery's method is that it depends on the memory and perceptions of the subjects, with no other check. Twenty-six per cent reported their family background as working-class, 22 per cent as poor and 44 per cent as middle-class; but Carl Lewis, for example, considered that being 'poor' was having only one car. More significantly, there seems little support for the 'hungry fighter' theory taken literally. Possibly distance lent enchantment, but overall, those who reported low financial status did not associate it with serious want. This seems related to the overwhelmingly favourable reports of home conditions. Well over 90 per cent reported home life as stable, secure and happy: 100 per cent thought their parents' behaviour was 'consistent' (presumably, both one parent with the other and over the period of childhood). Over 90 per cent thought the home environment supportive and encouraging, and not 'pushing'. Indeed, judging from the protocols this was an outstanding feature of the sample's home life. For example, Peter Rose (baseball):

Our family was poor but the home was very stable. I only saw my parents have an argument once. My older sister needed a pair of shoes. Instead of using the money that week for my sister's shoes, my father bought me a pair of boxing gloves. He said: 'She doesn't need no shoes, it's summer time!' (Hemery, 1986)

Shane Innes stressed her parents' support for all their children, not just herself as a record breaker.

Eighty-nine per cent thought that they had initially been 'shy and introverted'; 55 per cent thought they were assertive but not aggressive, 35 per cent neither aggressive nor assertive, and 10 per cent both assertive and aggressive. To some extent, perhaps, these may be 'socially acceptable' answers. Similarly 78 per cent reported getting on well with everyone; 88 per cent felt that what others thought of them was important and 92 per cent wanted to please others. Sixty-four per cent felt that their life had not been sacrificed, and 80 per cent considered it was not unbalanced. This may seem to shift us away from the origins of achievement, yet it is clear that such achievement at the highest level does indeed involve 'sacrifice' in some sense, and certainly imbalance as compared with the general population; and these factors become apparent very early on. On the other hand, there may be compensating rewards, financial or other: 'When O.J. Simpson (American football, and 440 yards relay world record) was asked about imbalance, he replied: "The opposite, sport led me to a more spiritual life" ' (Hemery, 1986). And it may well be possible to devote a very great deal of time and energy to one activity and yet have time for others also. Hemery quotes the coach and commentator Ron Pickering as saying that two hours' intensive training a day is sufficient to reach the top in athletics; but other authorities may disagree, and other sports may differ. We noted Boris Breskvar's view on the need for variety, and this seems true of prodigies in other fields such as John Adams and Ganesh Sittampalam.

The factor on which Hemery's subjects showed virtual unanimity (apart from rejection of drugs in sport) was the need for commitment. Thus the following: 'mind totally involved in playing your sport': 100 per cent; 'absolute or very high concentration': 97 per cent; 'emotional intensity plus control required': 100 per cent. This appears to be closely related to an urge to personal achievement. Thus 92 per cent considered they were most competitive against themselves, 89 per cent felt in control of their own destiny, 87 per cent were confident of producing their best. Eighty-eight per cent thought that increased financial rewards would have had no effect on their performances. Achievement, however, seemed not to be considered in terms of doing one's best – only 10 per cent – but of winning (53 per cent) or not losing (37 per cent). 'It matters not who won or lost, but how you played the game', as Newbolt had it, retains little meaning for top performers today.

Development of talent

Sixty-eight per cent of Hemery's subjects felt they could not have reached the top without a coach. Forty per cent had had one permanent coach, and only 11 per cent no regular coach. Several had coaches famous in their own right such as Percy Cerutty, Arthur Lydiard and Fritz Stampfl (all athletics). It seems generally clear that technical advice, while important, is far less so than the individual relationship, which is sometimes an emotional one. Peter Sterling (rugby league) said of the coach Jack Gibson: 'He was very good at reading the game, the opponents and us but the best thing I could possibly say about him was that he was more interested in you off the paddock than on'. This relationship is often crucial in the coach's getting the best from the performer, by whatever means.

A dramatic example from a different source is that of Mike

Tyson. He reportedly had his first fight at 11, when an older boy tore the head off one of his racing pigeons. He became a delinquent and at 13 was sentenced to the Tryon School, a tough reformatory. Here he met Bobby Steward, a counsellor and former professional boxer, who promised him tuition in return for overall effort. It was immediately apparent that Tyson was a natural boxer, and he made a rapid all-round improvement (Gutteridge and Giller, 1987). His subsequent triumphs and the complexities of his personal relationships are too well known to recount.

Clearly the first step in developing sporting ability is to identify it. Kane and Fisher point out that it is relatively easy to spot unusually good early performances, but that it is not always clear whether this indicates exceptional talent, or a temporary spurt due to opportunity, coaching, or early physical maturity. They quote figures from Zatsiorsky et al. (1973) showing that of the Soviet swimmers coming in the top six in all events in the Olympic Games between 1952 and 1978, none began serious training before 10, and some were as old as 13. In general, however Soviet swimmers are selected at 7 or 8. Kane and Fisher argue that an earlier start tends to be counteracted by a longer period of development, which shortens as the starting age rises, so that individuals tend to reach their peak at around the same age.

It is well known that certain countries have made very systematic efforts to identify and develop sporting ability on a national basis. The most complete examples of such efforts are naturally to be found in communist countries, where the interests of the individual are subordinated to those of society. From 1952, East Germany (German Democratic Republic) developed a system based on special boarding schools, which are designed to produce skilled people to meet the needs of the economy, science, sport and culture. Twenty of these schools are sports schools. Similarly in the USSR a complex system of specialized schools has been developed since 1962, of which thirty are sports boarding schools (Treadwell, 1987). The results of these programmes are readily apparent in international competition. In the 1988 Olympic Games the Soviet Union gained a total of 132 medals. Given the relative populations of 274.5 million and 16.7 million, even more remarkable is the

East German total of 102 medals. The United States (population 236 million) gained 94; West Germany (Federal Republic of Germany, 61.5 million) was fourth with forty. Great Britain (56 million) was twelfth with twenty-four.

It is generally recognized (e.g. by Sir Walter Winterbottom, opening address to the Guinness Conference of Sport, 1981) that at the highest levels of sport the days of the amateur are over in that, however they are supported, training and competing constitute a full-time occupation requiring almost total dedication. It is interesting that Treadwell found evidence that noted Soviet educationalists promoted the specialist school system after visiting selected English public schools, for long the home of amateur sport.

Given financial support, the general ways by which talent may be promoted are fairly clear (e.g. Thomson and Beavis, 1985), although as Humphreys (Guinness Conference) points out, the precise qualitative and quantitative changes that take place in the years needed for an athlete to reach world class performance are still not fully understood. Pressey (1955), reviewing early outstanding talent in music in the eighteenth and nineteenth centuries, and in sport in our times, identified some common factors: early opportunity and encouragement; superior early and continuing guidance and instruction; frequent and continual opportunity to practice and extend abilities; close association with others in the field, fostering abilities and providing stimulation; many and increasing success experiences, with general acclaim. Such a list maps well on to the recommendations of countless committees concerned with fostering talent. For example, the Yorkshire and Humberside Council for Sport and Recreation (1980) identified these factors: identifying talent; coaching; competitive opportunities; facilities and equipment; support services; educational and vocational guidance; parental backing; finance.

While all these might seem obviously desirable, the effects of the enormously increased pressure for outstanding performance need careful assessment. Fisher (1987) suggests that early intensive training may not produce the best athletes, and may in fact do harm. He quotes a survey by Atkin (1985) of young West German tennis players which found considerable evidence of long-term damage to spinal column, hips, knees and ankles, leading to drop-out before the age of 20. Because of such worries, the Sports Council commissioned in 1984 an extensive review of the evidence, the results of which are presented by Rowley (1986, 1987). Unfortunately, while the material is extensive, much of it is inconclusive; some studies have been poorly designed, while many have concentrated on the effects of competition rather than training. As Rowley points out, it is training that takes up by far the greater amount of time and effort, both for the athlete and for her/his family, and except in contact sports is by far the greater source of injury. It is important to remember that the possibly differential effects of various sports have yet to be sorted out, and there exist wide discrepancies in which groups of people take up which (if any) sport. For example, non-whites are disadvantaged in many activities, as are poorer groups; while women tend to be encouraged much more in sports thought to be 'feminine', such as swimming and skating, whereas men compete equally in all sports.

Overall, estimates suggest that in the UK about 80 per cent of all children between the ages of 5 and 15 years take part in some form of organized youth sport. A much smaller proportion train intensively. Rowley points to 'a widely held, though unsubstantiated belief that in order to achieve either national or international success . . . training and competition should begin before puberty'. As a consequence, even in this country, there is increasing pressure at younger ages. Research on the effects of this has concentrated on four areas: sports-related injuries; growth and development; physiological effects; and psychological effects. Injuries often result from over-stressful use of the still developing body, for example while bones are still growing, although if detected early this need not be serious. Most studies, however, merely list injuries sustained in particular situations, e.g. at a clinic or in a school, and it is impossible to draw general conclusions about the degree of risk.

It is similarly unclear what effects intensive training has on general growth and development. There is some evidence that in some sports young athletes tend to be more skeletally mature, for example males in both swimming and athletics. Girl swimmers, on the other hand, tend to have fewer than average adult bones. These are simply correlations, and it is difficult to draw conclusions. A rather more general finding is that, except for swimmers, menarche (onset of menstruation) tends to occur later in athletes than in the general population, and this is more marked at the higher levels of competition. Similarly, there is a higher incidence of menstrual disorders. Physiologically, it is generally accepted that intensive training has a stimulating effect on both the cardiovascular and muscular developments of the young athlete. However, the effects vary with the age, sex, maturation and level of activity of the individual. The most widely used measure of cardiovascular fitness is the maximal oxygen uptake (the amount of oxygen the body can utilize). This is increased most by endurance training at the time of the adolescent growth spurt, though the effects are greater for boys than girls due to physiological differences such as the latter's greater proportion of body fat, smaller heart, etc.

Some psychological effects are likewise linked to gender. One reason is the differential acceptability of sports for girls and boys, and greater pressure on girls to choose between sport and social activities. Delayed menarche obviously affects girls, who may suffer feelings of social inferiority as they lag behind their contemporaries. In some 'feminine' sports there is great emphasis on bodily appearance, and this may lead to such syndromes as anorexia (often foolishly called 'the slimmer's disease' – there is no disease, but a disturbed pattern of behaviour which may have serious consequences). Conversely, for boys there may be an emphasis on aggressive behaviour; for example Smith (1978) reports that young ice-hockey players are often chosen for their aggressive, even violent behaviour rather than for their skill. Proponents of sport often claim that it either allows for harmless 'letting off of steam' or teaches how to control aggressive impulses. The actual evidence is at best equivocal, and the models provided by many professional sportsmen unfortunately do not help to support the claims.

Evidence does suggest that serious participation in sport, with intensive training, tends to reduce helping and sharing behaviour and increase asocial or even antisocial aspects. Of course this is not to deny the potential benefits of social sport. Similarly, it is generally accepted that participants in school sports tend to produce better results in all areas than non-participants. This might be the sort of all-round superiority described by Terman so long ago; and it is less clear what are the effects of high-level activity. Young gymnasts and swimmers have reported difficulties with schoolwork due to tiredness and to the very long training periods required, so that homework has to be done late at night or early in the morning.

Chess

The chess, of all games wherein is no bodily exercise, is most to be commended; for therein is right subtle engine, whereby the wit is made more sharp and remembrance quickened. And it is the more commendable and also commodious if the players have read the moralization of the chess, and when they play do think upon it; which books be in English. But they be very scarce, because few men do seek in plays for virtue or wisdom. (Sir Thomas Elyot, *The Book Named the Governor*, 1531).

One who does is Tom Marjoram (1988), who specifically urges the merits of chess in teaching able children, although he does not mention Elyot. (The 'moralization' probably refers to writings by Caxton, and to a long tradition in which chess was held to exemplify proper behaviour, individually and in society; Goldstein, 1988.) As Elyot says, chess is one of those games which lack a physical dimension, so that young players do not risk the same sort of injury, or require the same bodily development, as do athletes. There are others, at least some of which produce prodigies. In 1981 Dongic Hsieh became the youngest life master at contract bridge, at the age of 11; the youngest female to have gained the title is Patricia Thomas, in 1982 at the age of 14. There may well be examples in other complex intellectual games such as Go; but it is in chess that youthful achievements have become most famous. In common with other sports, achievement has become an end in itself, or at least a means to financial security, rather than a training for life – for rulers, in Elyot's case.

In 1988, Matthew Sadler, aged 14, came to prominence when – indeed before – he became an international master, the third youngest in the world to do so. At his first major tournament, in May, international grandmaster Leonid Shamkovich, a guest commentator from New York, described Matthew as a genius and said he had every prospect of becoming World Champion. In June a £20,000 sponsorship deal was announced in which Matthew's chess fame would be used to promote Russian products in the West and vice versa (*The Times*, 31 May, 8 June, 20 June, 12 September 1988). As is well known, chess in the USSR is a national sport and attracts great popular enthusiasm and state support. Neither is the case in the UK (Matthew Sadler's previous support amounted to £100 from the local council), which is nevertheless ranked second in international terms. There is sufficient interest, however, to ensure that potential is probably encouraged if once it is sparked off.

Nigel Short is probably the best-known recent British chess prodigy. Currently rated world number three, he was first widely noticed in 1977 when at the age of 12 he qualified for the final of the British Championship, the youngest to do so by four years. He defeated the ten-times British champion Dr Jonathan Penrose. As seems fairly typical of chess prodigies (Collins, 1974), Nigel Short's enthusiasm for chess was intense once it began (Short, 1981). He did not quite equal the feat of Capablanca, who is reported to have beaten his father the first time he played him, which was only two days after watching a game, at the age of 4. Nigel Short was 6 when he watched his father and brother, aged 8, play, and begged to be taught. At 7 he followed the Bobby Fischer–Borris Spassky match at Reykjavik (which perhaps put chess on the mass media sporting scene) and started to play at a local club, as did his father. He read all the chess books he could get. At 8 his father started a chess club so as to bring playing opportunities within reach. Reviewing his progress later his father states:

He always accepted defeat gracefully, often giving his opponent a beaming smile even as he resigned. He showed no trace of nerves before a game, and almost never during a game. . . . Almost from the start we had adopted a deliberate policy of stretching Nigel's ability as frequently as possible, while occasionally slipping in a tournament we knew he could win. . . . Motivating Nigel to produce his best form against weaker opponents was always a problem, and his form was unpredictable against other juniors. (Short, 1981).

This sort of family support is, as we have seen, characteristic of other sporting achievers. Clearly Nigel's father played a significant role, but he also pays tribute to coach and organizer Leonard Barden, whose 'total dedication and enthusiasm' has 'helped immeasurably to put British junior standards on a par with the Russians':

Leonard not only manages to keep up to date with junior performances all over the country, but he also makes a point of getting to know as many parents as possible. His method is to goad the top junior players to greater efforts by a continual stream of information about their closest rivals.

Prodigy as he undoubtedly was, Nigel Short has not equalled the achievement of Gary Kasparov, a marginally later developer but the youngest ever world champion, at 22 in 1985. Short (1981) gives the early records of the most remarkable young players. Taking the first ELO world ranking he notes, 1,600 points, this was achieved by Karpov at 7; Spassky, Julian Hodgson (UK) and Short attained it at 9. Karpov reached 1,800 at 8, but this was exceeded by Reshevsky, who had done it at 7. In reaching 2,300 Reshevsky leads at 11, followed by Short at 12 and Kasparov, Pomar and Mecking at 13. Reshevsky was 19 before he reached the next benchmark at 2,400, which Fischer, Short and Mecking did at 14 (Fox and James, 1981; Winter, 1981). Such figures of course show little other than that individual progress is not necessarily steady. According to Reuben (*British Chess Magazine*, January 1989), of the many prodigies in chess history only Pomar failed to fulfil his early promise – he reached only the standard of a moderate grandmaster.

The most remarkable chess phenomenon must be that of the Polgar sisters. It is, to begin with, quite exceptional to find female chess geniuses, though it is far from clear why this should be so – there are no obvious physical disadvantages, for example. Second, it seems that Laszlo Polgar, a Hungarian educationalist, set out deliberately (as others have done) to show that normal children could reach exceptional heights given the right training and encouragement. This he did by immersing his three daughters in a chess environment from the age of 4 or so (*The Times*, 24, 31 October 1988). The result is that two, Zsuzsa and Zsofia, are 'just normally strong prodigies' expected to become grandmasters eventually, but the youngest, Judit, is ahead of all other recorded performances by at least two full years. In January 1989, still only 12, she won the Foreign and Colonial Challengers' Tournament at Hastings, an achievement unprecedented in the annals of chess. Matthew Sadler was second. Reuben (*ibid.*) states that Laszlo Polgar discussed with his future wife his wish to experiment with his children, and she agreed 'with some trepidation'. Zsuzsa's first interest was in mathematics, until at 4 she discovered chess. It is not clear whether it was her interest or her father's choice that chess should be the medium of the experiment. Once chosen, however, the family had resources only for that activity for all three girls.

Judit, already spoken of as a future World Champion, is described by Reuben as 'a true games player possessed by the steely determination and blinkered approach with which we are familiar in all individual sports'. How far this amazing child will go remains to be seen.

5 Calculators and Mathematicians

Newsworthy achievements

'PUPIL CRACKS MATHS RIDDLE' (*The Sunday Times*, 18 September 1988). The headline refers to Oliver Riordan, aged 16, of Ealing, West London, who 'confounded top international mathematicians and solved a riddle that was first thought to be impossible'. It seems that a Professor Conway of Princeton University had, at a New Jersey symposium in July, offered a prize of $10,000 for finding the hidden pattern in a sequence of numbers. Only one correct solution was forthcoming and that took three weeks. *The Sunday Times* publicized this on 11 September and offered a magnum of champagne for the solution plus a proof. Oliver came up with the answer in minutes, though the proof took longer. The champagne was actually won by a 38-year old father of two computer analyst from Coventry, who was first past the post.

Youngsters outsmarting their elders is generally good copy, and this partly explains the publicity mathematical prodigies, in particular, often get. In the 1980s three exceptional children have featured in this way in the UK. The first of these, Ruth Lawrence, passed O level mathematics at 9 and A level at 10. At that point her father, who had actively fostered her talent, was briefly in the news, protesting against the use of psychological tests by Kirklees education authority to determine whether Ruth could attend a part-time physics course (*The Times*, 14 September 1981). This difficulty passed, Ruth entered Oxford University, took a first in mathematics at 13 and the same in physics a year later, then went on to do research.

This rate of early progress was exceeded by John Adams. He

80

passed O level at 8 with a grade B in 1986. The fourth of seven children, he could read newspapers and tell the time at 2, and was using a computer at 3. He attended a village school in Asfordby near Melton Mowbray in Leicestershire, and prepared for the examination with half an hour's extra work a night with his father, a teacher of mathematics, and his mother, a former bank worker (*The Times* 21, 22 August 1986). At 9 he got a grade C at A level. The Associated Examining Board was described as 'sparing no expense' in arranging a press conference to announce the result (*The Times,* 14 August 1987). A press release from the Board supplied some of the above details and added that John loved sport and played for the school football team and was also very interested in snooker, athletics and cricket. " 'He's no swot' says John's mother Pat, 'although he did have to work hard for his A level – but then that is what he wanted to do' ". The Board believed John to be the youngest ever to get either an O or an A level. That year the Board also gave one O level in mathematics to a 10 year-old and 2 to ll year-olds; as well as one in language to a 10 year-old and six in languages and two in art to 11 year-olds.

Like many records, that of John Adams was short-lived. In February 1988 Ganesh Sittampalam got a grade A in mathematics at O level, and in August a grade A at A level, having been aged 9 years and 4 months when he took the examination, three months younger than John Adams (*The Times,* 23 February, 19 August 1988). Ganesh was coached by his father, an investment expert with a Ph.D. in mathematics. His head teacher at Surbiton High School, London, described him as 'pleasantly mischievous' and added: 'genius is not a word to be used lightly, but in this case it completely fits the bill.' His mother stated that Ganesh was 'a lazy baby' who walked and talked late but suddenly shot ahead at 2. According to *You Magazine,* 11 September 1988, his parents first noticed his ability at 5 when he spontaneously remarked on what happens if you take one, add a half, then a quarter, and so on: you get closer and closer to two, but never quite reach it. Strictly, one cannot speak of records in public examinations. John Adams and Ganesh Sittampalam took those of different Boards, at different times, and though the Boards go to immense trouble to ensure that standards are consistent, it is not possible to establish absolute equivalence. In taking at 9 examinations intended for 18 year-olds, these children might be compared to Goethe, who at their age is said to have done the same schoolwork as boys twice as old (Cox, 1926).

It is noticeable, at least if press reports can be relied on (and in the main they are consistent), that all these three very remarkable children are happy and well adjusted, with friends and 'usual' interests outside study. All of them were coached by their fathers. Dr Arjuna Sittampalam is quoted as saying: 'I felt it was very important that he didn't learn anything by rote. He had to understand the conceptual and logical structure behind the whole thing. I made sure that he thought for himself and I always stopped short of telling him what the next step was.' James Mill might have agreed, though he would probably not have added: 'It was totally voluntary. Basicially, I told him, "Whenever you feel like learning more, come and ask me. If I'm free, I'll teach you" ' (*You Magazine*, 11 September 1988).

Like Ganesh, Adragon Eastwood DeMello is described as liking roller skating, cycling and normal activities for his age; which was 11 when he graduated in mathematics at the University of California (*The Times*, 6 January 1987; *The Times Higher Education Supplement*, 17 June 1987). Named after the Chinese year of the dragon in which he was born, and film star Clint Eastwood to whom he is distantly related, Adragon spoke his first word, 'Hello' at 7 weeks (6 in some reports). His father gave up a career as a science writer to educate him. According to one teacher whose school he attended for eight months in 1985: 'The only way he could perform was when his father sat in the classroom next to him. From a very young age his father has trained him like a monkey'. While there may be something in the latter remark, it is, even on the scanty information available, quite obviously far from the whole truth. Adragon has successfully passed university examinations and is reported as doing exceptionally well in classwork in English as well as in mathematics, computer studies and astronomy. He has had articles and poems published, with which his father might have helped, but there can be no doubting an extraordinary ability. Once again an unusual parent is part of the picture. Augustine DeMello appears to be ambitious for his son, speaking of a possible Nobel prize by 16, suggesting that no test can measure Adragon's intelligence and complaining that in America giftedness is not easily recognized, which is perhaps a little unfair.

There are of course many well-known historical examples of the early emergence of mathematical talent. Probably the youngest person ever to be appointed a full professor was a mathematician, Colin Maclaurin (1698–1746), who did significant work before he was 14 and gained his chair, at Marischal College, Aberdeen, when he was 19. In the 1745 Jacobite rebellion he organized the defences of Edinburgh (recalling Archimedes at Syracuse), but unfortunately died from illness brought on by his exertions *(Dictionary of National Biography)*.

Perhaps the most famous mathematical prodigy is Karl Friedrich Gauss (1777–1855), often considered along with Archimedes and Newton, one of the three greatest mathematicians. The early history of Archimedes is not known. Newton as a boy made sundials and water clocks, entered university at a normal age of 19, and then produced his epoch-making discoveries at 23. The story of Gauss is that before he was 3 he noticed and corrected a mistake in the weekly payroll which his father was making up. According to Bell, 1937 (quoted by Burt, 1975), Gauss was born in poverty, to a father who intended his son to follow him as a bricklayer and thus provide for his old age, and accordingly did everything he could do thwart the child's intellectual interests and prevent him obtaining an education. This is an example of the difficulty of being certain of the facts in many famous cases: a bricklayer would have to be quite prosperous to be operating a payroll, and other authors give the father as an accountant. Gauss seems to have learned early to read and count, probably with little formal teaching at the local school, and soon excelled at arithmetic and languages. Luckily a young man named Bartels joined the school as a pupil-assistant; he shared Gauss's interest in learning, mathematics in particular, and between them they created the environment both needed.

Burt (1975) considered the most remarkable attainments of any young person he had heard of to be those of Sir William Hamilton (1805–55). Hamilton read Hebrew at 7, and by 12 knew also Latin, Greek, French, German, Italian, Spanish, Syriac, Persian, Arabic, Sanskrit, Hindi and Malay. His father hoped he would obtain a clerkship with the East India Company. At 10 he was matched in public with the calculating prodigy Zerah Colburn, who was one year older; he lost, but 'not without honour'. At about the same time he came upon a Latin version of Euclid, and by 12 was reading the works of Newton. Entering Trinity College, Dublin at 18, he subsequently came first in all subjects at all examinations. While still an undergraduate he was appointed Professor of Astronomy, and shortly afterwards Astronomer Royal for Ireland. He published many scientific works and was twice gold medallist of the Royal Society (*Dictionary of National Biography*).

Here is a case of brilliance at both languages and mathematics. However, mathematics has certain features which make it a likely vehicle for precocity. Some of these were described by Mitchell (1907) in a study of exceptional calculators. Mathematics, or, as Mitchell says, arithmetic, is 'the most independent and self-sufficient of all the sciences'. One does not need quantities of facts to pursue it. Furthermore, much can be done by exploring basic methods: '. . . addition is only a shortened form of counting'. The same is true of multiplication 'which seems to be the basis of many calculating feats'. This enables the individual to go a long way on his own, or, very rarely, her own – Mitchell mentions only one female. Then again, one can practise mathematics with few resources of books or laboratories, and in any spare time, anywhere. The interest which often seems to drive exceptional performers on can be said to be intrinsic, lying in the properties of numbers themselves; understanding is itself rewarding, even without the incentive of examinations or other external reinforcement.

Exceptional calculators

The ability to calculate without external aids such as paper and pencil or machines, whether ancient like the abacus or modern, is possessed in some degree by anyone who has grasped elementary concepts of number and can add one and one. A very small number of individuals have been recorded as taking this particular skill to the point where it excites wonder or can be shown by way of professional entertainment. Smith (1983) set out to review all such cases, and though he modestly states that he failed in this, he must have included the greater part of those known, which come to only a few dozen (although as usual it depends where you draw the line). In most of them the ability appears at an early age.

There are inevitably some exceptional calculators from the past about whom it is difficult to establish the facts. For example, one of the first to be recorded was Thomas Fuller, an American negro slave who had been brought from Africa at the age of 14 and whose abilities were not well known until he was 70. He was illiterate but could perform such feats as reducing seventy years seventeen days twelve hours to seconds, which took him two-and-a-half minutes; the sort of rather pointless calculation often posed by curious audiences. He died in 1790.

Perhaps the first calculator to be definitely known as a child prodigy was Zerah Colburn (1804–1840). A farm boy from Vermont, he was regarded as backward until nearly 7, when after six weeks at school his father overheard him repeating multiplication tables. He may have learned from older brothers and sisters, but his father thought to test him further and was amazed when he correctly multiplied thirteen by ninety-seven. Colburn's abilities developed rapidly and he was soon able to solve such problems as the number of seconds in 2,000 years, the product of 12,225 and 1,223, or the square of 1,449. At 7 he took six seconds to give the number of hours in thirty-eight years two months and seven days (Howe, forthcoming). His father soon began to capitalize on this by taking Zerah round the country, and then abroad, giving demonstrations and, rather unsuccessfully, seeking patrons to sponsor his education. As a result Zerah was educated very spasmodically, though he showed a particular talent for languages. In Paris in 1814 he was examined by Franz Josef Gall, the inventor of phrenology, who located his faculty of calculation on either side of his eyebrows. Without a secure means of livelihood Colburn was at various times a mathematician working on astronomical calculations, a teacher of languages and literature, and a preacher, though without any great success in any of them.

A more successful boy from the same state of Vermont was Truman Henry Safford (1836–1901). He showed all-round precocity, and excelled in calculation at the age of 3. At 10 he performed such feats as mentally squaring a number of eighteen digits. He was interested in science, philosophy and history as well as mathematics, and eventually became a professor of astronomy.

A very direct contrast with Zerah Colburn was his contemporary George Parker Bidder (1806–1878), 'the calculating boy' (Clark, 1983). The son of a stonemason at Moretonhampstead in Devon, Bidder became interested in mental arithmetic at the age of 6. He used to play in the workshop of an elderly blacksmith neighbour, where on a certain occasion someone mentioned a sum, to which he gave the correct answer. As with Colburn this caused surprise and further questions were put; later his fame began to spread, and his ability began to earn him small sums of money. By 9 he was being demonstrated all over the country, before large audiences as well as nobility and even royalty. Queen Charlotte, consort of George III, asked: 'How many days would a snail be creeping, at the rate of 8 feet per day, from the Land's End, in Cornwall, to Ferret's Head, the distance by measurement being 838 miles?' One hopes she found the answer, 553,080, useful. Sir William Herschel, then Astronomer Royal, put the following:

Light travels from the Sun to the Earth in 8 minutes and the Sun being 98 million miles off, if Light would take 6 years and 4 months travelling at the same rate from the nearest fixed star, how far is that star from the earth, reckoning 365 days and 6 hours to each year, and 28 days to each month?

Bidder took one minute to solve this. Such a feat is not only remarkable for a child, of course: it would be so for anyone. And in times before computers, such abilities had considerable value. In his early years George Bidder received little formal education, partly because of his public engagements, but eventually he was sponsored by a wealthy Scottish lawyer to prepare for University. He entered the University of Edinburgh at 14, not then an exceptionally early age, and became a civil engineer. In this career he waas outstandingly successful, building among other things the first Norwegian railway and the Victoria Docks in London.

In some ways, as Howe (forthcoming) points out, the early lack of education was a help, in that Bidder developed for himself methods of rapid calculation quite different from those of school. Bidder later wrote and spoke about his methods; he stressed, for example, the need to reduce the burden on memory. Thus in multiplying 279 by 373, he would start with 200 x 300 (=60,000); then 200 x 70 (=14,000; total 74,000); 70 x 300 (=21,000; total 95,000) and so on; in this way only a running total has to be remembered, plus the original problem. A somewhat similar modern case is described by Hope (1987): a 13 year-old girl who claimed to be largely self-taught and who had developed a number of ingenious methods for herself.

Bidder was a mathematician as well as a calculator, and this seems to be more common (as far as one can tell from the very small number of cases) than a mere calculating ability on its own. There are also calculating 'idiots savants', and because of the contrast between one intellectual ability and general back-wardness it has sometimes seemed that they are the more remarkable. In fact it appears that their abilities are much more limited, even in calculation, than those of people like Bidder or indeed Colburn; some seem to depend largely on remarkable memories. For example, Jedediah Buxton (1702–72) was able to square a thirty-nine-digit number in his head, but it took him two-and-a-half months. He also kept a mental record of the number of free pints of beer he was given, running into thousands.

Another feat of idiots savants is calendrical calculation; usually, telling the day of the week on which any particular date fell, or will fall, and doing so very quickly. This feat does not necessarily appear in childhood, nor is it confined to the mentally retarded. Nevertheless it raises questions about the structure of mental abilities somewhat similar to the questions regarding those of mathematical child prodigies. O'Connor and Hermelin (1984) and Hermelin and O'Connor (1986b) have shown in a series of convincing experiments that idiot savant calendrical calculators do not depend on memory alone, but also employ rule-based strategies. Howe and Smith (1988) conclude, from a review of the literature and a study of one individual, that such individuals are self-taught; that they use methods other than the published methods (O'Connor and Hermelin found that they did use the conventional methods, at least to some extent); and that they cannot express the rules or methods that they use. They also found that the ability is restricted to certain periods of time, which of course is consistent with a partial use of rules – if the rules were fully understood they would apply to any period. Where mistakes occur they are likewise related to lack of knowledge of the principles of calendar construction. Calculators do have considerable knowledge of days and dates, and they devote a great deal of time and effort to this. It may be that this is a hobby which can be pleasantly pursued in isolation, yet which at the same time, when practised in public, brings social approbation. A similar sort of activity is seen in learning the complexities of the London transport system, or comparable masses of information.

More mathematical precocity

Calculating ability does not necessarily show itself early. For example Pericles Diamandi, born in 1868, was good at mathematics at school but only discovered a talent for mental arithmetic when he entered his father's grain business where it was useful. Salo Finkelstein (born 1896 or 1897) began at 23. Hans Eberstark (born 1929) as a child was exceptionally gifted at languages, later working as a simultaneous translator into German or English from either of those or from French, Spanish, Italian, Portuguese or Dutch. At 22 he heard of some calculations being demonstrated and immediately showed he could do as well.

It seems that more typically there is an early interest in numbers, sometimes associated with the individual being relatively isolated. Mitchell noted several who had been shepherd boys, such as Henri Mondeux (1826–1862). He learned to calculate by playing with pebbles, did acquire some general education, but showed no other ability. Another was Jacques Inaudi (1867–1950), whose interest was aroused in much the same way at the age of 6. By 7 he could multiply two five-digit numbers. He too showed no other particular ability, and made a living as a professional calculator, typical feats being naming the day of the week of any date, and reducing periods of years to seconds. He also performed memory feats such as repeating correctly series of up to thirty-six digits. He and Diamandi were the subjects of some of the very few experimental investigations carried out on mental calculators, at least until very recently, those by Alfred Binet, the pioneer of intelligence tests. An interesting finding was that when Inaudi was compared both with students and with restaurant cashiers, on tasks of a kind to which the latter were accustomed, that is rapidly totting up small sums, he was much faster than the students but no more so than the cashiers, perhaps a little slower.

Mitchell concluded that 'precocity is unmistakably the rule' in exceptional prowess at mental arithmetic or mental algebra, and this seems to be generally consistent with the larger number of cases described by Smith. In some of these the early history is obscure, such as in the case of the Indian Shakuntala Devi, or as in that of Hans Eberstark, for whom other interests took precedence. Perhaps the most successful professional calculator described by Smith was Wim Klein (born 1912), a Dutchman, whose interest began at 8 when he discovered factoring. He was stimulated by his elder brother Leo whose talent lay more in a remarkable memory.

A particularly interesting case is that of Professor Alexander Craig Aitken, FRS (1895–1967), a very distinguished mathematician. As a boy in New Zealand he was not exceptional at a very early age; it was not until he was 13½ that his interest was aroused, when algebra was introduced at school and he at once saw how powerful and general a method this was for calculation. For the next four years he 'underwent what can only be described as a mental Yoga'. 'I tried harder and harder things until, in the end, I was so good at arithmetic that the master didn't allow me to do arithmetic.' This had a general effect on his development:

I was interested in literature just as much, Latin, French and English. But this greater freedom suddenly encouraged me to think I had a memory and a calculative power capable not only of arithmetic but also capable of, for instance, literary memory. I suddenly moved away.

He did so to such effect that he won every school prize except that for chemistry, which was boringly taught and for his lack of interest in which he was caned; of note to those who still believe in the efficacy of that method. Aitken was also a very good athlete, had an exceptional memory and a great knowledge of literature, wrote poetry and played the violin (Hunter, 1962, 1977; Smith, 1983).

An indubitable mathematical child prodigy was Norbert Wiener (1894–1964), already mentioned as the contemporary of William Sidis. Wiener's father Leo was an excellent linguist, speaking German, French, Italian, Polish, Serbian and Greek, as well as being a good classical scholar and amateur mathematician (Howe, forthcoming; Wiener, 1976). Leo Wiener in fact became professor of modern languages at the University of Missouri, later moving to Harvard, and Norbert grew up in a highly intellectual atmosphere, amply supplied with books and among distinguished academics. Leo Wiener also had very specific views on education, which derived partly from those of Karl Witte, an Austrian cleric who set out to make his own son Karl, born in 1800, into a 'superior man'. By the age of 16 the boy had gained two doctoral degrees and later became a distinguished literary scholar, an expert on Dante. Wiener translated Witte's account of his methods into English. Wiener's education of his son is reminiscent of James Mill:

> Every mistake had to be corrected as it was made. He would begin the discussion in an easy, conversational tone. This lasted exactly until I made the first mathematical mistake. Then the gentle and loving father was replaced by the avenger of the blood. The first warning he gave me of my unconscious delinquency was a very sharp and aspirated 'What!' and if I did not follow this by coming to heel at once, he would admonish me, 'Now do this again!' (quoted by Howe, forthcoming)

The similarity extends to the fact that both John Stuart Mill and Norbert Wiener were required to teach their younger siblings, 8 and 1 respectively. None of these seems to have become remarkable. Leo Wiener was evidently a demanding and difficult man, with little insight into the needs of others, but at the same time one of great knowledge and, even more importantly, of great enthusiasm for learning and for life. Thus he was also an inspiring model to his son. Norbert's mother supplied some emotional support in his early years, but later both parents were over-possessive as well as being prejudiced against minority groups – including Jews, which they themselves were – in a way which their son came to find intolerable. Although Norbert Wiener enjoyed academic success both early and continued, he perhaps never fully overcame the emotional residue of his childhood.

A happier childhood, at least in the early years, was that of Bertrand Russell (1872–1970). Having lost both parents he was brought up largely under the influence of a grandmother of forceful character whose somewhat unusual regime nevertheless resulted in good health, plenty of enjoyment and short lessons for fear of overwork. Russell almost spontaneously developed precocious intellectual interests, but it was the effect of mathematics that was most dramatic:

At the age of eleven I began Euclid, with my brother as my tutor. This was one of the great events of my life, as dazzling as first love. I had not imagined there was anything so delicious in the world. After I had learned the fifth proposition, my brother told me that it was generally considered difficult, but I had found no difficulty whatever. This was the first time it dawned upon me that I might have some intelligence. From that moment until Whitehead and I finished *Principia Mathematica,* when I was thirty-eight, mathematics was my chief interest, and my chief source of happiness. Like all happiness, however, it was not unalloyed. I had been told that Euclid proved things, and was much disappointed that he started with axioms. At first I refused to accept them unless my brother could offer me some reason for doing so, but he said: 'If you don't accept them we cannot go on', and as I wished to go on, I reluctantly accepted them *pro tem.* The doubt as to the premisses of mathematics remained with me, and determined the course of my future work. (Russell, 1967)

Mathematical ability

Mitchell concluded 'Skill in mental calculation is, owing to the isolation of mental arithmetic already noted, independent of general education; the mathematical prodigy may be illiterate or even densely stupid, or he may be an all round prodigy, and veritable genius'. It would now seem to be more accurate to say that greater skill in calculation is attainable by the more mathematically gifted, who are interested in method rather than mere feats. Wherever on a scale of general ability a prodigious calculator may come, however, it seems clear that intensive practice is necessary in order to develop the talent, and that this in turn depends on strong motivation, which often seems to be fired by a particular incident, as in the case of Aitken, Eberstark or Klein. Smith (1983) suggests:

Calculating prodigies cannot be easily created for the same reason they appear so infrequently in the population – motivation. Children are not surrounded by people doing mental calculation as they are by people talking. Therefore, a strong interest in numbers is required of the child, and a willingness to isolate himself from the typical amusements of his peers. Calculating prodigies remark again and again that numbers are their friends. One suspects that a child with many human friends is less likely to find solace among numerical acquaintances.

Smith (1988) repeats his view that every child has the capacity to become a calculating prodigy, but that few have the motivation; but by this he seems to mean, not that all could become Aitkens, merely that all could develop the ability to some extent. George Bidder also considered how to encourage mental arithmetic, which he thought superior to the ordinary sort in its ability '. . . to strengthen the reasoning power of the youthful mind; so as to enlarge it, as to ennoble it and to render it capable of embracing all knowledge, particularly that appertaining to the exact sciences' (Bidder, 1856, quoted by Smith (1983)).

Mental arithmetic is not now much in demand, and lonely children if mathematically inclined are more likely to make friends with their computer. It may also be said that while the feats of young calculators have often been astounding, and far beyond the reach of most adults, they have not exceeded or perhaps matched those of adult calculators. This is also true of mathematics (and indeed, as far as one can see, of all fields of intellectual endeavour with very few exceptions). Lehman (1953), in a very extensive survey of *Age and Achievement*, found many instances of important contributions by young mathematicians, but none were below 18. Where calculating ability falls off, it may well be due to loss of motivation and hence failure to keep in practice. Aitken reported this of himself (Hunter, 1962).

Smith (1988) distinguishes several components of mental calculation: basic operations of arithmetic; more complex rules of procedure; special memorized data, such as logarithms; and memory. The fundamental operation is multiplication; but this is done differently according to whether the calculator visualizes the numbers he or she is working with or hears them. Auditory calculators typically work from left to right;

visualizers use cross multiplication. Both typically develop more economical ways of working, as Bidder did; and much of the skill tends to become unconscious so that as Aitken put it, sometimes 'I have had an answer before I even wished to do the calculation'. Many calculators have been professional entertainers, concerned to put on a good show. It is not suggested that they cheat; but Barlow (1952) shows how, for example, time can be gained for calculation by writing figures on a blackboard, ostensibly for the benefit of the audience.

Hunter's (1962) account of Aitken is of interest, although it was descriptive rather than experimental. Hunter concentrated on one task, that of decimalizing fractions. Given, say, two divided by sixty-three, Professor Aitken paused for four seconds, during which he repeated the problem, then said, 'Point 0, 3, 1, 7, 4, 6, then the whole thing repeats', giving the numbers one every two seconds. Hunter describes the experiential characteristics, how it seemed to Aitken himself. First of all there was the non-sensory nature of numbers; Aitken's experience was more like that of someone expertly playing a fast ball game, in which one does not consciously think out each move. This meant, of course, that it was very difficult for him to describe his process of thought: 'From moment to moment, he intends in schematic fashion to do this or that. He can describe what he intends to do but . . . he cannot give what an observer would regard as an adequate description of the intending as such'. Secondly, his mental processes seemed to Aitken to be complex rather than one single stream of calculation: 'I seem to move on several different levels'. At least since Ulric Neisser's *Cognitive Psychology* of 1967, this would be recognized as multiple processing. Thirdly, there was what Hunter calls 'onleading by leaps', in at least three ways. Aitken would immediately see the properties of even very large numbers, rather as one immediately knows, on hearing 'twelve', that it is three times four and two times six. Then there was the ability to make procedural judgements, deciding on a method that was likely to be productive; and recognizing an answer as right, or likely to be right. Hunter compares these to decisions by chess players, based on a repertoire of game situations. If this is a good analogy, it would be one reason why older, more experienced calculators should be better than the very young.

While an understanding of mathematics may make better calculators, it seems that great mathematicians are not necessarily fast or accurate at calculating, although some have been child prodigies in this respect, such as Gauss and Ampère. Mathematical ability does often seem to show itself early, as with the current GCE stars as well as older cases such as Blaise Pascal (1623–62) who, like them and as already noted, owed much to his father, himself a gifted mathematician. The most famous instance usually quoted of the opposite, that is of mathematical ability only appearing quite late, is probably Einstein. He did not shine at school and was not considered exceptionally promising. But as Howe (forthcoming) describes, he certainly had by the age of 12 or 13 exceptional intellectual interests and was avidly studying mathematics and physics on his own, soon outpacing a friend, Max Talmey, who later gave an account of his progress. By 16 he had produced a brilliant paper on electromagnetic phenomena.

Marjoram and Nelson (1986) quote the findings of V.A. Krutetskii, who between 1955 and 1966 studied a group of 192 children aged 6 to 16, 34 of whom were judged to be mathematically gifted. He reported that, as compared with the less gifted, they shared the following characteristics.

1. They view the mathematical content of a problem both analytically and synthetically.
2. They are quick to generalize the content of a problem and its solution.
3. They exhibit curtailment when solving problems of similar type: i.e. after relatively short exposure, they come to regard certain steps in the solution as obvious and use abstracted abbreviated forms of reasoning, omitting intermediate steps.
4. They are flexible in their thinking and can change easily from one cognitive process to another even if it is qualitatively different.
5. They are not tied to techniques of solution that have been successful in the past, and can re-adjust when these fail.
6. They look for simple, direct, elegant solutions.
7. They can easily reverse their train of thought.
8. They will investigate aspects of difficult problems before trying to solve them.

9. They tend to remember the generalized, curtailed structures of problems and their solutions.
10. They tire less when doing mathematics than in other classes.

They are also described as preferring either a visual/spatial or a logical analytic mode of thought; and as not just having better memories and working faster but as thinking about mathematics in qualitatively different ways and already possessing some adult mathematical problem-solving skills.

A number of studies (e.g. Benbow and Stanley, 1983a) have shown that girls tend to be better at computation, boys at application and problem solving. Girls tend to be superior in mathematics at primary school level, but boys then increasingly draw ahead, as they do in spatial ability. The differences become very marked at the extreme upper end; thus thirteen times as many boys as girls score at the level of one in 10,000. There seems to be some association between languages and mathematics, although factorial studies of intelligence commonly distinguish between verbal and numerical ability. And there is some association with music, according to Marjoram and Nelson, but it is one-way: Révész (1925) found a 'significant' bias towards music in mathematicians, but only nine per cent of musicians had any talent or interest in mathematics. Music, even now, is part of general culture in a way that mathematics is not.

The causes of superior ability are still obscure. The role of a father, already mentioned in individual cases, was demonstrated in a well-known study by Carlsmith (1964). Taking a sample of 1,460 American college students born between 1941 and 1945, and alike in every respect except that the fathers of some had been away on military service, he established quite clearly that early and long separation resulted in relatively greater ability in verbal areas than in mathematics, while no separation resulted in greater mathematical ability. It has also been suggested that there are physiological factors. Benbow and Stanley found that in the one in 10,000 class of mathematically gifted boys, twenty per cent were left-handed, roughly twice the U.S average. It is also the case that more boys than girls are left-handed, and more boys than girls dyslexic. This suggests that the right-hand half of the brain tends to be more dominant in boys, and it has been argued that this is due to increased exposure to the hormone testosterone in the womb (see Chapter 10).

Special mathematical training

Partly because mathematical ability often seems to show itself early, and partly because it is so fundamental to other studies, especially science, a lot of attention has been paid to identifying and encouraging it. There are more methods than relying on having an unusual father, although it is plausible to suggest, as Howe does, that the really outstanding early performance, the prodigy, nearly always seems to involve a dedicated adult. Sometimes, as we have seen, such a person believes that his methods alone are responsible. Ken Adams, father of John, has called his book *Your Child Can be A Genius - And Happy!* (1988). If this is so, one must wonder why we have not heard much of John's six siblings.

In fact, parents of mathematical prodigies usually report noticing something exceptional in their child early on. Straker (1983) has summarized the likely signs in pre-school or infant school children (cited by Marjoram and Nelson, 1986):

(a) a passion for counting;
(b) a liking for numbers, often including them in stories and rhymes;
(c) the use of logical connectives: if, then, so, because, either, or;
(d) a delight in making patterns, showing balance and symmetry;
(e) neatness and precision in arranging toys;
(f) the use of sophisticated criteria in sorting and classifying;
(g) a pleasure in jigsaws and constructional toys.

Perhaps the most extensive attempt to identify and encourage mathematical talent is the Study of Mathematically Precocious Youth (SMPY) based at Johns Hopkins University at Baltimore, U.S.A., originated and directed by Julian C. Stanley. Projects more or less deriving from it also exist at Duke,

Arizona State, and Northwestern (Illinois) Universities, and taken together these were in 1983 identifying some 70,000 talented students each year. The origins of the SMPY lie first in Stanley's interest as a high school teacher in the late 1930s, but specifically in the identification of a computer prodigy aged 12, named Joe, who a year later, in 1969, entered Johns Hopkins University, and at 17 obtained a master's degree in engineering. The SMPY began officially in 1971. As Benbow and Stanley (1983b) point out it is still too early to evaluate the long-term results, for which one must wait until several cohorts have reached middle life. They do mention that 'a number' have already been author or co-author of scientific publications, including one at 15 and two at 16.

The SMPY seeks first to identify mathematically gifted children, essentially by standard school attainment tests. It then adopts a policy of selective acceleration. Stanley (1977) gives the rationale for this, contrasting it with the method of enrichment. Enrichment programmes, in his view, may involve:

(a) 'busy' work, i.e. merely giving the child more to keep it occupied;
(b) irrelevant academic work;
(c) general cultural activities;
(d) relevant academic work – not more advanced, just more of the same.

Only (c) is of any use to the mathematically gifted, but it does not meet their specific mathematical needs. Acceleration, on the other hand, offers clear advantages:

(a) increased zest for learning and for life, better attitudes to education and other activities;
(b) enhanced feelings of self-worth and accomplishment;
(c) reduction of egotism and arrogance;
(d) better educational preparation, especially in mathematics which is basic to many disciplines;
(e) better preparation for selective colleges, i.e. those hard to get into;
(f) accelerated career, giving more time for other activities;

(g) more chance to explore specialities and hobbies;
(h) more time to explore careers before marriage;
(i) less cost;
(j) greater chance of career opportunities through being noticed;
(k) the possibility of greater success in life, both professionally and personally.

What selective acceleration involves in practice is a 'smorgasbord' of opportunities, often at several different institutions, together with a programme of counselling and guidance, and at the same time skipping grades whenever appropriate. In this way the students can pursue each ability as far and as fast as they are able, or wish to. Benbow (in Benbow and Stanley, 1983b) reports that questionnaire responses from 1,896 SMPY students showed them, as compared to control groups, to be superior in both ability and achievement, to express stronger interest in mathematics and science and to be more strongly motivated educationally; also, 'the majority of the students felt that SMPY had helped them educationally while not detracting from their social and emotional development'.

It might be said that this is, in effect, what the parents of Ruth Lawrence, John Adams and Ganesh Sittampalam have done on an individual basis; and Stanley (in Benbow and Stanley, 1983b) gives three examples from SMPY. Colin Farrell Camerer, born 1959, tested in the sixth grade (i.e. at 12), missed out the seventh grade, meanwhile taking a computer science course at Johns Hopkins. He then omitted grades nine to thirteen, enrolled at Johns Hopkins and took a BA at 17 . He did this 'through a combination of college courses taken for credit while still in high school, Advanced Placement Programme examinations, and heavy course loads in college'; but he still found time to be in the college television quiz team, to be active in wrestling, golf, and writing for the college newspaper; and to tutor other mathematical prodigies. At 17 he entered the Chicago Graduate School of Business, taking his master's degree at 19. Chi-Bin Chien, born 1965, at the age of 10 scored in the verbal part of scholastic aptitude tests as high as the average Johns Hopkins student of 17–18, and in the mathematical part a little higher. She omitted grades 6, 7, 9, 10, 11 and 13, and in 1981 became the youngest ever baccalaureate of Johns Hopkins, beating the previous holder, Charles Homer Haskins (1887), by seven months. Nina Teresa Murishige, born 1963, won the Oklahoma high school piano contest when in the tenth grade; she also played the flute and violin. Skipping the twelfth grade, she took a BA in mathematics (with minor piano) at 18, and was awarded both a Churchill scholarship to Cambridge and a Rhodes scholarship to Oxford, accepting the latter. 'We know of quite a few more as remarkable in their own ways', remarks Stanley.

6 Precocious Artists

Adult versus child

Talent in any of the arts can, and perhaps most often does, show itself early. Pressey (1955) lists, among the most prominent classical composers, the following as having been precocious: Berlioz, Chopin, Debussy, Dvořák, Handel, Haydn, Liszt, Mendelssohn, Mozart, Rossini, Schubert, Verdi, Wagner. Barlow (1952) adds Brahms, Meyerbeer, Richard Strauss and Weber. Mahler began composing at 4, fascinated by the military music at a barracks in his village and by the folk songs of the local people. But there is certainly not a simple prediction from early to later performance. Rosamund Shuter-Dyson (1986) mentions that Charles and Samuel Wesley (nephews of John) were playing on their mother's harpsichord before they were 3, and their precocity can be compared with that of Mozart; yet their ultimate achievement, while not negligible, was far less than his. She notes that Leopold Mozart devoted his life to his son's career, while the Wesleys' father tended to regard music with suspicion unless it was religious. No doubt this was just one factor.

The precise relationship between early and later performance is unclear in the arts, as in other areas. What is expected of a child artist may be different from what an adult has to do; rather as with the Quiz Kids. An interest in creativity and free expression has led to children being encouraged in schools to produce big splotchy paintings, and being given such coarse brushes that they can scarcely do anything else. (I once came across a genuine, though not good, primitive artist, an elderly lady who painted like a child. She had been asked to teach in the local primary school.)

There is always a place in the entertainment world for a good boy soprano, especially around Christmastime. Repertoire, style and voice in particular are naturally quite different from those of an adult, and relatively few such stars become outstanding adult performers. Even a simulation of childhood can appeal. In a perhaps less sophisticated time than ours, although extending into the age of television, 'Wee Georgie' Wood worked the variety theatres for over fifty years in the character of a precocious small boy, at his best topping the bill with a mixture of comedy and pathos. One of the most remarkable of effectively pre-Freudian works, J.M. Barrie's *Peter Pan* (1904), is still revived annually with 'the boy who never grew up' played, more or less improbably, by an adult actress.

An interesting example of how young people can produce what is in demand is given by Kunkel (1985). The city of Venice was for many years renowned for its music. Between about 1650 and 1800 four of the several orphanages developed a policy of encouraging their girls to perform music, by a system of rewards and privileges, better prospects of marriage, etc. Eventually, each was giving up to seventy public concerts a year and the best, La Pietà, up to ninety. Contemporary accounts agree on the high standards. At a time when, as with pop music now, concerts consisted mainly of new music, Vivaldi was a regular composer for La Pietà, and gave the girls some of his most complex pieces. Yet these girls can hardly have been other than a cross–section of the population, biased if at all towards the lower end of the social scale. After 1800 the decreasing prosperity of Venice led to a falling-off in demand and a disappearance of talent.

What differentiates the child from the adult performer is often spoken of in terms of depth of feeling or understanding, of painterly quality, musicality, or the like. Techniques can be mastered quickly but more profound qualities take time, not just for more work but for greater personal development. In cultures still possessing live traditions of folk music, such as Bulgaria, it is held that singers are at their best between 35 and 60. Earlier, they lack experience of life; later, vocal powers start to diminish, so A.L. Lloyd (1908–82), the great collector and singer, used to say. Révész (1925), in his study of the musical prodigy Erwin Nyiregházi, distinguished between technique and musicality, stressing '. . . the need and capacity to understand and to experience the autonomous effects of music'. Bamberger (1982) suggests that it might be possible to relate the transition from early to later musical performance to Piaget's distinction between sensory-motor and formal thought processes, but this does not as yet seem to have been worked out in detail.

It is thought particularly remarkable when a young artist shows such qualities, as in the case of Corey Cerovsek, a Canadian who made his British début at 14 playing Mozart's A major violin concerto. His conductor Rudolf Barshai is quoted as saying: 'His imagination is like an adult's. His style is that of an experienced artist'. Barshai compared Corey to Mikhail Goldstein, whom he had heard at 12; Goldstein had played a public concert in Odessa at the age of 5. Corey Cerovsek was given a miniature violin at that age. He is reported as being also excellent at mathematics and languages, but disliking to be called a genius or prodigy: 'They make me sound like a different species. I play the violin because I love it' *(The Times,* 27 December 1986).

Csikszentmihalyi and Robinson (1986) make the general point, not confined to the arts, that both individual capacity and cultural demands change within a life-span, and thus it is unreasonable to expect talent to be a stable trait. It cannot be assumed that a 5 year-old prodigy will necessarily be an outstanding teenager or adult. The closest match will be where 'talent' is defined in terms of scores on psychological tests, such as intelligence tests. Such scores do show considerable consistency over long periods, partly due to the way they are constructed, but they are not the same thing as real-life performance. It is also the case that prodigies necessarily are marked out as such by their current performances; in the arts especially these are not always the same as lasting reputations, at any age.

Before the footlights

'This, sir,' said Mr Vincent Crummles, bringing the maiden forward, 'this is the infant phenomenon – Miss Ninetta Crummles'. . . .

'May I ask how old she is?' inquired Nicholas,
'You may, sir,' replied Mr Crummles, looking steadily at his questioner's face,
as some men do when they have doubts about being implicitly believed in
what they are going to say. 'She is ten years of age, sir.'
'Not more?'
'Not a day.'
'Dear me!' said Nicholas, 'it's very extraordinary.'
It was; for the infant phenomenon, though of short statute, had a compar-
atively aged countenance, and had moreover been precisely the same age – not
perhaps to the full extent of the memory of the oldest inhabitant, but
certainly for five good years. But she had been kept up late every night, and
put upon an unlimited allowance of gin-and-water from infancy, to prevent
her growing tall, and perhaps this system of training had produced in the
infant phenomenon these additional phenomena. (Dickens: *Nicholas
Nickleby*)

Miss Crummles might have done well in the Hollywood of the
1920s and 1930s when there was something of a vogue for child
stars: the age of Shirley Temple, Judy Garland and Mickey
Rooney, to name perhaps the most famous. Their subsequent
careers diverged widely: Shirley Temple, the youngest ever
Oscar winner at 6, left films for marriage and politics; Judy
Garland was greatly successful as an adult performer but
ultimately a tragic figure, dying at 47; Mickey Rooney is, at the
time of writing, starring in the West End. Groups of children
featured also, as Our Gang, and the Dead End Kids, some of
whom, such as Gabe Dell and Huntz Hall, made the transition
to adult acting, though with modest fame. Perhaps none was
quite so put upon as Joey Cooley, the Idol of American
Motherhood:

'The party of the second part, hereinafter to be called the artist, shall abstain
from all ice-creams, chocolate creams, nut sundaes, fudge, and all-day suckers,
hereinafter to be called candy, this to be understood to comprise doughnuts,
marshmallows, pies in their season, all starchy foods and twice of chicken.'
Can you imagine my lawyer letting them slip that over! (P.G. Wodehouse:
Laughing Gas)

All these and many more played child parts. It was far
different with the remarkable William Henry West Betty (born
1791), called The Young Roscius. His mother reputedly began
to instruct him almost from infancy: in what, is not clear, but at
some point in childhood he learned Wolsey's speech from
Henry VIII after hearing his father recite it. His family having

moved to Belfast, he there at the age of 10 saw Mrs Siddons on the stage and declared he would die unless he too could be an actor. Accordingly, he made his début on 19 August 1803 as Osman in an adaptation of Voltaire's *Zaïre*. The house was crowded and his success complete. He was promptly engaged for four more nights in four parts. November saw him in Dublin in more new roles, one of which, the famously long Hamlet, he is said to have learned in three hours. This was followed by Cork, Waterford, Glasgow, Edinburgh and Birmingham. In December 1804 he appeared at Covent Garden, drawing such crowds that on one occasion troops had to be called out to restore order. In the same month he was also at London's other great theatre, Drury Lane, and the next (winter) season appeared alternately at both at a fee of fifty guineas a night. On a famous occasion the Prime Minister, Pitt, adjourned the House of Commons so that members might be in time to see his Hamlet. He then toured provincial theatres, returning to London in 1805–6 but to diminishing acclaim, though still immensely popular elsewhere. In 1808 he left the stage and two years later entered Christ's College, Cambridge, but left again following his father's death in 1811. In 1812 he resumed his acting career, but with only limited success. He continued to appear at intervals until 1824 when he finally retired, to live quietly for the next fifty years on the large fortune he had acquired. He is said to have acknowledged that the enthusiasm of his early supporters was mistaken *(Dictionary of National Biography)*.

Perhaps no other actor, at least of classical parts, has enjoyed such acclaim at such an age, though public enthusiasm is a doubtful measure of talent. Many later distinguished entertainers have made an early start: Mary Pickford was on the stage at 5, and Elizabeth Taylor gave her first Royal Command performance at 3, dancing with her ballet class. There are also, however, cases of child stars who faded, and of adults who started late. Until recently, entertainment was one avenue of escape from indigence, as with, for example, Charlie Chaplin and W.C. Fields, or from genteel poverty, as with Noel Coward (Coward, 1937). Chaplin first appeared professionally at 8, one of the clog-dancing 'Eight Lancashire Lads' (Baker, 1983). Coward was 10 when he appeared in *The Goldfish*; the age at which a more recent child star, Tatum O'Neal, won an Oscar for her part in *Paper Moon* (Morris, 1983). Fields ran away from home to work in vaudeville at 11. What impresses in such histories is not perhaps so much early talent, of which in any case there is no reliable record, as determination. Fields is said to have practised juggling standing by his bed so that he would fall into it when too exhausted to continue (Taylor, 1949).

I have not come across any systematic examination of precocity in this area. A particularly interesting example (to me anyhow) is that of Leonard, Adolph, Julius, Milton and Herbert Marx; better known as Chico, Harpo, Groucho, Gummo and Zeppo. The story is familiar but worth recalling. Sons of a poor and by all accounts incompetent immigrant tailor, they had little or no education, but a remarkable mother.

She was a lovely woman, but her soft, doelike looks were deceiving. She had the stamina of a brewery horse, the drive of a salmon fighting its way up a waterfall, the cunning of a fox, and a devotion to her brood as fierce as any she-lion's. Minnie loved to whoop it up. She liked to be in the thick of things, whenever there was singing, storytelling, or laughter. But this was in a way deceiving too. Her whole adult life, every minute of it, was dedicated to her Master Plan. . . . Minnie's Plan was simply this: to put her kid brother and her five sons on the stage and make them successful. (Marx, 1976)

The plan involved the sons becoming performers in their early teens, with varying fortune and talents but eventual financial success. Under Minnie's direction, all six made at least passable entertainers; brother Al Shean was a prominent variety artist and three sons in the top class of comedians. At the same time, despite virtually identical backgrounds and Minnie's impetus, the five sons could hardly have been more different in personality: Chico a spendthrift, gambler and womanizer, Groucho complex, scholarly and eventually a cantankerous old man, Harpo gentle and universally liked, and so on (Adamson, 1973; Eyles, 1966). Such an example almost makes experiments redundant as proof of the roles of both inheritance and environment.

Musicians

Young musical virtuosi are, if not commonplace, not infrequent. Solomon Cutner, known professionally as Solomon, died in 1988. Born in 1902, he appeared in public in 1911, playing Tchaikovsky's first piano concerto 'with a fire and fluency that astonished laymen and professional colleagues alike' and showing equal skill with Mozart and Beethoven. By 1919, a life devoid of normal childhood interests, devoted solely to the piano – originally under a particularly zealous teacher – had brought him near to collapse. The great conductor Henry Wood advised a two-year break. He took it, returning to music in 1921, and his career was successful and distinguished until prematurely ended by a stroke in 1956 (*The Times*, 24 February 1988). Jascha Heifetz (1901–1987) 'will be remembered as the most securely brilliant of modern violinists'. He began to learn the instrument at 3, from his father, himself an accomplished player. Like Solomon he began to play in public at 8, later developing into one of the greatest of classical players (*The Times*, 12 December 1987). Yehudi Menuhin at 7 gave a performance of Mendelssohn's violin concerto 'that was, by all accounts, unbelievably mature and spiritually wrought' (Andrew Stephen, *The Sunday Times*, 20 April 1986).

A particularly unusual history is that of Erwin Nyiregházi (born 1903), who was studied for six years, from 7 to 13, by the psychologist G. Révész (1925). His father, a singer in the Royal Opera Chorus in Budapest, was apparently encouraging and caring, but died when Erwin was 12. He reported that his son tried to sing before he was 1 year old; before 2, reproduced tunes correctly; by 3, played on the mouth-organ everything he heard. At 4 he began to compose. Révész found that at 7 Erwin could name any note or chord played, and could adjust a 'sound variator' to notes that differed only slightly from international pitch. By 9, he learned Beethoven sonatas and Bach fugues after hearing them three or four times. His playing was admired not just for technique but for musicality; and his compositions, according to Révész, were 'at the same time, tender, powerful, placid, passionate, joyful, and melancholy'. Révész found that on tests of general intelligence Erwin was at least two to three years above average, he was eagerly interested in all sorts of knowledge, while in personality he was 'a child in the full sense of the word; a clever, gay, friendly, charming boy'.

Débuts in Berlin at 15 and New York at 17 were enthusiastically received. But a first marriage ended in a stormy divorce case, and in his wife attacking him with a knife, forcing him to flee to Los Angeles. There he worked for film studios, eventually leading the life of a near-vagrant. Although he continued to play, for forty years he did not own a piano. A concert and an amateur recording in 1973 led to two professional records being issued, bringing him again before the public, only to disappear once more. Nyireghāzi died in 1987, survived by the last of ten wives (Gabriel and Shuter-Dyson, 1981; Shuter-Dyson, 1986 ; *The Times,* 18 April 1987).

The most famous of musical prodigies is without doubt Mozart (1756–1791), whose story is well known. His father Leopold was likewise a musician. Wolfgang Amadeus began to play the harpsichord at 3, and at 5 composed an *Andante and Allegro* and gave his first public performance. Whether his father should be said to have encouraged or to have exploited such a talent is perhaps open to question. Certainly in the next few years Mozart was exhibited throughout Europe, amazing connoisseurs and musicians alike as performer and composer. Although he died at 35, Mozart's career cannot be regarded musically as other than a triumph; indeed it is perhaps the supreme example of extraordinary precocity being followed by the highest achievement. There is little doubt either that both talent and hard work contributed to his early development. This is also true of Felix Mendelssohn (1809–47), often referred to as almost Mozart's equal as a prodigy, if not as an adult composer. Mendelssohn came of a wealthy family, which allowed him a general education as well as skilled music tutors. At 10 he was translating Caesar and Ovid, but he had already given his first concert as a pianist at 9. He studied composition with a distinguished musician, Carl Friedrich Zeher, and his exercises for one year, between the ages of 10 and 11, have been preserved:

[they are] the record of a prodigy, to be sure, but also the record of a child laboriously applying himself to the traditional disciplines of music theory. . . . Zeher led his pupil systematically through chorale, invertible counterpoint, canon and fugue. . . . Mendelssohn's progress during this time was truly remarkable (Todd, 1983).

Shuter-Dyson (1986) quotes evidence that musical talent

characteristically appears early. Scheinfeld (1956), investigating forty-seven outstanding instrumentalists, found that their ability had been noticed at an average age of 4 years 9 months (cited by Shuter-Dyson, 1986). For students of the Julliard School of Music the age was 5 years 6 months. Manturzewska (1979) reported that entrants to an international Chopin piano competition, and piano students at the Warsaw Academy of Music, had started lessons typically between 5 and 7 (cited by Shuter-Dyson, 1986). Révész (1925) suggested that early development might be partly due to music depending less than other arts on general mental development. Many of the arts are to some extent solitary pursuits and can, like mathematics, be practised alone, though instruction and guidance are also essential.

Pianist Artur Rubinstein (1973) tells us that as an infant he identified people by the songs they sang to him. Walton, Handel and others sang before they talked. The musical child typically attends to and delights in music. At 2 or before, such a child sings tunes accurately or picks them out on a keyboard. Often there is 'perfect pitch': Rubinstein noticed wrong notes at 2. And there is often a strong sense of tone: Rubinstein rejected, and Yehudi Menuhin actually broke, toy violins because their tone was so disappointing. Memory too is often remarkable. The pianist Dimitri Sgouros was reported to have thirty-five concertos in his repertoire at 13. And self-initiated learning is characteristic. Shuter-Dyson quotes the composer Peter Maxwell Davies, who passed GCE A level music virtually unaided. On the other hand, Sloboda (1988) has found that concert pianists are not necessarily or even generally outstanding at early ages.

Musically gifted children are typically ordinary in other respects. They show a measure of superego strength and personal control, necessary for prolonged and steady practice. They typically come from homes where at least one parent is musical. Scheinfeld found that 75 per cent of the fathers, and 50 per cent of the mothers, of his instrumental group had some musical talent. Freeman (1979) concluded that, whereas for children with talent in the visual arts a favourable environment in both home and school were equally important, for the musical child the home was of supreme importance.

There would seem to be a complex link between musical aptitude and general intellectual abilities, which would include perceptual, memorial and kinaesthetic aspects. Pupils at the Yehudi Menuhin school of music were found to have IQs in the range 93–166, with a mean around 130. This is well above average for the population as a whole (100), but the range is very wide. The student with the lowest IQ, who was at remedial level in reading and arithmetic, gained an award for advanced music study (Shuter-Dyson, 1986).

The complexity of this link is forcibly shown by the existence of musical 'idiots savants', a term referring to generally retarded persons who excel at one activity. An outstanding case is described by Sloboda, Hermelin and O'Connor (1985) under the initials NP, though in a televized 'QED' programme NP was identified as Noel Patterson. NP was born in London in 1962. An only child, he lived with his mother and stepfather until 1979, when he was admitted to a residential home for the autistic, where he still was at the time of the report. Autism is a complex condition, not well understood, but generally characterized by more or less complete withdrawal from social communication, and by behaviour, both in general and on any psychological measures, which indicates extreme mental retardation. NP, for example, scored a verbal IQ of 62 and a performance IQ of 60, levels at which other than institutionalized life is not possible. NP plays an extensive repertoire of classical pieces on the piano. Unable to read music, he could learn a new sonata-length piece in three or four hearings. He also plays popular music and hymns, and despite being generally withdrawn enjoys playing in public.

Hermelin and O'Connor investigated NP's abilities more systematically, first of all to confirm his learning capacity. They found that he could indeed rapidly memorize a tonal piano piece almost note-perfectly. They were particularly interested, however, in the mechanisms underlying this. It appears that it cannot be simply a question of remembering a sequence of sounds; NP's performance involves memory for tonal structures and relations. This is indicated by the facts that mistakes were such as not to impair the musical structure; that the ability did not extend to an atonal piece; and that NP's memory for verbal material is below average. His ability, then, consists not just in an unusual memory, but is akin to that of skilled musicians, although in many respects much more limited. NP's playing, for example, generally lacks expression. It does seem, however, that he must have perfect pitch. N.P. attended a day nursery until 5, and a day school for the educationally subnormal until 17, where he would have heard some music. He listened obsessively to music on the radio from an early age, and tape recordings between 5 and 8 show his ability already developing; but he had no musical instruments at home.

Hermelin, O'Connor and Lee (1987) give an account of five further similar individuals, all severely retarded, whom they tested for ability to carry out five sorts of musical activity: to continue a tune, invent a phrase or tune, improvize an accompaniment to a tune, invent a piece having melody as well as accompaniment, and improvize in jazz or contemporary idiom. These subjects were 18, 19, 31, 36 and 58 years old. All showed musical ability as children except the last, for whom information is lacking. They were compared with six normal children who had all received special musical tuition for at least two years, these being a closer match than adult musicians. The retarded subjects were far superior in both musical competence and musical inventiveness. (For further cases see Charness, Clifton and MacDonald, 1988; Lucci, Fein, Holevas and Kaplan, 1988.) The general conclusion which O'Connor and Hermelin draw is that one has to conceive of some form of 'musical intelligence' which is at least partly independent of general intelligence.

Judd (1988) concludes that if any cluster of skills is central to musical talent it is musical memory. This seems to be a trait of both orchestral musicians and idiot savants; it would seem to help to account for the ability of composers – Beethoven is the most famous – who continued to work successfully after becoming deaf. Conversely, poor-pitch singers are deficient in melodic memory, which improves if their singing is improved through training. Although it may be central it is only part of a complex interaction of many capacities which make up musical ability, including sensory, motor, mathematical, linguistic, reading, spatial, sequential and social skills.

Graphic artists

A similar conclusion seems to follow from studies of idiot savant artists. A remarkable case is that of Nadia (Selfe, 1977, 1983). She was born in 1967, and at the age of 6 was referred to the Child Development Research Unit at the University of Nottingham. At 7, her language was limited to about ten single-word utterances. She gave an overall impression of lethargy and impassivity; she was very clumsy, poorly co-ordinated, and excessively slow in her movements. She could not hop, or walk up stairs one at a time, or use a knife and fork together. She did not respond to questions or commands, but it was not clear whether she failed to understand or was unwilling to co-operate; either way, of course, this renders psychological testing difficult. At 3½ Nadia suddenly displayed an extraordinary ability in drawing, marked from the outset by an outstanding manual dexterity which was quite lacking in other areas. Her drawings were remarkable for their almost photographic realism. They were in conventional perspective, the proportions between and within elements were accurate, and there was occlusion (elimination of hidden lines when objects overlap). The drawings gave an impression of movement and vitality, and were in this and in technique totally different from the drawings of normal children of the same age. Nadia seldom drew from life and never copied pictures directly. Her method was to study pictures in a book, and then at some later time produce her own version with many changes and embellishments, for example presenting the subject from a new angle.

Young children are often said to draw what they know to be the case rather than what actually meets the eye, though there is evidence that even below the age of 10 they can be taught to draw what they see (Freeman and Cox, 1985). Artistic sophistication involves (among other things) developing a method of representing or projecting the three-dimensional visual world on a two-dimensional surface, by means of a 'drawing system', as Willats (1985) terms it. Willats showed that children typically progress through a series of such systems, starting with no projection, then orthographic projection (an adult example is an engineer's plan), until eventually conventional perspective is reached, though of course not all attain that level of skill. Since the Renaissance this has been the prevailing convention in Western art, to such an extent that it commonly appears the only natural one – pictures that fail to use it look 'wrong'. In fact it is culturally determined; other societies have used other systems. It is thus of great interest that Nadia correctly applied this convention, presumably learned from other pictures, even when changing them. She was not just reproducing from memory.

Lorna Selfe in 1983 reported on eleven further cases. These were mostly autistic children and all had severe mental retardation. Like Nadia, their drawings all showed marked differences from those of normal children. In particular, they employed photographically realistic proportions; they represented three dimensions; they showed distance by diminishing size; and they used occlusion. Selfe theorizes that these differences are related to the children's lack of language. She argues that normal children learn to draw through verbal mediation, typically speaking aloud a list of features while drawing. They 'attend to objects as representatives of classes'. Thus a horse is given four legs no matter what angle it is viewed from, because horses have that number. Children with very little language cannot do this, but instead attend to the spatial relationships in what they see and represent these in their drawings. They thus have a more advanced visual understanding, but it is limited, being 'concentrated into spatial awareness'; 'social, conceptual, and symbolic communication', writes Selfe, 'is absent'.

O'Connor and Hermelin (1987a, 1987b) have also studied such artists, one of whom, Stephen Wiltshire, appeared in the 'QED' programme already mentioned. As with the musicians, they were compared with a control group. In this case each artist was matched with another mentally handicapped subject without special ability. Five tasks were used: the Goodenough–Harris 'Draw a Man' test (which is held to be an index of general mental development); the Rey–Osterrieth test, involving copying a complex abstract design, which is used to assess possible neuropsychological malfunction; a short-term visual memory task, using Persian letters; reproducing line drawings, both concrete and abstract, from memory; and identifying incomplete pictures (progressively more of a drawing of an everyday object is shown until the object is identified).

O'Connor and Hermelin are cautious about drawing inferences from what were in fact quite complex results, but they do feel justified in suggesting that here too is an ability which is relatively independent of general mental development. It seems that the artists may have a richer and more accessible store of visual images or forms, a 'picture lexicon'. These experiments are among the first to attempt a systematic investigation of such exceptional performances (see also Waterhouse, 1988), and they may well shed light on normal development also. Rosenblatt and Winner (1988) conclude that superior visual memory is an essential component of superior drawing ability. But artists must also have greater facility in output, in drawing skill. Just how this comes about remains unclear.

There is a great deal of interest in the normal development of ability in the visual arts, (e.g. Freeman and Cox, 1985), but when it comes to exceptional precocity we are to some extent back in the area of anecdote. Sir Alfred Munnings, the former President of the Royal Academy, is said by his biographer to have made his first sale at the age of 6 (Goodwin, 1988). The ability of Millais was noticed at about the same age, and he entered the Royal Academy schools at 11½, exhibiting at the Academy at 17. Michaelangelo, although the son of relatively poor parents, was put to a wet-nurse, then the practice of rich families. She was the daughter of a stonemason and the wife of another, leading Michaelangelo to remark later, perhaps with some truth, that he took in carving with his mother's milk. It seems that his visual memory was noticed early (Gardner, 1983, quoted by Hermelin and O'Connor, 1987). He started in an artist's studio at 13, but this was in fact three years later than the normal age, and Michaelangelo was paid, rather than paying for his training, suggesting that his work was already advanced. Salvador Dali was not only precocious himself but had an older brother who died young, who he was always convinced, despite lack of evidence, had been an outstanding genius; but Dali's accounts of his past inextricably mingle fact and fiction.

Pablo Picasso (1881–1973) is generally said to have been a child prodigy. His father was a painter of still lifes, 'the kind with pheasants and pigeons, hares and rabbits: fur and feathers'. Picasso later recorded: 'My father would cut off the claws of a dead pigeon and pin them to a board in the position he wanted; then I would have to copy them very carefully until the result satisfied him' (Daix, 1965). It seems that this was so successful that when Picasso was 13 his father turned over his own brushes and colours to him and never painted again. As well as painting his father had always liked making things, colouring and transforming sculptures, making paper and cardboard cut-outs; and Picasso did so too 'as far back as anyone could remember'. At 14 Picasso applied for entry to the Barcelona Academy of Fine Arts, where his father now taught. According to Daix, it took the other candidates a month to do their examinations drawings, whereas Picasso recalled: 'I finished mine the first day. I studied it for a long time, and I carefully considered what I could still add to it, but I couldn't see a thing. Absolutely nothing'. Daix says: 'What impresses us most in Picasso's earliest surviving works [that is those done at the ages of 12 or 13] is not merely their technical precociousness, but the capacity to choose and make decisions, the maturity and intelligence of a boy on the threshold of adolescence'. Of course it is easy to read such ability back into the past history of the famous, but this is consistent with many such accounts, not only in the arts. A remark of Picasso's is of interest. Visiting an exhibition of children's drawings he said: 'I could not have taken part. When I was 12 I drew like Raphael.' Taken literally this must mean, among other things, that he used the drawing system of conventional perspective.

Pariser (1985, 1987) has examined in detail the juvenile work of Klee, Toulouse-Lautrec and Picasso. He concluded that each of them struggled with standard graphic-developmental problems, in the same way as less gifted artists. Their early works were not always outstanding, but

by early adolescence they had finished experimenting with isometric and nonperspectival systems of representation and had mastered one-point perspective. By mid-childhood they had also acquired a sense of conventional compositional structure.

None of them actually started out drawing like Raphael (Picasso only claimed to have done so at 12). It will be interesting to see what the future holds for Wang Yani, who when in London at the age of 11 already had a portfolio of more than 4,000 paintings in watercolour and had toured China, Japan and West Germany, having started painting when she was 2. The paintings were for sale at between £300 and £400 (*The Times*, 11 February 1988).

Poetry and prose

As yet a child, nor yet a fool to fame,
I lisp'd in numbers, for the numbers came.

So at least claimed Alexander Pope (1688–1744) in later life. ('Numbers' is used in the archaic sense, meaning 'rhythm; metrical feet, verses' (OED).) Undoubtedly he was precocious, though in his life of the poet Samuel Johnson, ever judicious, says 'The earliest of Pope's productions is his 'Ode on Solitude', written before he was 12, in which there is nothing more than other forward boys have attained, and which is not equal to Cowley's performances at the same age'. The work of Abraham Cowley, now probably forgotten except by scholars, had the advantage that it was published when written; with Pope there was always some suspicion that pieces might have been touched up later. For example, Pope's *Pastorals*, his first major work, though much admired when he first produced them at 16, were not actually printed until five years later. Johnson was in no doubt as to the need to bring on young talent, and in a sentence disposes of one of Pope's tutors who miserably failed: 'How Mr Deane could spend, with a boy who had translated so much of Ovid' he remarks magisterially, 'some months over a small part of Tully's *Offices*, it is now vain to inquire' (Johnson, 1777).

Johnson (1709–84) was himself a youthful prodigy, with an exceptional memory and an immense if erratic capacity for concentration. He himself accounted for his learning more simply: 'My master whipped me very well. Without that, sir, I should have done nothing'. This was the scholarly but cruel Joseph Hunter, who habitually beat his pupils when they failed to respond correctly, whether or not they had any chance of knowing the answer. Such arbitrary punishment is likely to produce strong emotional reactions and very likely high, if anxiety-laden, motivation. In rats the result would probably be experimental neurosis. It is not dissimilar to some of the techniques of so-called brainwashing, nor to those of Zen Buddhism. A Master is reported as saying: 'If you answer incorrectly I shall give you fifty blows. If you answer correctly I shall give you fifty blows. Speak!' At any rate, Joseph Hunter's small school produced, at the same time as Johnson, a bishop, an archdeacon, a chief justice, a poet and a celebrated doctor. In Johnson's subsequent life, periods of furious work alternated with guilty inactivity, though one would not be justified in attributing this entirely to Mr Hunter (Boswell, 1792; Hibbert, 1971).

The greatest literary prodigy of the eighteenth century, indeed of English letters, must be Thomas Chatterton (1752–70), the 'marvellous boy'. He was the posthumous son of a Bristol schoolteacher, poor but of some culture, and was at first regarded as stupid. At 4 he knew only one or two letters; at 5 he was rejected by a day school as dull; at 6½ he was said by his mother to be 'little better than a fool'. About this time he became fascinated by the illuminated capitals on some old manuscripts which his mother was tearing up as waste paper. He quickly learned to read and by 7 was thought remarkable for his brightness. By 8 he was so insatiable a reader as to forgo eating and drinking. Chatterton became obsessed with medievalism – old manuscripts, heraldry, statuary. In 1762 he was greatly affected by his confirmation, celebrated by the Bishop of Bristol, and following it produced his first poem, *On the Last Ephiphany, or Christ Coming to Judgment,* which was shortly afterwards published in a local paper. During the next year he filled several notebooks with poetry and prose, some of which was published. In particular he produced a poem in the 'medieval' style that was then fashionable, a spurious genealogy of a local worthy (perhaps as a joke) and an extensive glossary of 'old words'.

In 1767 Chatterton was apprenticed to an attorney, but his time was largely occupied in writing; above all a series of poems supposedly written by twelve different – in fact fictitious – medieval authors, centred round an imaginary monk of the fifteenth-century, Thomas Rowley. At different times Chatterton seems to have wished to present his works as copied from old manuscripts or as his own. He certainly asserted their historical origin to the dilettante Horace Walpole, who concluded, however, that they were modern – as, to today's eye, they quite patently are. Chatterton now became involved in lengthy negotiations with publishers which came to nothing, although some other works appeared. Disappointed in this, and with his indentures cancelled, in 1770 he left Bristol for London, where he led a life not then unusual for a struggling writer – Johnson's was very similar – writing furiously, selling sometimes, starving usually, and refusing charity. Chatterton did not survive the life of Grub Street, but on 25 August 1770 killed himself with a dose of arsenic, having first destroyed such of his work as was to hand.

Walpole later remarked: 'I do not believe there ever existed so masterly a genius', though he had hardly recognized it at the time, while Johnson considered: 'This is the most extraordinary young man that has encountered my knowledge' (*Dictionary of National Biography*). Chatterton has come to seem almost an archetype of the brilliant young artist destroyed by society. This romantic glamour may distort the view of Chatterton, whose surviving works are hardly read; on the other hand they are certainly extraordinary for his years. It is dangerous to read too much into a life only scantily known, but his initial 'dullness', his obsessions, his creation of elaborate fantasy, his inability to survive a life which, however hard, was survived by others, are reminiscent on the one hand of the idiot savant, on the other of such a present-day prodigy as Feldman's 'Adam'.

By way of contrast there is Daisy Ashford (1881–1972), author of *The Young Visiters* and a number of other stories. What is remarkable about this long life is that her masterpiece was written at the age of 9, and after 13 she produced no more; perhaps a record literary retirement. The vogue for her work may owe something to a liking for childish naïvety and innocence – a preface was contributed by J.M. Barrie – but there is also an undoubted gift for words, if not always for spelling, a sharp observation and real humour. Daisy Ashford's father encouraged her in story-telling, taking down her first efforts from dictation and writing out a fair copy. Storytelling was by no means unusual among Victorian children, at least the better-off, in an age without radio, films or television. One sister painted, another was musical, and it seems that Daisy had a serious ambition to be an adult writer. But a convent school, and above all, perhaps, a harsh reception by family and friends of her cherished and ambitious *The Hangman's Daughter*, put an end to it (Carpenter, 1982).

Daisy Ashford's stories, like those written as children by such popular authors as Mrs Ewing and Frances Hodgson Burnett, were adult romantic novels in miniature, emulating current fashion. In this they resemble one of Feldman's children, 'Randy McDaniel', who at the even more remarkable age of 4½ was producing creditable imitations of 'Dr Who' and 'Hammer horror' film scripts. He began to write at 3, having taught himself to type with one finger – the equivalent of Daisy Ashford's amanuensis father. As mentioned above, when last reported on by Feldman (1986b), at 14, he was writing lyrics for rock music.

As with Picasso drawing like Raphael, all the arts involve the learning of adult techniques. That this is so in the case of words, in particular poetry, has been stressed by M.C. Livingstone (1984). Livingstone's emphasis is on 'the tradition of poetry . . . which pays attention to form and uses poetic devices', the need for control, craft, revision and structure: '. . . children do not naturally write in the poetic line; they must be taught to do so'. This may seem at variance with the emphasis often placed on 'free expression' and 'creativity', but these characteristics are really at one end of a pendulum swing. More typically, artists in all fields have begun by imitating existing techniques, as Gombrich (1977) has shown convincingly with reference to visual art. Too rigid an adherence to academic rules results in lifeless art, in whatever field, but all art depends upon rules, or at least conventions. But to explore this here would lead us too far afield.

7 Young Leaders

Social skills

Why is the office of President of the United States of America 'not more frequently filled by great and striking men'? This question, Winkler (1988) notes, could be as well asked today as it was by James Bryce in his classic analysis *The American Commonwealth* a century ago. In a country above all where talent could rise, 'it might be expected that the highest place would always be won by a man of brilliant gifts'. But, Bryce observed, the men of most ability tended to enter business rather than politics. Moreover, outstanding men make more enemies than the mediocre; and

the ordinary American does not object to mediocrity. He likes his candidates to be sensible, vigorous, and above all, what he calls 'magnetic', and does not value, because he sees no need for, originality or profundity, a fine culture or a wide knowledge.

Whether this holds in the 1980s I leave to others. It is certainly not inconsistent with psychological research suggesting that effective leaders, while needing intelligence, are not too far ahead of those they lead, at least intellectually (Brown, 1965). One might expect from this that future leaders would not be exceptional as children. On the other hand, Bryce also remarked that the qualities one requires to gain office are not necessarily the best when one is in it. Historians identify many examples of the *arriviste*, more successful at getting to the top than at performing when there: Napoleon III, Prime Minister Harold Wilson and President Jimmy Carter might qualify.

The second volume in Lewis Terman's *Genetic Studies of*

Table 7.01: Average IQ of eminent people at ages 7 and 26 (after Cox, 1926)

	Average IQ (7)	*Rank*	*Average IQ (26)*	*Rank*
Philosophers	170	1	180	1
Writers EHCS	160	2	170	3.5
Writers PND	160	2	165	6
Revolutionary statesmen	160	2	165	6
Scientists	155	4.5	175	2
Statesmen	155	4.5	165	6
Religious leaders	150	6	170	3.5
Musicians	145	7	160	7.5
Artists	140	8	160	7.5
Soldiers	125	9	140	9

(EHCS = essayists, historians, critics, scholars; PND = poets, novelists, dramatists)

Genius was a highly original study by Catherine Cox (1926), who attempted to assess the intelligence of the most eminent persons (nearly all men) of the past four centuries. This she did by having judges rate their youthful performances against those of contemporary children whose intelligence could be tested. Cox was well aware of the limitations of this method. For one thing, the attribution of 'eminence' is to some extent an arbitrary decision which depends largely on writing about, or by, the subject being available. Then again, it may be the result of accidents of birth. For this reason Cox excluded hereditary aristocrats; but this had the effect of reducing the numbers of soldiers and statesmen. Cox also recognized that the rating of intelligence was only an approximation. Nevertheless she ended up with a main sample of 282 eminent persons about whom she was reasonably confident. There were for each person two estimated IQs, one based on performance up to age 7 and one up to 26. Subjects were classified by the main area in which they achieved fame as shown in Table 7.01.

From this it would appear that philosophers are outstandingly intelligent as children, and soldiers – perhaps the most direct form of leadership – least so. Religious leaders and statesmen are in the middle. Even an IQ of 125, however, is far above average. But there are some reservations. Apart from the fact that intelligence, and the IQ which is an index of it, is no longer thought of as being so fundamental and fixed as it was in

Cox's day, these figures necessarily come from what children were actually recorded as doing. Thus Cox's highest IQ of 195–200 goes to John Stuart Mill, whose childhood was largely devoted to intellectual pursuits. Given a more normal upbringing, he would presumably have been just as able, but would have been rated lower. Conversely, Mozart's activities were largely musical, and were thus difficult to equate with test performance. Cox eventually estimates that:

An IQ of 150 is probably not too high for a youth who combines with superior general ability grasp of life situations and a far-sighted fidelity to sustained effort, remarkable (though peculiarly auditory) memory, and the ability to analyse, to synthetise, and to create harmony.

Future leaders may have shown early signs of leadership quality, but these would not contribute directly to intelligence as rated by Cox's judges.

More research attention has been paid to youthful intellectual and artistic talents than to those that might mark future leaders. Abroms (1986) points out that there is no general agreement on what leadership is, or on whether there are general qualities of leadership across different situations. In North America, at least, gifted leadership implies superior role-taking skills, elevated moral reasoning, and prosocial behaviour (helping others). Abroms quotes research by Karnes and Shwedel (1981), who found that children rated high for leadership behaviour such as being sought out by others to become involved in activities, being joined by others and assigning roles to others were not necessarily the most intelligent. Leadership may be linked to verbal ability, but Abroms (1986) found that too high levels of knowledge and verbal skills, and lower levels of role-taking skills, may put other children off. Other studies have found that while there may be some relation between intelligence and leadership, too highly intelligent children may not be good at offering advice, or may be domineering.

Such research as there is tends to support Terman's early finding that the intellectually gifted are more mature in respect of personality, for example in making moral judgements, in social skills and friendship. Janos and Robinson (1983a) compared a group of twenty-four markedly accelerated university students aged from 11 to 18 with students on average four years older. On the whole the younger students appeared as mature as the older, though slightly lower in self-confidence and assertiveness (quoted by Janos and Robinson, 1985). Similarly, intellectually gifted children tend to be above average in such qualities as self-sufficiency and independence, energy and enthusiam, and sociability (Janos and Robinson, 1985a,b). All these are qualities which may contribute to leadership in any sphere.

   If instruction in social skills were sufficient to create leaders, Philip Dormer Stanhope (1732–1768) would be remembered as more than the illegitimate son of the Earl of Chesterfield to whom the famous *Letters* were addressed. Although in Dr Johnson's well-known opinion they taught 'the morals of a whore and the manners of a dancing master', they were intended as part of a system of education designed to fit a young man for a role in both polite society and, what was much the same thing, public service. As one of the letters remarks, 'Never were so much pains taken for anybody's education, and never had anybody so many opportunities for knowledge and improvement.' Chesterfield began when his son was barely 5, writing at first elaborate essays in French and English, on classical history, mythology and composition; but the ultimate aim was to make his son as perfect as possible in the social graces of the day. Advice ranged from leaving off 'greasy, heavy pastry, fat creams, and indigestible dumplings' (Philip being then 20) to the proper use of a handkerchief, and to the art of flattery: no woman is so ugly as not to accept flattery on her looks, but a beauty must be flattered on her understanding. But as is well known, the whole system produced only a pleasant undistinguished young man who died not very long after secretly marrying a wife with neither looks nor position. The Earl of Chesterfield supported her and her two sons, and transferred his letter-writing to his godson and heir, but to no greater effect. Admonition alone produced unexceptional early performance.

Business and enterprise

William Morris (1877–1963), later Lord Nuffield, the most successful British industrialist of the twentieth century, was 16 when he opened his small bicycle shop in Oxford in 1893 with a capital of £4 – a few hundreds now. He first repaired bicycles, the coming fashion (H.G. Wells thought they would produce a mobile infantry), then raced them, then built them, then designed them himself. Next he made motor cycles, and then motor cars. It was Morris's foresight and quick grasp of new methods of production that gave him dominance, rather than engineering skills. At the same age of 16 Cornelius Vanderbilt (1794–1877), the poorly educated son of a farmer, bought a ferry boat with which he carried farm produce and passengers between his Staten Island home and New York. Within two years he had bought three boats, and went on to become the greatest transport magnate in the United States, leaving a fortune of $100 million when he died. Thomas Alva Edison (1847–1931), probably the most prolific of all inventors with over 1,300 patents to his name, as a boy sold newspapers on a train, soon employing two others and producing a newspaper on the train itself, all before he was 15. Edison was essentially interested in the practical applications of inventions rather than in scientific principles, and was equally successful in marketing and making money from them. Haroldson Lafayette Hunt (b.1889), at one time considered the richest man in the world, is said to have been reading the financial pages of the newspapers at the age of 3 (Baker, 1983; Morris, 1983).

There are many contemporary examples of youthful enterprise. John Broome, creator of Britain's most successful leisure park at Alton Towers, and currently redeveloping Battersea Power Station for the same purpose, at 16 bid £4,000 for a house at an auction, having just £122 in his Post Office account at the time. It also happened to be illegal to own property under the age of 21. Fortunately his parents honoured the bid and Broome spent his evenings working to convert the house into flats, eventually leaving the property business with some £15 million (*The Sunday Times,* 12 June 1988). Similarly, Richard Branson, of Virgin Records and Airways, was an entrepreneur while still a schoolboy (at the prestigious public school Stowe). Growing Christmas trees and breeding budgerigars were not particularly successful, but a magazine, *Student,* was, with contributions obtained from such as John Le Carré, David Hockney and Jean-Paul Sartre. Articles from Robert Graves and Yehudi Menuhin were rejected as too boring (Brown, 1988). Sir James Goldsmith is said to have decided to get rich at the age of 8 (Wansell, 1988). *You Magazine* for 11 September 1988 reports on Cyrille de Vignemont, aged 17, a French prodigy who at 13 created and marketed a sophisticated and best-selling business programme, *Chargé de Mission.* At 15 he was appointed head of a think tank at the Ministry of Planning.

Something can be learned about conditions predisposing to leadership from studies of the successful. Cox and Cooper (1988) investigated in some detail the careers of forty-five chief executives of large British companies, using interviews and various psychological instruments. They point out that successful management is only one form of business leadership – entrepreneurs are slightly different. This particular sample were marked by the following characteristics: determination; learning from adversity; seizing chances when presented; ambition and the need to achieve, though in the long rather than the short term; high self-confidence deriving from 'a very clear internal map of how the world is and ought to be'; well-integrated value system; effective management of risk (this is where they differ especially from entrepreneurs – they were moderate risk-takers, with chances of success well-calculated); clear objectives; high dedication to the job; intrinsic motivation – all found their work completely 'involving and enjoyable'; well-integrated life – little conflict between work and home; pragmatic approach; sound analytic and problem-solving skills; and high level of innovation. These managers had often achieved, or been given, high responsibility at an early age. Although this usually means here in their 20s, and thus is outside the 'child' range, Cox and Cooper see the origins of many of the traits in childhood. For example, eight of the sample suffered the death of their father when they were under 16, and ten more were separated from their parents when quite young, usually by being sent to boarding-school or being evacuated in the Second World War. Still others had fathers who were absent for long periods in that war. In many cases it seemed the result had been the development of independence and a sense of responsibility: some actually were responsible for themselves and for others at an early age. When parents were present they often stressed achievement and success.

Almost all the respondents saw their childhood in retrospect as normal and happy. By contrast, a sample studied by Cooper and Hingley (1985) of more entrepreneurial individuals responsible for major changes rather than for management had seen themselves as loners (cited by Cox and Cooper, 1988).

Mickie Most, pop music entrepreneur worth £50 million 'first million made by 24', advises us to set goals early, to start young, determined to be confident and ambitious, and waste no time on books; he has never read one (*You Magazine*, 19 February 1989). Cease, reader, while there is yet time.

Two notions which run through much research on outstanding achievement are those of self-concept and locus of control. Locus of control refers to an individual's generalized expectation as to whether success or failure is due to internal or external factors; self-concept refers to the set of beliefs people have about themselves. Many studies show that a positive self-concept tends to go along with internal locus of control, and it is frequently suggested that both are related to achievement, perhaps causally. Keith, Pottebaum and Eberhardt (1986) attempted to elucidate these relationships, though achievement was academic rather than in business or entrepreneurship. This did have the advantage that an unusually large sample could be studied: 27,718 American high-school seniors. Such a sample, with a range of achievement, would probably be impossible outside of education. The results showed that locus of control had a positive and important influence on academic achievement; high-school seniors with a more internal locus achieve at a higher level, even when other important variables, such as intellectual ability, are held statistically constant. On the other hand, self-concept had no direct effect on achievement. It may however have an indirect effect, in that a more positive self-concept does seem to lead to a more internal locus of control. Keith *et al.* are careful to point out the limitations of this study, arising from the method of analysis and the particular nature of their sample; furthermore, it is not clear just how internal locus affects achievement – do these students work harder, believing that their efforts will give better results? (See also Pottebaum, Keith and Ehly, 1986.)

It would be quite a jump to infer something about achievement in general from this. Keith et al. suggest that it may be more effective to seek to raise academic achievement directly, or through variables, such as work methods, that are known to affect it, rather than, as has been popular, through improving self-concept. This would be consistent with a fairly general finding that it is better to address behaviour directly rather than indirectly; you should teach what you want people to learn, rather than hope it will somehow rub off in the course of learning something else. It is not unreasonable to conclude that if one wishes to increase leadership or business skills, as anything else, then these should be practised.

Rulers, villains and heroes

When power is hereditary it naturally sometimes devolves on the young, with varied consequences. James V became King of Scotland at the age of 1 year and 5 months (1513), and his grandson James VI was four months younger at his accession (1567). Frederick II of Sicily was king at 3 (1198), and Louis XIV, the 'Sun King', of France was 4 when he succeeded his father in 1643. K'ang Hsi became Emperor of China at 6 in 1661. The last three all count among the most remarkable of monarchs, though the usual fate of crowned infants is to be pawns in a power struggle. Edward VI (1537–53) inherited the throne of England from his father Henry VIII at 9. He is said to have shown a cold shrewdness in his short reign, acquiescing in the execution of his uncle and 'protector' the Duke of Somerset, whose successor the Duke of Northumberland persuaded the King, on his death-bed, to nominate as heir one of the most tragic of young sovereigns, Lady Jane Grey. She was the same age as he, known for her beauty, piety and intelligence (she spoke five languages, including Greek and Hebrew), but survived the dynastic struggle only until the following year, when she was executed along with her husband and her father, having been Queen for nine days. The next sovereign but one, Elizabeth I (1533–1603), although she did not succeed until 1558, by the age of 6 was proficient in both Latin and Greek, could speak and write French fluently, play the lute and the virginals, and was an accomplished needlewoman. Such attainments today would rank her as a prodigy, but then were no more than what was expected of a royal princess.

Few if any monarchs succeed in exercizing real power before their early teens. Frederick II was 14 when he became effective ruler. Edward III and James IV were 15 when they became King of England (1327) and Scotland (1488) respectively; both were able to establish themselves as dominant rulers. So was Ivan IV, 'The Terrible', who became Tsar of Russia at 16 in 1547, and Nero, who became ruler of Rome at the same age in AD 54. At Nero's birth an astrologer prophesied that he would become Emperor but murder his mother, Agrippina. She reputedly accepted the one at the cost of the other. In the event he did murder her, but not until he was 21. Henry VIII of England and Hussein of Jordan both became king at 17, in 1509 and 1952 respectively, the latter surviving successfully, to date, in a world that has rapidly lost faith in monarchs (Baker, 1983; Morris, 1983).

Legal and moral responsibility are generally set at specific years, even if arbitrarily. In the UK it is legal to drink alcohol in private at 5, but illegal to buy liqueur chocolates before 16. At that age one can consent to sexual intercourse, marry (with parental consent), enter, or live in, a brothel, sell scrap metal or buy fireworks. Not until 18 can one get tattooed or take part in an exhibition of hypnotism, or of course vote. In recent years, in the UK and perhaps world-wide, there has been a steady increase in juvenile crime, both male and female. Methods of reformation have in general rather low success rates, so that once started many delinquents repeat offences. There must, then, be record-holders for numbers of convictions; but these perhaps fall outside our present interests. For one thing, delinquents do not show outstanding ability, even at crime. If there are some who do, presumably they are less likely to be convicted. Those that do get caught tend to be of lower than average intelligence, and generally possess lower self-esteem and confidence in themselves and in society (Hoghughi, 1983). It is theoretically possible that there are unknown young master criminals, but on the whole it is more likely that the archetypal 'Napoleon of crime', on the lines of Professor Moriarty, the brilliant mind that goes wrong, is a myth, at least as far as juvenile delinquency is concerned. Young children can and do commit serious crimes, including murder. In October 1988 Ciaron Collins was convicted of killing Sharona Joseph; she was 2 and he was 12 at the time. Twenty years before that Mary Bell, aged 11, was found guilty of killing two boys. These are the youngest recent cases in the UK, but though exceptional are perhaps hardly to be regarded as achievements.

Nor does it seem as though those world leaders of our time who far outdo the worst of criminals have been noted for exceptionally vicious childhoods: Stalin, responsible for the death of countless millions of his fellow citizens, heads the list, at least statistically, followed by Hitler. No one could have predicted the career of either from his childhood. For youthful prodigies of depravity on a grand scale one has to turn, briefly, to history; for example, to the Julio-Claudian dynasty of the early Roman empire, of which Nero (37–68) was a teenage member. Readers of Robert Graves's *Claudius* novels or of his classical sources such as Tacitus and Suetonius will have a vivid idea of Nero's crazed iniquities; according to the latter Nero's later personality showed itself already by the age of 11.

While crime is at least possible in early years, military command is less so, though there may be indications of future martial prowess. Ferdinand Foch (1851–1929), Marshal of France and allied Commander-in-Chief in the First World War, is said to have begun his military career at the age of 6 in that he became fascinated by descriptions of historical battles. Military careers could formerly begin much earlier than they can now. Horatio Nelson (1758–1805) went to sea at the age of 12, and had a command by 24. In the British navy of the eighteenth-century a line-of-battle ship might carry fifty or more boys of 6 to 18 (Rodger, 1986), leading a life in which elements of 'normal' childhood were strangely mingled with great hardship and danger. Yet personal accounts then and for another hundred years and more give an impression also of fun, comradeship, patriotism, *esprit de corps,* duty, courage – such now quaint expressions (Baynham, 1969, 1971). Perhaps the most famous young British naval hero was Jack Cornwell, who was 16 when his ship, the light cruiser *Chester*, took part in the battle of Jutland in May 1916. Cornwell was a sight-setter on the forward 5.5 inch gun. The gun was put out of action and the rest of its crew killed early in the battle, but although fatally wounded Cornwell remained at his post, only being discovered much later. As with many military exploits this was in fact quite pointless since there was nothing he could possibly do there. However, Admiral Beatty in his citation referred to 'outstanding devotion to duty in the presence of the enemy', Jack Cornwell was posthumously awarded the Victoria Cross and became the object of national hysteria of pop star proportions; a national day, now lapsed, was named in his honour.

Jack Cornwell was not the youngest VC. Two boys have gained it at 15. Thomas Flinn was an Irish drummer boy at the siege of Cawnpore in India in November 1857. In a charge against the enemy guns his officer Major Stirling was shot dead, and he was wounded, but he carried on up to the battery, where he took on two men single-handed. Flinn's subsequent career was inglorious. Two days after the medal award ceremony at Karachi he was arrested for being drunk and disorderly, and this set the pattern of a long catalogue of offences. He was finally discharged in 1869, retired to his native Athlone, and died at 50 a pauper in the workhouse. Thomas Fitzgibbon, the youngest VC, was a hospital apprentice with the East India Company, attached to the sixty-seventh regiment which was engaged in the 'Opium' wars designed to force the Chinese to accede to the Company's profitable drug trade. In August 1860 a British and French force was attacking the Taku forts at the mouth of the Pei-Ho river, which blocked the way to the Chinese capital. The regiment had advanced to within 500 yards of the forts when an Indian stretcher-bearer was shot. Fitzgibbon went out to help him, and then another man, in the face of heavy fire and without any cover; he himself was badly wounded (Percival, 1985).

Undoubtedly young people caught up in the wars of the present century will have demonstrated equal if unrecorded bravery. One example that has been documented is the defence of the Cavalry School at Saumur in France in June 1940, when a force largely of cadets in their teens, plus their officers and instructors, held out for nearly three days against a German division (Macnab, 1988). Similarly there have been many examples, some of them famous, of less dramatic but not less remarkable heroism, resistance and survival. The story of Anne Frank (1929–45) is too well known to recapitulate, due to her diary written when she and her family spent three years in hiding in German-occupied Amsterdam. While the diary is unique the example, sadly, is not.

The youngest recipient of the Albert Medal for gallantry was Anthony Farrer who in 1916, aged 8, fought off a cougar to save the life of another child. Since 1774 the Royal Humane Society has been making awards for bravery in the saving of human life (Bishop, 1974). In 1971 its highest award, the Stanhope Medal, went to Thomas Nicol of Aberdeen, aged 13, when he rescued a 5 year-old girl from drowning. SALVOR (as the Society still calls its heroes) dived over thirty feet into a dangerous flooded quarry, found the child under water and with his brother dragged her up the cliff face to safety. The Society believes its youngest medallist ever was Frederick T. Kirby, who in 1904 clung to a boy of 8 who had fallen through ice when skating at Burin, Newfoundland, until help arrived and they were got out. SALVOR was 5 years old.

Werner (1984) reviews research on the characteristics of young people who are able to cope effectively with stress or who have shown an unusual degree of psychological strength for their age. Such resilient children generally have temperamental characteristics that elicit positive responses from both family members and strangers, and they tend to establish a close bond with at least one caregiver from whom they receive attention during the first year of life. Resilient children have four central characteristics in common: an active approach towards solving life's problems; a tendency to perceive their experiences constructively; the ability to gain others' positive attention; and the ability to use faith to maintain a positive vision of a meaningful life. Werner argues that those who care for or work with children can tilt the balance from vulnerability to resiliency if they: accept children's temperamental idiosyncrasies; allow children to have experiences that challenge rather than overwhelm their coping abilities; encourage children to develop special interests and activities; model the conviction that life makes sense; and encourage children to reach out beyond their nuclear family for interpersonal contacts. Two other general points may be noted: resilient children had at some point been required to carry out a socially desirable, helping task (compare Cox and Cooper's subjects); and they showed a central trait of confidence that things will work out, that odds can be surmounted.

The young idea

The notion that personalities are or can be shaped in early childhood long precedes Freud, though he gave it added force. Plato (428–348 BC) remarked:

The first step, as you know, is always what matters most, particularly when we are dealing with those who are young and tender. That is the time when they are taking shape and when any impression we choose to make leaves a permanent mark.

St Francis Xavier's (1506–52) view is equally well known: 'Give me the children until they are 7 and anyone may have them afterwards'. The aim of both was the popular but misguided one of creating adults in a certain mould. Plato's hope in *The Republic* was to construct a system for producing leaders – the Guardians of the state. The qualities required were a philosophic disposition, high spirits, speed and strength, and these were to be developed through appropriate literature, music, a physical and military education, and mathematics. One reason that this now seems curious is that current ideas of education centre on content rather than on development of skills, still less character and personality. As of 1988, the ghost of Mr Gradgrind walks in the (British) National Curriculum. By contrast, 'The aim of practically all Greek educators was the production of citizens able to take their part in the civic community' (Beck, 1964). Some Greek educational theorists assumed an authoritarian, some a democratic society, but all aspired to create leaders within it. The origins of Greek education were aristocratic, and the development of democracy largely involved making education available on the basis of merit rather than birth, together with the acceptance that these two do not inevitably go together: a fact which was irrefutably shown by plebeian victories in the Games.

Today the dominance of black athletes provides a striking parallel, but education too has followed a similar pattern. In Mr

Gradgrind Dickens caricatured the schooling thought fit for the lower classes. In the nineteenth century, indeed both before and since then, education for the more privileged, at least in Britain, has been concerned to produce leaders and rulers, mainly through the medium of the public schools. It may not be quite true that the battle of Waterloo was won on the playing fields of Eton, which at that time hardly existed in any organized form (and in any case Napoleon was outnumbered two to one); but the anarchic tumult of Eton (especially) in the eighteenth century seems no bad preparation for war. That the schools at least from the time of Arnold developed an ethos of public service and public leadership can hardly be doubted. Nor can the persistence of that ethos: in 1980 61.7 per cent of senior civil servants, 82.5 per cent of High Court judges, 67.4 per cent of bishops and 79.9 per cent of bank directors had been to public schools (Richards, 1988). Of course, a large part of the explanation lies in the fact that parents have to be wealthy to send their children to such schools, and that wealth also opens many career doors. It is also probably true that, on the whole, the better off will be endowed with above-average abilities, and will tend to transmit these to their children. Nevertheless, the schools themselves clearly have a profound effect. Home Secretary Douglas Hurd remarks: 'I dream of Eton'. General Sir David Fraser:

I loved it [Eton] from the very beginning. The thing I felt at once was that it was an adult place. You had to find your own way about. You were left to sink or swim, which I think is the definition of liberty.

No doubt some have sunk, but the swimmers remain. Benedict Taylor, actor, who as a boy spent ten days at Eton on an exchange with his comprehensive school:

I thought the uniform made a hell of a lot of difference. Wearing a stiff collar you'd suddenly be walking with your head in the air because you had no choice. You would be strutting around and feeling a million miles taller than everyone else in the street. It is an environment in which you feel special, unusual, and that gives you confidence. You feel that you are being groomed for something. (Danziger, 1988).

Attitudes are inculcated by, expressed in, a multitude of

ways many as small as stiff collars; others as obvious as a prefectorial system. General Fraser's remarks are, interestingly enough, almost identical with those of some eighteenth century Etonians, long pre-dating the 'traditional' (really Victorian) model of the public school (Chandos, 1984).

Likewise, attitudes can be developed with varying degrees of explicitness: most successfully, perhaps, with a variety of modes. The most dramatic attempts to change attitudes and even personality have gone under the popular title of 'brain-washing' or thought reform. These perverted programmes, combining traditional and scientific techniques in the service of an ideology usually more concerned with suppressing individuality than with developing leadership, have nevertheless shown the effectiveness of what is termed 'milieu control': the creation of a total environment within which all information and social pressure is directed to one end (Lifton, 1961). A boarding-school can have some of these attributes. In more normal circumstances, generally admired qualities will be the most likely to develop.

In the nineteenth-century heyday of British leadership, by far the most popular author of stories for boys was G.A. Henty (1832–1902). Henty, who could write a book of 140,000 words in twenty days, had sales perhaps reaching 25 million (Arnold, 1980). Although set in a variety of historical periods, his stories nearly all featured a hero who was the epitome of the young leader:

manly, straighforward, could give and take punishment . . . fearless, never lying, resourceful, [they] almost always develop strong physiques, they usually learn to box. . . . Normally they are from sound middle-class families; sometimes from the gentry. Whatever their starting point improvement is the objective: of fortune and status. (Arnold, 1980).

Henty's sales were dwarfed by those of his counterpart in the USA, Horatio Alger, Jr (1832–99), with an estimated 400 million (Hoyt, 1974). Like Henty's, Alger's writings featured a youthful hero, but a prodigy not of manly leadership but of self-made commercial success. Alger's ideal came from a poor home mortgaged to a pinch-penny squire, made his way to the big city, where he was swindled out of his small resources, but then luckily got his foot on the ladder and by hard work and acumen accumulated a handsome fortune on which to retire, a pillar of society, while the squire got his comeuppance. Easy to caricature though their writings are, Henty and Alger provided what boys wanted to read; and presumably, to be. At the time of writing, the most popular fare of British teenagers is reported to be the Australian soap opera 'Neighbours'.

Leaders, as already noted, tend to be ahead, but not too far ahead, of those they lead. Maslach, Stapp and Santee (1985) review the literature on readiness to act differently to others, and find that people usually feel most comfortable with a moderate degree of difference from the norm. Difference is found when positive rewards are possible; and individuals vary greatly in their willingness to stand out. Most research has been on negative aspects of being different, but Maslach et al. point out that there is also a more favourable side.

Altruism and spirituality

Joanne Gillespie, aged 10, was not expected to survive the cancer from which she was suffering, yet found strength to write and illustrate a book, *Brave Heart*, in the hope it would help other children. At the time of the report she herself was making a remarkable recovery, was back at school and attending ballet and tap-dance classes. Her mother said: 'She urges other children not to give up, that life is worth fighting for. I felt so proud of her doing something positive after all she had been through' (*The Times*, 17 October 1988). Such courage and concern for others are extraordinary but not unique, even at so young an age. Indeed research suggests that what is broadly termed altruism begins very early in life. In the first few months a child confuses distress in others with distress in itself; it is not able clearly to distinguish itself from others. From about 10 or 12 months the child can distinguish another's distress from its own, but does not fully realize the cause of it, so that it will try to help by giving what it would itself want. For example a child seeing another cry may seek its own mother rather than that of the other child. The earliest reaction to signs of distress in others is usually crying or other indications of sadness. At about 18 months there is 'an explosion of prosocial behaviour'. Children are seen to 'help, share, protect, defend, comfort, console, give simple advice and mediate fights. . . . Most of these different forms of prosocial behaviour have in common an apparent attempt to set things right for the victim' (Bales, 1984, cited by Raaheim and Radford, 1984).

Many religions accept the possibility of extraordinary spiritual qualities in children. Joan of Arc (*c* 1412–31) at about 13 began to hear mysterious voices which she was convinced were those of St Michael, St Margaret and St Catherine, teaching her self-discipline and telling her to rescue France from the English. She was of course executed for her beliefs but the verdict was reversed in 1456 and she was eventually canonized in 1920. St Agnes was martyred at the age of 13 in AD 304, but precisely why has become confused over the years. The story is that she refused to marry the son of the Prefect of Rome, stating that she was the bride of Christ alone. For this, she was thrown into a brothel. In one account, the only youth who would touch her was struck blind, and she then healed him; in another he was struck dead; while in yet another she was burnt at the stake but the flames did not consume her and she was eventually beheaded. St Bernadette (1844–79) was 14 when she had her famous visions of the Virgin Mary at Lourdes over a period of five months. These were declared genuine by the Pope in 1862, Bernadette was canonized in 1933, and nowadays some 3 million people visit Lourdes each year in hope of a cure for various illnesses. There are many other examples from the past and indeed from the present. In 1985 it was reported that more than 2 million pilgrims had already been attracted to the small Yugoslav village of Medjugorge, in the belief that the Virgin Mary appears there at a quarter to seven each evening to a group of young people; a quarter to six in winter. This began in June 1981 when two girls, Ivanka Ivankovic (15) and Mirjana Dragicevic (16) saw 'a bright shining figure of a smiling young woman in the sky'. Later the same day other children saw the same sight. Subsequently some of them spoke to the vision and she replied. This was followed by the miraculous cure of a paralysed deaf mute boy of 3. In the next few years life in the village changed completely, organized now around both the spiritual and logistic aspects of becoming a place of pilgrimage.

The phenomena have attracted not only religious but also political (Yugoslavia is communist) and scientific interest. Unlike in the past, numerous scientific investigations of greater or lesser thoroughness have been made, but with, apparently, little definite result. All that seems clear is that some young people experience something unusual, something that to them is the Virgin (*The Sunday Times*, 6 October 1985).

As is well known, the spiritual leader of Tibetan Buddhism, the Dalai Lama, was before the communist destruction of that country's culture traditionally chosen as a small child. The present incumbent, Lhamo Dhondup, was nearly 4 years old when various tests, including his having to choose certain items belonging to the thirteenth Dalai Lama, showed him to be the right person (Goodman, 1986). Few people who have seen or heard the Dalai Lama can fail to be impressed by his spiritual authority. Either the tests are valid in their own religious terms; or the selectors are outstanding predictors of child development; or the child was remarkably adaptable. A comparable case in some ways is that of Jiddu Krishnamurti (1895–1986), who at the age of 13 was picked out as a future great spiritual leader by C.W. Leadbeater, then one of the two leaders (along with Mrs Annie Besant) of the Theosophical movement. Krishnamurti, a thin and weakly boy who was considered dim-witted, was to be the 'Vehicle' for the incarnation of the Lord Maitreya, the World Teacher, also identified with Christ (an event still being predicted in 1988 by a man called Benjamin Creme). Krishnamurti was accordingly carefully prepared for this role, but eventually rejected the whole apparatus of Theosophy. Nevertheless, he did indeed become a spiritual leader, revered by many thousands for his concepts of freedom from spiritual authority and for opposing the narrowness of race, nationality, and formal religion. Leadbeater, for his part, throughout a long life found other boys to share his bed and his bath, more or less platonically – there is no suggestion that Krishnamurti did so – but no more spiritual prodigies (Lutyens, 1975; Tillett, 1982).

It will be interesting to see what is the future of Osel Iza Torres, the child of a Spanish couple converted to Buddhism, who at the age of 23 months was confirmed, by the same sort of tests as were applied to the Dalai Lama, as the reincarnation of

Yeshe, a Tibetan lama who died in San Francisco in 1984. Osel
was about to leave Spain for a monastery in the Himalayas,
according to *The Times,* 4 February 1987; see also Mackenzie
(1988).

Modern spiritualism likewise begins with children, in this
case the Fox sisters. In 1848 Katherine, aged 11, and Margar-
etta, aged 13, were living with their parents at Hydesville,
Arcadia, New York. In March the family began to be disturbed
by raps and knockings in the night. Mrs Fox apparently formed
the idea that some disembodied intelligence was at work. The
next step was to pose questions, which were readily answered
by raps. Before long the neighbours were at it, and the thing
became a sensation. An older sister, Leah Fish, saw possibilities
in promoting the powers of the two young girls, and a long and
complex career as mediums began. Years later they explained
how apples tied to strings had produced thumps, how toe joints
could be cracked to make raps, how with practice a questioner's
face could be read to reveal which answer was the one desired
(Brandon, 1983). Certainly deceit may be the explanation of
apparent childhood wonders. A once-famous example was that
of the Cottingley fairies. Frances Griffiths was 9 years old and
her cousin Elsie Wright 15 when in 1916 they brought home
photographs showing themselves with a number of tiny
winged creatures exactly like the fairies of a child's picture
book. This was not surprising, since that is what they were – cut
out and included in the photograph. What is interesting is
firstly the ingenuity of the girls; secondly their persistence with
the story for seventy years until Elsie finally revealed the trick
in 1983 (for her part Frances maintained that one photograph
was genuine); and thirdly the fact that what look now such
obviously faked pictures took in large numbers of people,
including the admittedly gullible Arthur Conan Doyle (*The
Sunday Times,* 13 July 1986). One more aspect of the case is
that it is only quite recently, since belief in fairies ceased to be
general, that they have been pictured as gauzy things a few
inches high. The 'little people' were just that – like us, but
smaller, which is how, presumably, they would photograph.

One should not entirely dismiss the notion that Frances saw
something: according to her daughter she saw a fairy as late as
the Second World War. Nor is it quite impossible that the

Foxes at first produced spontaneous phenomena, supplementing them with more reliable methods. A similar puzzle surrounds poltergeists, so often associated with a young person, frequently an adolescent girl. The curious thing here is that apparently identical effects are reported from a wide variety of times and places, contact between which is virtually impossible (Gauld and Cornell, 1979). Even when allowance has been made for ingenious trickery and the fallibility of witnesses, there remains something to explain: at the least, there is an exceptional achievement of some kind, whether occult or fraud. Perhaps the same might be said of the young 'metal-benders' who proliferated in the wake of Uri Geller (Taylor, 1977). Amid the welter of largely unsupported claim and counter claim (Frazier, 1981), two common findings recur: one is that the phenomena are remarkably elusive in any form of properly controlled investigation, and the other is that over a period of time they tend to disappear. Thus it is effectively impossible at present to reach any valid conclusion.

8 Prodigy and Genius

Early lives of geniuses

illud ingeniorum velut praecox genus non temere umquam pervenit ad frugem.

With a line from Quintilian, James Sully (1886), perhaps the first British developmental psychologist, introduced a discussion of the early talents of geniuses. For the non-classical reader he translated: 'That is to say, the early blossom of talent is rarely followed by the fruit of great achievement'. That might seem to be supported by Terman's longitudinal studies: his gifted children were successful but not at the very highest levels. We have already suggested some reasons for this, and have described the opposite technique used by Catherine Cox, namely looking backwards at the childhood of the eminent. This had been done before, though far less systematically, one of the first studies being by Galton (1874), who was particularly interested in the origin of the bent for science among the most distinguished. Asking a sample of 180 by questionnaire, he found that about 60 per cent showed what he called strong innate tastes; but by this he did not mean hereditary, merely natural or spontaneous. The next strongest factor (twenty-four cases) was professional duty: the need to take up science as part of earning a living, such as academic teaching. Twenty thought the influence and encouragement of private friends the vital factor; nineteen named indirect opportunities and indirect motives (whatever they were); thirteen encouragement by teachers; eleven fortunate accidents; eight travel in distant regions; leaving three giving residual unclassified influences. While this was rather unsystematic, it did show that the topic was amenable to statistical treatment, and it is interesting that these as it were naïve responses, made before the age of psychological investigation altered our expectations, show up already many of the factors that have subsequently appeared.

Sully's own enquiry was based on published biographical material on seven categories of distinguished persons. Of forty musicians, twenty-nine showed ability as children and another twelve by the end of childhood. Fifteen painters and sculptors out of fifty-eight showed decided skill by the age of 15, and about fifty by 20. Thirty-nine out of fifty-two poets were distinctly precocious, while of twenty-eight novelists, twenty-one showed imaginative power before 20. Among thirty-six scholars, historians and critics, thirty exhibited preternatural ability in childhood or early youth; half in the area in which they later became famous, half either in some other area or generally. Twenty-seven out of thirty-six scientists showed a bent for science by 20, and seven did their first significant work by that age. Twenty-five out of thirty-seven philosophers showed marked philosophical inquisitiveness by 20, but only two did important work by then. In total, Sully concluded that in a sample of 287, 231 showed clear evidence of talent before the age of 20. He added: 'I doubt, indeed, whether one could find in the lists of musicians, artists and poets, a single clear instance of a man of supreme genius having failed to give these early indications'. Musicians are the most precocious, artists almost equally so. Both depend on a 'special and restricted sense-endowment'. Poets are the most precocious writers, and similarly depend on the senses – an ear for rhythm and musical sounds – plus a romantic imagination. Scholars come next, which Sully attributed to their use of memory, a precocious trait. The early development of scientists was largely due to mathematicians being included in that category. Overall, there is a less than perfect match between early promise and later achievement. The explanation for this is that genius is:

essentially a native quality. A truly great man is born such . . . he is created with a strong and overmastering impulse to a definite form of origination. And hence he commonly gives a clear indication of this bent in the first years of life. On the other hand, actual production presupposes other conditions as well.

Added to this, there may be cases of late development. Sully's subjects overlap to a large extent with those later studied by Cox, as, inevitably, do his conclusions.

Another two major early studies were those by Havelock Ellis (1904), of 975 men and 55 women drawn from the then recently published *Dictionary of National Biography*, and by J. McKeen Cattell (1906), a follower of Galton, of American men of science. Both concluded that ability showed itself early. Ellis thought precocity was the chief feature of his data, but it could show itself in various ways: some individuals were exceptional at ordinary subjects, some were engrossed in a specialized subject, while some were unusually physically active, even brutal. It was also the case that some subjects showed outstanding early general ability which was much greater than anything achieved later. Where Sully put this down to extraneous factors, Ellis attributed it to two different sorts of ability.

Cox's work has already been described. A more detailed study of her top twenty individuals was made by McCurdy (1957). These were as shown in Table 8.01.

'Fame' refers to the estimated rank for fame in Cox's original sample of 282. On this basis the correlation of childhood IQ and fame among the top twenty is effectively zero, though the average rank for fame is, at 105, well above the midpoint for the whole sample, 141.

McCurdy distinguished three related factors which often appeared in the childhood of these twenty. Firstly, there was an exceptional degree of attention given to the child, often because it was an only or a first offspring, or else came late in the father's life (Coleridge), or was sickly (Voltaire). Or, in the case of William Pitt, attention was given because of the peculiar circumstance of being second born. This meant that Pitt would not inherit the title of his father, the Earl of Chatham, and thus could follow him into politics by way of the House of Commons. Pitt is said to have announced at the age of 7 that he was glad of this. Certainly he entered the Commons at the age of 21, admittedly through patronage. More remarkably, he was Chancellor of the Exchequer at 23 and Prime Minister at 24. This was received by the House with derisive laughter, but Pitt became one of the greatest to hold the office. Incidentally, he too was seriously ill as a child, at 14, but recovered through the

142   *Child Prodigies and Exceptional Early Achievers*

Table 8.01: Twenty most outstanding individuals (McCurdy, 1957, after Cox, 1926)

		IQ	Fame	Birth order	Age at marrying
1. MILL, J.S.	1806–1873	190	103	1/9	45
2. LEIBNIZ	1656–1717	185	19	1/1	—
3. GROTIUS	1583–1645	185	72	1/5	25
4. GOETHE	1749–1832	185	4	1/6	39
5. PASCAL	1623–1662	180	35	2/3	—
6. MACAULAY	1800–1859	180	53	1/9	—
7. BENTHAM	1748–1832	180	181	1/2	—
8. COLERIDGE	1772–1834	175	157	10/10	23
9. VOLTAIRE	1694–1778	170	2	5/5	—
10. LEOPARDI	1798–1837	170	280	1/5	—
11. CHATTERTON	1752–1770	170	170	3/3	—
12. NIEBUHR	1776–1831	165	135	2/2	24
13. MIRABEAU	1749–1791	165	30	?9/11	22
14. ADAMS, J.Q.	1767–1848	165	274	2/5	30
15. WIELAND	1733–1913	160	152	1/?	32
16. TASSO	1544–1595	160	48	3/3	—
17. POPE	1688–1744	160	50	1/1	—
18. PITT	1759–1806	160	9	2/5	—
19. MUSSET	1810–1857	160	261	2/2	—
20. MELANCHTHON	1497–1560	160	77	1/5	23

copious use of port wine prescribed by his doctor: the childhood of genius is not what it was. McCurdy found a 'very strong positive parental interest' in the cases of Mill, Liebniz, Grotius, Goethe, Pascal, Macaulay, Bentham, Coleridge, Niebuhr, Adams, Wieland, Pope, Pitt and Melanchthon. In the cases of Mill, Goethe, Pascal, Bentham, Niebuhr, Adams, Wieland, Tasso and Pitt, this led to them being subjected to remarkable and intensive educational programmes. Pitt's father trained him as an orator – then an indispensable technique for a politician – by having him recite and translate the classics at sight (*Dictionary of National Biography*).

Secondly, such attention meant that the child was very much in the company of adults, and relatively cut off from other children. However, several developed an intense affection for a sister: McCurdy lists Goethe, Pascal, Macaulay, Voltaire and

Mirabeau, in whose case it seems to have extended to incest. Musset was devoted to an older brother. It is noticeable that more than half the twenty were unmarried. Thirdly, no doubt related to the isolation, there was a marked tendency to develop a rich fantasy life. The most outstanding case is that of Chatterton, whose imaginary character of Rowley, the central figure in his pseudo-medieval romances, may have represented the father who died before Chatterton was born. This might account for the emotional involvement in what the author himself knew to be his own work, and his distress when it was rejected by critics (principally Horace Walpole) as forgery. We have previously noted a fourth factor, that with few exceptions all enjoyed a favourable educational environment.

Background to talent

Goertzel and Goertzel have followed in the tradition of biographical research presenting for example (1962) a sample of 400 eminent persons who lived into the twentieth-century. Their main findings were these. Most had not been born in metropolitan centres: (stage celebrities were the most likely exceptions). Of fewer than 10 per cent could it be said that neither parent showed some strong interest in learning, and this trait of parental interest was often accompanied by physical exuberance and a persistent drive toward goals. Three-quarters of the subjects had had a troubled childhood in some way: poverty; broken marriage; rejecting, over-possessive, estranged or dominating parents; financial ups and downs (about half); physical handicaps (about a quarter); parental dissatisfaction over school failures or vocational choice. Half the parents held strongly some unpopular view subsequently accepted – such parents reared nearly all the statesmen, humanitarians and reformers. Twenty-five per cent of the mothers, but only 5 per cent of the fathers, were described as dominating. Dictators, military men and poets had the highest percentage of dominating mothers; the over-possessive parent of a peer-rejected child, especially a mother who dislikes her husband, is the most likely to rear a dictator or military hero. No poet was the child of a poet. Seventy-four of eighty-five writers of fiction and drama, and sixteen out of twenty poets, came from homes where they regularly witnessed tense psychological dramas between parents. Lawyers, physicians and scientists tended to be adventurous, outdoor children; explorers and adventurers 'almost always' had a history of accident proneness. Of the 400, 358 came from families in the business or professional classes, some being wealthy. Only one had been on public assistance; one subject was reared in a workhouse and two in orphanages. Nearly half the fathers had been subject to traumatic vicissitudes in their careers. Twenty-three were alcoholics and of these, fourteen children became humorous writers or performers. In the whole sample there was a very low incidence of hospitalization for mental illness. In general the children enjoyed being tutored by parents or professionals, but often disliked school, especially secondary school; college was more satisfactory, especially if prestigious. Although 60 per cent expressed dissatisfaction with schools and schoolteachers, 80 per cent showed exceptional talent there.

Some more detailed work has been done by Berry (1981, 1988). He took as his sample Nobel prize winners, particularly in science (over 300 from the establishment of the prize in 1901). As he points out, although the criteria used by the Nobel committees are not revealed, they probably remain stable over long periods. And Nobelists are almost universally accepted, certainly in science, as worthy of the award (there may also be others as worthy who fail to gain it). The detailed facts of winners' lives can be established reliably, if with some trouble. In general talent appeared early, but Berry's main interest was in the cultural background. Consistent with other findings, the fathers' occupations show that prize winners have come overwhelmingly from professional and business families, and this is so regardless of country. But within this there are significant groupings: for example, about 20 per cent of the Nobel scientists are the children of university professors, and a further 19 per cent of doctors. Splitting the 'professional' group into those concerned with education, research and scholarship on the one hand, and everything else on the other, it appears that the children of the first group achieve success overwhelmingly in the sciences and hardly at all outside them, whereas the children of non-academic professionals contribute equally to all areas. Perhaps even more striking is the effect of religious and cultural backgrounds; winners come overwhelmingly from 'radical protestant and Jewish family backgrounds'. This is not so much, if at all, a matter of religious observance, rather of cultural values such as the value of education and knowledge for their own sake. One could add such 'protestant ethic' traits as ambition and expectation of success on the part of both families and children. Such values are likely to be transmitted largely within the family, though there is also a tendency for those sharing cultural values to be grouped geographically. In the USA, for instance, the Nobelists come mainly from two areas, Jewish New York and Protestant, small-town Midwest.

Anne Roe's article (1952), based on a study of twenty distinguished biologists, twenty-two physicists and twenty-two psychologists/anthropologists, gave a famous generalized portrait of the 'average' eminent scientist as:

the first born child of a middle class family, the son of a professional man. He is likely to have been a sickly child [Berry found no evidence at all to support this] or to have lost a parent at an early age. He has a very high IQ and in boyhood began to do a lot of reading. He tended to feel lonely and 'different' and to be shy and aloof from his classmates. He had only a moderate interest in girls and did not begin dating them until college. . . . Not until his junior or senior year in college did he decide on his vocation as a scientist. What decided him (almost invariably) was a college project in which he had the opportunity to do some independent research, to find things out for himself.

Berry, however, in his much larger samples, found smooth progress through school and university to be an almost universal characteristic of distinguished scientists, though not of engineers and mathematicians. Precocity is common, but mathematicians in particular, contrary to some notions of 'genius', often also show early evidence of ability to take social responsibility.

Walters and Gardner (1986) describe what they term the 'crystallizing experience', a turning-point in development at which a vocation is realized. They studied biographies of eminent persons in art, music and mathematics, and interviewed teachers of gifted children in the same fields. They concluded that such points do occur, but not with equal frequency in the three areas, visual arts having least. 'The crystallizing experience is a fragile phenomenon that occurs principally when circumstances combine inborn talents, self-teaching, and proper exposure to a set of materials, in a particular way.' It would be difficult to show that such experiences when they do occur actually cause an individual to take a particular line; they may be more in the nature of a recognition of where interest already lies.

Bertrand Russell's discovery of mathematics has been mentioned, but here is a description of a similar discovery in sport, from one of the greatest heroes of cricket's golden age, then 7 years old:

About this time I used to watch net practice exhibited on a tennis lawn by two of the best local cricketers. I could see from a top window in our house. I can remember the peculiar attraction, amounting to a thrill, of the sound of willow against hard leather. Psychologists will note that this thrill released some impulse in the small boy, who for the life of him could not have restrained himself from running down the garden the first time, and always afterwards, whenever he heard that sound, to watch the game over the thick quickset hedge. I had never had a bat of my own, or a ball, or played cricket; but the appeal was immediate and irresistible. (C.B. Fry, 1939)

Family influences

Irresistible as cricket is, perhaps more frequent than the crystallizing experience is the effect of one important individual, often of course within a family. A rather curious family phenomenon which almost qualifies as a natural experiment is that of the British Nanny, well documented by Gathorne-Hardy (1972). For something over a century, nearly all upper and upper-middle class British (and many other) children were effectively reared not by their own parents but by a surrogate of very variable quality but undoubted influence. There can be no question that for many children Nanny was the most significant person in their lives, often with a lasting effect. Winston Churchill (1874–1965), in extreme old age, in lucid moments would refer to his love for Nanny Everest, whose sole and loving care he had been for the first years of his life. Churchill was not intellectually an outstanding child, but he was early remarkable for strength of character.

Indeed, Nanny often fitted Torrance's description of the

mentor, though in other cases she was far less benign. Among Gathorne-Hardy's many examples of eminent persons influenced by their nanny, that of Lord Curzon (1859–1925) is particularly dramatic. Curzon was one of the grandest of Victorian/Edwardian grandees – Privy Councillor, Foreign Secretary, Viceroy of India, Knight of the Garter, Earl, Lord Privy Seal – yet ultimately disappointed, never to attain quite the highest office or quite the power he longed for. He was certainly a child prodigy, at Eton winning all available prizes with exceptional marks. Then and later his capacity for work was phenomenal; yet it was allied to an obsessional quality which made him quite unable to delegate even the trivial; a hoarder of power, of knowledge and even of objects. Gathorne-Hardy traces much of this to the monstrous Miss Paraman who became his nanny when he was 5.

In her savage moments she was a brutal and vindictive tyrant; and I have often thought since that she must have been insane. She persecuted and beat us in the most cruel way and established a system of terrorism so complete that not one of us ever mustered up the courage to walk upstairs to tell our father or mother. . . . I suppose no children well-born and well-placed ever cried so much or so justly.

Gathorne-Hardy argues:

As an infant and child minute attention to detail, an intense punctiliousness, an absurd sense of personal duty had been savagely beaten into him. All his life Miss Paraman brooded over him, daring him to let others do what he should do himself. He never dared.

It is plausible; yet at the same time we must note that Curzon's ten siblings had unexceptional careers.

Nevertheless, if even a substitute parent can have such effects, how much more the real one? – many examples have been given. In few areas is this more apparent than show business. Sinclair (1988) describes the family background of many girl film stars, and Edwards (1988) that of perhaps the most famous of all, Shirley Temple. As so often, an ambitious mother created the phenomenon, out of a musically gifted small child who was spending several hours a day at dancing school before she was 3, who at 5 was getting 500 fan letters a day and who before she was 6 had made twenty-seven films.

Howe (forthcoming) points to two main ways in which families can affect the chances of their children excelling. The first way is the specific teaching of skills and knowledge, the second is the transmission of values and attitudes. (In practice, it is often not easy to separate these: for example, scholarship involves all of them.) Again, we have seen these in many examples of precocious children. Howe adds the sort of general expectations shown by Berry as among contributing factors. He quotes research by Bloom (1985), at the University of Chicago, on the family backgrounds of highly talented young adults in several different fields, including mathematics and science, the arts and sport. While there were differences between families, there were also many similarities. All the parents seem to have been keen for their children to succeed, and prepared to go to great lengths to encourage this. They would supervize and check homework, arrange for extra tuition and co-operate in it, including extra-curricular activities such as music or sport, giving time, energy, praise. The whole emphasis of the family, which was seldom a broken one, was on activity, work, success, responsibility, efficient use of time. Howe also quotes some earlier research by W.T. Root, who found, in a sample of gifted children aged between 6 and 13, that 37 per cent had been given an exceptionally large amount of training at home by their parents. Parents were typically ambitious for their children and willing to spend time and energy in encouraging them. They tended to treat their children in a more adult way as rational and intelligent beings rather than talking down to them.

Yet, apparently consistent though family influence may be, children manifestly diverge. The Marx Brothers have been mentioned; another example is the Mitford sisters, whose adult political orientations ranged from communist through neutral to extreme fascist (of course these extremes are alike in their authoritarianism). Perhaps less known are the Knox brothers, Edward, Dillwyn, Wilfred and Ronald, gifted sons of an unworldly scholar and bishop, who became respectively editor of *Punch*, a wartime code-breaker, a priest and teacher, and a Roman Catholic dignitary and translator of the Bible. As children they played self-invented games one of whose rules was 'nothing is impossible' (Fitzgerald, 1977).

Apart from anecdote, research bears out such diversity. The

intelligence even of identical twins reared together, although it correlates very highly, is not identical. Correlations reported range from less than 0.60 to about 0.95, with a median at 0.85 (Bouchard and McGue, 1981). After childhood such twins diverge more. When it comes to personality traits agreement is even lower. In these cases the hereditary endowment is the same, and the environment is as closely similar as one can well get. Identical twins brought up together tend right from birth to share almost the same circumstances, often being dressed alike and even being taken for each other, at least by those who do not know them really well. Considering this and much other evidence, Plomin and Daniels (1987) ask, why are children in the same family so different? Their answer essentially is that, no matter how similar the environment may seem to be, it must be experienced differently. 'Non-shared environment' is the most important source of environmental variation for personality, psychopathology and intelligence after childhood. This means that 'what parents do that is experienced similarly by their children does not have an effect on their behavioural development'; the effects of parents on their children 'lie in the unique environments they provide for each child'.

This would probably not come as too much of a surprise to parents, who well know that their children react quite differently to the same situation. It does mean, however, that it is virtually impossible to prescribe specific rules for creating a particular sort of child, such as a prodigy. It is possible to say what works in general; but individual development remains unique. This is another reason for being sceptical of the claims of those who, on the basis of one (or even two or three) outstanding children, suggest that all children can develop in the same way. As G.W. Allport (1961) put it in a bit of folk wisdom, 'the same fire that melts the butter, hardens the egg'.

As far as cognitive development is concerned, evidence shows that it can certainly be greatly impeded by disadvantageous circumstances but that, within a normal range of environments, environmental effects are relatively modest. Rutter (1985), for example, concluded this from an extensive review; but it does not quite answer the question as to whether there can be exceptionally advantageous circumstances which would reliably bring about great advances in manifest ability. Nor does it attempt to deal with larger cultural issues.

Brownell and Strauss (1984) point out that the premise that development can be significantly improved by early environmental stimulation rests on a number of assumptions; for example that development is more influenced by environmental factors than by biological and genetic factors; that development is linear and continuous; that early experiences determine later development; and that the normal social environment may be inadequate for optimal development. These assumptions are not necessarily false, but nor are they necessarily to be taken for granted. Caruso (1984) shows how, historically, most research attention has been paid to the effects of parents on children, the effects of infants on care-givers, and the reciprocal nature of the interactive process. Only recently has there been much concern with the effects of forces external to the parent–child dyad. Clearly all these aspects need to be taken into account.

Problems of development

In another examination of the early days of genius, this time concerning education, Sully (1891) concluded: 'It cannot be said that the boys who afterwards proved themselves to have been the most highly gifted shone with much lustre at school, or found themselves in happy harmony with their school environment'. Considering the nature of some of those environments, it would be rash to take this as generally true; and indeed later research gives, as we have seen, a much more optimistic picture. Nevertheless there is clearly a less than straightforward relationship between early and later achievement. Some of the reasons have been mentioned. There are also some general assumptions that should be made explicit, as Brownell and Strauss do.

One of the most complex is that of universality, particularly in respect of cognitive development, though the problem runs throughout psychology. The first experimental psychologists, Wundt and his followers, assumed that the mechanisms of the mind can be studied in any healthy specimen, rather as a physiologist does with the body. Freud, trained as a physiologist and a doctor, made just the same assumption; and so, indeed, did the behaviourists, for whom the conditioned reflex explored by Pavlov, another physiologist, seemed the basic unit on which all behaviour was built. The psychometric tradition from Galton on has indeed tried to deal with variations between individuals, but this still leaves the question as to whether the ways in which individuals are compared with each other are universally valid. It is a simple matter to say, for example, that the population of Japan is on average of less stature than that of the United States (whatever the reasons). It is quite another thing to say that one group is less intelligent or more dominant than another. Some would argue that such qualities can in principle only be defined in terms of their context, and thus can never be universal. Others take the view that at least some psychological characteristics, usually intelligence, can be defined independently of context. Thus Spearman (1904), in his famous two-factor theory, claimed to have identified the essential nature of general intelligence, valid in all circumstances: briefly, the ability to see relationships. A similar, though more sophisticated, line is taken by H.J. Eysenck (e.g. 1986): in effect, that intelligence can be defined biologically. However, even if it is possible in principle to establish a universal trait of intelligence, relatively few scientists would agree that it has actually been done. The more optimistic believe that it can be. For example, J.W. Berry (1984), while accepting that there are wide variations in what counts as intelligent in different cultures, argues that 'pancultural characteristics' of intelligence must also be sought.

In the present context, Feldman (1980) holds that developmental psychologists have been unwisely preoccupied with studying what all individuals have in common (even if to varying degrees). He wishes to move 'beyond universals' to qualities that may be unique, or shared by only a few. This is brought out in his later (1986b) account of child prodigies. A prodigy, on his view, is not just someone who remarkably excels at something, such as mathematics or chess, which everyone can do to some extent however small, but one who reveals talents 'out of the usual course of nature'. Since there is, in fact, no general agreement as to what constitutes the usual course of nature as regards human abilities, this too remains an assumption.

An assumption that has usually been linked with universality is that of statistical normality. As mentioned earlier, Galton had noted that many physical characteristics, such as height, tend in a given population to follow the bell-shaped 'normal' curve of distribution, with many individuals clustered towards the centre – the average – and fewer and fewer the further away one gets from it. Since abilities must, so he thought, depend on some physical quality, presumably of the brain, they too are likely to follow this pattern. And indeed many measurements do yield such results. It is also the case, however, that tests of intelligence in particular have come to be constructed on the assumption that this must be so. This view has been challenged, for example by Walberg; see Chapter 10.

A third issue is that of continuity. It has been generally assumed, at least since Freud, that present behaviour can be largely explained in terms of the past. Again this assumption is shared by Behaviourism, the past being the learning history (or history of conditioning) of the organism. Explanations in terms of the present, for example those of the Gestalt psychologists, have found less favour; while those in terms of the future have generally seemed quite unscientific. Yet it can be argued that in many ways it is more sensible, and helpful, to say that a tennis player practices hard because she wants to win than because she has been conditioned to do so. The dominance of historical explanations means that it is important to establish how far the past can in fact predict the future. The answer is, to a limited extent. Thus Clarke (1979), in an extensive review, concludes that, except for extreme conditions such as autism, long-term predictions of human development tend to be rather poor. This is particularly so with personality characteristics, while intelligence is rather more consistent. The reasons for this do not lie in inadequate methods of measurement, but in the nature of development itself. The adult cannot be a simple extrapolation from the child, because many adult qualities do not exist at an earlier age. This is so whether they are genetically pre-programmed, like sex, or the result of interaction between constitution and environment, like social and moral attitudes. Furthermore, no science can predict the chance encounters, opportunities or calamities of future years, which may determine the course of individual development. Then, too, individuals vary not only in their circumstances, but in their capacity for change. At the same time, this capacity is generally greatest in the young, and declines with age, meaning that the younger the child, the less easy it is to predict. This is certainly not to deny continuity of development; but the degree of consistency from child to adult is moderate (Bornstein and Sigman, 1986). One must point out that this judgement depends on what one considers 'moderate'.

Such at least is the current view. Clarke points out that at the beginning of the century a much more deterministic view was widely held, largely in the form of a belief in heredity. J.S. Bruner refers to three changes in generally held views of the child's mind in recent years: the child is seen as active and intentional rather than passive; it is assumed that the mind has structure at each stage – it is never a 'blank slate', or like unformed Plasticine; and it is from the start – birth or before – open to education and learning (in Bronfenbrenner, Kessel, Kessen and White, 1986). Hareven (1986) describes historical changes in the family and the course of development, and shows that the stages of life, such as childhood, adolescence, youth, which we distinguish have not always been seen in the same way. Aries (1960) went so far as to claim that childhood as a distinct experience and stage of life was only discovered in the eighteenth-century. This is over-simple, and all periods must have recognized the course of development, though in different ways: Shakespeare had his seven ages of man (in *As You Like It*), which were astrological in origin; medieval writers were more inclined to discern three, four or six, from the biology of birth, maintenance and decay, or different combinations of the four humours, or from six periods of world history (Burrow, 1986). Hareven summarizes different accounts of the emergence of the modern, private, nuclear, domestic, child-centred family; the sort of family described in so many accounts of gifted children.

Ability and achievement

As Caruso (1984) points out, the family is set in a cultural context. D.K. Simonton (e.g. 1978) has made several studies of the cultural features that have historically been associated with the emergence of eminent persons. Among them are, he suggests, formal education, role-model availability, *zeitgeist*, political fragmentation, war, civil disturbance and political instability. This is reminiscent of Harry Lime's remark in the film *The Third Man* about the disorder of Renaissance Italy producing Leonardo da Vinci while Switzerland's three hundred years of peace gave us the cuckoo clock. One problem with this is that different periods cannot easily be equated. War is now a far different phenomenon from what it was a century ago. It is plausible to argue that some periods have produced many creative persons, or at any rate many creative achievements, and others fewer, but the reasons must surely be extremely complex, involving genetic, economic, geographical, political, social, religious and many other factors. One of the most obvious examples is that of classical Greece; see for example Vernant (1962).

Within our own culture, Havighurst (1961) suggested some ways in which the numbers of children of superior ability might be increased. These were as follows: remedying deprivation, so that deprived groups will produce their full share of the more able; counselling and guidance; more emphasis on 'need for achievement' in both home and school, particularly in terms of motivation for intellectual activities; widening the concept of giftedness from just 'intelligence'; and improvements in teaching so that learning is made more attractive to children.

This would probably still hold good. Such measures might well increase the chances of outstanding ability appearing, but the course of individual development remains relatively unpredictable. Agassi (1985), for example, criticizes what he sees as the 'myth' that genius necessarily appears before maturity. Some geniuses develop late and some prodigies fail. It is not entirely clear who is supposed to believe in this myth, since as we have seen the evidence from Terman onwards shows that the growth of talent is general but not universal. Whether potential comes to fruition is certainly partly a matter of circumstances, but the precise nature of the interaction is still unclear.

It is less contentious to assert that great achievement seems to involve great personal involvement, to put it in general terms. Those who reach the top in any field seldom, if ever, seem to do so without the greatest efforts of which they are capable. Examples have been given from many fields. Aspy and Aspy (1985) offer evidence, admittedly largely anecdotal, that intensity of involvement lies at the heart of the thinking process. Similarly in the case of such odd skills as calendrical calculating (O'Connor and Hermelin 1984; Howe and Smith, 1988; Obler and Fein, 1988). It is clear that this is partly the result of continued practice which to many would seem too boring or pointless to pursue. It is of the nature of skills, whatever the natural talent, that they require time and effort, and thus commitment (see Chapter 10). Dr Johnson explained that he had not mastered the violin because: 'I found that to fiddle well, I must fiddle all my life; and I thought I could do something better'.

There is another puzzle here. It might seem obvious that one cannot expect to win without trying as hard as, or harder than, the next person, yet it is difficult to see why in principle an individual could not by chance occur who was sufficiently talented to make great effort unnecessary. Indeed in particular circumstances this does happen; the local champion may be locally unbeatable. As he or she ventures further afield competition becomes more intense, but this is only a matter of relative probabilities. If no worthy opponent appears, less than the best may suffice. Bertrand Russell (1967) tells how as an undergraduate he went around Cambridge looking for the clever men, that is cleverer than he, but could not find them; at least until he met John Maynard Keynes. (The future economist at 4½ explained the nature of interest to his father, and at 6 was greatly interested in his own brain. 'Just now', he remarked, 'it is wondering how it thinks. It ought to know' (Harrod, 1951).) But biographies also show rather convincingly that it is not competition alone, at least directly, that motivates great achievement, but rather the desire for mastery of the art or discipline. Just why music or mathematics should seize so strongly on the imagination of one individual but not another is not yet fully explicable. Talent and commitment are probably correlated, but far from completely; it is quite possible to be devoted to a sport without being much good at it.

On the other hand, although G.K. Chesterton remarked that

if a thing is worth doing it is worth doing badly, it is probably more rewarding to do it well. Indeed, substantial research on learning shows fairly conclusively that positive reinforcement is in general more effective than negative. Such reinforcement may be either intrinsic or extrinsic. Waterhouse (1988) speculates as to possible physiological mechanisms (see Chapter 10); but it is easy to see that doing what one is good at is likely to be enjoyable. This is likely to be strengthened if one also has a strong desire to excel. Certainly some prodigies at least have felt this, for example Chatterton, Goethe, Boris Becker. Polit and Falbo (1987) reviewed 141 studies of only children for evidence of 16 personality traits, and concluded that they scored significantly higher on achievement motivation than did others. It is not unreasonable to suppose that first-borns would share some of this also; and even those in other isolated positions. It will be recalled that ten of Cox's top twenty were first-born.

One reason for such achievement traits is presumably the extrinsic motivation supplied, in the first instance, by parents or parent substitutes. As we have seen, this is true of groups of gifted children, and in some cases to an extreme degree – Johnson's Mr Hunter, James Mill, Boris Sidis, Leo Wiener, Miss Paraman, for example. Such persons, having either no knowledge or an idiosyncratic knowledge of learning theory, rather obviously mingled positive and negative reinforcement somewhat haphazardly and arbitrarily. Such a regime, as already suggested, especially if conducted in a closed and emotionally charged environment, is likely to have a powerful effect even if the motivation produced is accompanied by personality problems – as in many cases it undoubtedly has been.

Less dramatically, it is possible to become habituated to different regimes, within limits. It is, for example, relatively easy to get used to an increased or decreased amount of regular sleep, to the extent of two or three hours, with apparently no long-term ill effects (Horne, 1988). Anyone who has been a serious part-time student knows how what for ordinary undergraduates supposedly takes all day can be accommodated in a life already fully occupied by employment and domestic concerns. Children are not only even more adaptable, but have less reason to suppose their regime unusual especially if, like J.S. Mill and others, they are relatively isolated. Even where this is not the case, as with the recent mathematical prodigies, it is likely that, as with most children, their own family arrangements would constitute what is experienced as normal.

The experiments of Rosenthal (e.g. Rosenthal and Jacobson, 1968), although subsequently criticized, seemed to demonstrate that, at any rate to some extent, children's performance can improve if their teachers are led to believe they have superior ability. Gruber (1986) argues that the main force in the development of an extraordinary person is that individual's own activity and interests; although at the same time the meaning and value of any particular kind of extraordinariness depends on the historical and social circumstances in which it appears. Scarr and McCartney (1983) propose a theory of 'how people make their own environments'. Given that certain characteristics, or at least potentials, are inherited, these will interact with the environment in three ways: a passive way, through environments provided by the biologically related parents; an evocative way, through responses elicited by the individual from others; and an active way, through the selection of different environments by different people. It is not too difficult to see these mechanisms at work in the lives of exceptionally gifted individuals for whom we have biographical data, and whose gifts came to fruition to varying degrees and at various stages of life.

9 Intelligence and After

The search for intelligence

It has often been assumed that prodigies are, in some sense or other, exceptionally intelligent; indeed this has sometimes been taken as the defining characteristic. To psychologists, 'intelligence' has come to seem something of a Frankenstein's monster; originally conceived as a great scientific advance, it has run out of control, epitomizing the dire consequences that follow when man 'aspires to become greater than his nature will allow' (Mary Shelley; *Frankenstein, or the Modern Prometheus*, 1818) – that is, in the present case, to understand ourselves in a scientific sense and hence ultimately even to alter our natures. However this may be, few words or concepts arouse greater controversy than does 'intelligence'. The controversy is partly scientific, but very largely political.

Intelligence has become a political issue partly because it has seemed to provide a scientific way of differentiating individuals and groups, and then of justifying differential treatment for them; partly because this has become linked with other bases of differentiation such as class, race and colour, which are themselves controversial and are in turn linked to prejudiced attitudes; partly because intelligence as measured by psychologists is as a matter of fact linked to various indices of success such as education, higher social status and higher income; and no doubt partly because of numerous other complexities. None of these links is inevitable or necessarily causal. Put more simply, attitudes and policies come first, and 'intelligence' has been pressed into service to support them.

This has been the easier since many scientific issues remain unresolved. The psychological concept of 'intelligence' arises from the attempt to investigate scientifically the obvious fact that human beings vary very widely in performance; both in the range of things that they do and in the success with which they do them. It is natural to ask first how performances can be classified; then whether they can be grouped into categories; then whether any common factors can be identified, and if so, measured; and finally what might be the origins of such factors. Essentially these are the questions that have been asked by psychometricians, though not necessarily in this order, and not often with generally agreed answers.

The first problem arises from the fact that human behaviour is not a fixed and defined entity given to scientists to study. This is a basic difficulty of all science, as has been generally accepted following Karl Popper (e.g. 1963). All observation presupposes a decision as to what to observe. In the case of behaviour the problem is compounded by the facts that the observer is herself part of what is to be observed, and that behaviour is not static but constantly changing (partly, just to add to complexity, because it is being observed). Thus if behaviour is to be studied, the first question is, which behaviour? Alfred Binet (1857–1911) devised what came to be the first intelligence test of the modern type, for the practical purpose of identifying children who needed special education. One of his items was describing a route across Paris. Clearly this would be a completely different task today, even for a child born in Paris, while for one reared elsewhere it would be meaningless. But it was a perfectly sensible sample of behaviour at that time and place; one on which children could reasonably be compared with each other and which could be expected to correlate with future performance on other tasks. (Though this has to be established empirically, it is not a matter of intuition.)

It is practically, indeed logically, impossible for an investigator to study behaviour other than that which has meaning for her. Psychometrics has developed in particular (closely related, Western) cultures, and for the practical purposes of those cultures. Thus performances have been selected on the basis of success in those societies. It has been found that they do, in fact, tend to group together, as Terman showed. Theories of intelligence have been developed in the attempt to identify some common factor or factors in these correlated performances; and tests of intelligence have been devised in the attempt to sample behaviour in a more systematic and standardized way, and to allow prediction over a wide range of activities. It remains the case that the best test of any particular activity is that activity itself: by 1985, one could say confidently that Boris Becker was a very good tennis player; when coach Breskvar took him on, it was only a prediction – based, as we saw, on a number of observations.

It is important to realize that although all theories and tests of intelligence have been developed in particular cultures, they are not *necessarily* restricted to them. At a simple level, it is a matter of fact that one culture, broadly defined, is now dominant in the world, and success in practical terms means success in that culture. It is also true that, genetically, human beings are much more similar across the world than they are different, and there is no reason in principle why a theory developed in one context should not turn out to be generally useful. Nevertheless no theory of intelligence has so far been conclusively demonstrated to be universally valid. Part of the problem here is that there is no agreement, not just on 'what intelligence is', but on what sort of a concept we ought to be considering.

It is possible to conceptualize behaviour at one or more of three levels, as was realized by Thomas Hobbes (1588–1679); physiological, individual and social. Diamond and Scheibel (1985, cited by Waterhouse, 1988) analysed sections of the brain of Albert Einstein and found them significantly different to control brains; for example, greater numbers of glial cells (the function of this type of cell is as yet unclear). Similar differences were found in the brains of rats which had been reared in an enriched and stimulating environment. This suggests that, whatever the original endowment, the brain (like every other aspect of living things) develops in interaction with the environment. Nevertheless one could reasonably speak of a brain at any particular point as being more or less capable of sustaining high level, 'intelligent' behaviour. It would be odd, though, to speak of Einstein's brain, even before dissection, as intelligent. It was Einstein, not his brain, that was the genius. This is because intelligence is a term descriptive of behaviour, that is, of living individuals. Some would argue further that the behaviour it describes only has meaning with reference to other individuals or groups. On this basis, Einstein set down in the Australian bush a century ago would no longer be a genius, since he would not be very good at finding witchetty grubs and water-holes. If this conclusion seems perverse, it may be because we assume Einstein's frame of reference, which is almost the same as our own, to have priority.

Ideally, the reference group would be the whole human race. This in essence was Galton's standard of comparison, though it led him into value-judgements about the worth of the activities of different groups which are currently unfashionable – classical Greece was as far above Victorian England as the latter was above contemporary Africa. This sort of difficulty is still with us. Furthermore, we can only sample what the human race is capable of; the past is largely out of reach and the future wholly so. Other problems arise, first, when attempts are made to define the ability that is a common factor in superior performances. Since these can only be a selection from what is possible, it always turns out that the definition excludes things that someone wishes to call 'intelligent'. In general, the selection has emphasized intellectual/cognitive/scholastic activities as seen in Western society. Ryle (1949) argued that intelligence cannot be defined by a list of tasks, since it refers, rather, to the way in which tasks are carried out – quickly, accurately, adaptively, etc. Thus it makes sense to speak (as we do) of boxing or playing the piano intelligently or unintelligently, as well as, say, doing mathematics. But it would be unusual to assert that boxing, or washing the dishes, could be done as intelligently as mathematics.

Secondly, there is a tendency to turn what has been defined from a shorthand description into an explanation. Howe (1988a) attacks this on the grounds that intelligence has not been shown to be reliably related to other variables, such as physiological mechanisms or basic mental processes. Ryle pointed out the real fallacy, which is that to suppose that 'intelligence' is the cause of behaving intelligently is like saying that speed is the cause of a car going fast. It has seemed that (for example) a child's good or poor performance at school is explained when its intelligence is measured, and an IQ established which is much above or below average. An IQ, however, is only a quick way of saying that certain tasks have been carried out in a certain manner. Its virtue is that it allows, within limits, comparison with other individuals, and prediction of performance on other activities.

The varieties of intelligent behaviour

Partly due to psychologists' attempts to avoid some of these problems the term 'giftedness' has become popular. In practice, it is often almost equated with 'intelligence'. Humphreys (1985), for example, takes 'gifted' to mean 'intellectually gifted', and posits that the fundamental basis of giftedness is 'a high level of general intelligence'. He does not deny that athletes, musicians and graphic artists can perform at 'gifted' levels, but argues that the talents involved 'are not primarily intellectual'. Feldman (1986a) distinguishes between the prodigy and the individual of high intelligence, on the grounds that the former are 'on the whole, extreme specialists' whereas a high IQ implies generalized intellectual abilities 'that seem to permit high levels of functioning in a wide range of environments'. Why such a child should not be called a prodigy is not clear. Feldman's own definition does not help: 'I think of a prodigy as a child who is able to perform at or near the level of an adult professional in an intellectually demanding field' (Feldman, 1986b). Almost by definition, one can hardly excel in an intellectually demanding field without a high level of intelligence, and the introduction of the adult professional standard merely confuses the issue. In many cases, such as exceptional language development, it is difficult to see what it means. And it has been assumed here that most people would want to speak of prodigies in fields which are not primarily intellectual, such as sport or the arts, in addition to those children who have displayed a range of talents.

   Distinctions between specialist and generalist, and between intellectual and non-intellectual, may not reflect the real way in which human abilities function. Dr Johnson's definition of genius as 'a mind of large general powers, accidentally determined in a particular direction', although merely intuitive, is perhaps a better starting-point. Just what characterizes those 'general powers' is among the still unresolved issues. All the answers involve making judgements. The judgement may be simply of what is thought to be the essence of 'intelligence'; or more systematically, it may be of what sorts of performance to measure and analyse, and then of how many factors it makes sense to accept as accounting for the variance. Suppose one were to analyse sporting ability; it would probably be the case that there is something in common between all sports, so that a professional in one would be likely to perform better in any other than would a person picked at random from the general population. But equally, sportspeople would fall into groups, with relatively little overlap in ability between, say, moving-ball-game players and horse-riders. Footballers (especially in running-with-the-ball rule games) would have something in common with track athletes but much less with snooker or pool players, and so on. One might well conclude that there was something that could be called 'general sporting ability', and a range of more specialized abilities – some of them possibly very specialized indeed. But the conclusion might be that it was more sensible to speak of a number of relatively independent abilities. And one would have to recognize that what constitutes a sport is largely arbitrary, and that levels of skill may not be equivalent, as different sports gain or lose in popularity.

It is similar with intellectual ability. Many of the earlier theories of intelligence stressed one major factor, such as the 'innate general cognitive ability' – 'g' to its friends – of Cyril Burt (1883–1971), plus further specialized abilities. L.L. Thurstone (1938) on the other hand distinguished seven, possibly eight, 'primary mental abilities', while J.P. Guilford (1982) proposed 150 factors. Currently, Howard Gardner (e.g. 1983) takes the line of separate abilities considerably further with a theory of 'multiple intelligences' of which he distinguishes six: linguistic, logico-mathematical, spatial, musical, bodily-kinaesthetic and personal. Two aspects of this account make it particularly relevant to the consideration of prodigies. One is that it considers a much wider range of behaviour than most previous theories. The first three of Gardner's 'intelligences' cover much the same ground as before, except that they are seen less as aspects of intelligence and more as separately

164   *Child Prodigies and Exceptional Early Achievers*

functioning abilities. The other three have seldom been considered as 'intelligence' in any shape. Musical intelligence involves the ability to perceive pitch and rhythm and is the basis of musical talent. Bodily-kinaesthetic intelligence concerns control over one's own body, as seen in gymnasts and mime artists; and control over instruments, as in engineers, surgeons, and tennis players or golfers. Personal intelligence has two aspects: an intrapersonal component concerned with self-perception and the monitoring of one's own thoughts and emotions, and with the use of this information to guide one's own actions; and an interpersonal component to do with showing sensitivity to others discerning their feelings and intentions and acting appropriately.

It will be obvious that this account can accommodate such exceptional behaviour as that of Mozart or Maureen Connolly or Ganesh Sittampalam as well as those at the head of Cox's list of youthful genius. It is also more consistent with the 'idiot savant' cases inasmuch as it is less surprising, in Gardner's view, that a particular talent can develop apparently in isolation. One still has to deal with the difference between the case of an exceptional but limited technical capability to draw or play an instrument and that of the creative or interpretative genius; between Noel Patterson and Yehudi Menuhin. And it would be misleading to suggest that Gardner's theory explains either case better than does 'g' or the like; rather, it is a more comprehensive description.

However, it may yet be not comprehensive enough. Taking only cognitive functions (approximately, those concerned with information processing), Caroll (1988) concludes that research to date shows that they can be represented by some forty to fifty dimensions, grouped together in a hierarchical fashion (in contrast to Gardner and more consistent with the older views). The pattern is approximately as follows. *Fluid intelligence* is a term introduced by R.B. Cattell (e.g. 1963) to include something like 'g'; general ability at reasoning, understanding complex problems, use of rules and procedures, judgement, planning. Cattell distinguished this from *crystallized intelligence*, the use of learned skills, verbal comprehension, numerical facility. Caroll uses the labels *Gf* and *Gc*. *Gv* is a group concerned with spatial understanding – spatial relationships, orientation, estimation of size, perceptual speed. *Ga* is to do with sound patterns – judgement of sound intervals, loudness, pitch quality. *Gm* is different aspects of memory – associative, meaningful, numerical. *Productive factors* involve different sorts of fluency such as associational, expressional, ideational, verbal; and flexibility of use. *Speed factors* probably have several aspects concerned with the swiftness with which information can be dealt with. *Psychomotor factors* include such things as dexterity, aiming, psychomotor co-ordination, reaction time. Finally there is an *affective* group where cognition interacts with feeling or motivation; such things as attention, carefulness, persistence. Caroll is careful to state that this scheme (which is very crudely sketched here) is not all equally well-supported by research. Nevertheless, it is plausible to suggest that one needs something of this kind to describe the abilities of, say, outstanding games players, and to distinguish one from another. One may have exceptionally quick reaction times, another better judgement, and so on. Similarly for artists, scientists, and others.

A one-paragraph summary such as the above may risk seeming to state the obvious; in fact the complex patterns and relationships of abilities can only be established by extensive empirical research, which is itself only one step in discovering the factors governing their development. It is a truism that by far the greater part of psychological research has been carried out on American college students. There is no reason in principle why these should not be typical examples of the human race; but it is equally the case that nearly all psychological functions exist in a social context. Students or anyone else cannot be taken as pure laboratory specimens. Even the apparently homogeneous group 'students' is variable. Alexander (1985) found that whereas more gifted students tended to define intelligence in terms of cognitive processes such as understanding, reasoning and problem solving, the less gifted more often referred to social and academic attributes. Similarly other cultures have been found to have different concepts of 'intelligence'. For example, Cole, Gay, Glick and Sharp (1971) found that the Kpelle people of Liberia were accustomed to apply the equivalent of 'clever' to skill in social relationships, rather than to such activities as rice farming or car repairing.

Berry (1984) argues that both local and universal features of cognitive functioning must be included in any complete account, and is optimistic that this can be done. It would be premature to assume it has been achieved as yet. Fry (1984) describes some of the ways in which the concept of 'intelligence' changes even within our own culture, while Goodnow (1984) urges that we need to explore, not just the definitions of intelligence, but the ways in which the judgement is made that someone is 'intelligent', whether that judgement is based on test results or everyday knowledge. Fitzgerald and Mellor (1988) found that implicit theories of intelligence, the view of the man in the street, are much simpler than most formal theories used in psychology, which may account for some of the popular confusion.

The growth of intellect

Whatever pattern intellectual excellence takes, there must be questions as to its limits, both in speed of development and in ultimate capacity, and these must be closely linked to conditions of growth. It has long been fairly well established that intelligence can be retarded by numerous factors, both physiological – inborn and acquired – and environmental (see, for instance, Vernon, 1969). Correction of such factors can produce improvement. It would seem to follow that it should be possible to specify ideal, or at any rate adequate, conditions for normal development. One is drawn almost irresistibly to a horticultural metaphor. It is not too difficult to arrange for adequate normal growth of plants. Some gardeners go further and produce leeks (for example) of colossal dimensions, or amazingly early blooms. It is done by a combination of breeding and cultivation – feeding, pest control, etc. Human beings are clearly more complex, and, in particular, to an extent create their own environment; by the same token they have more potential. On the other hand they are not, in general, amenable to selective breeding. It is far from clear what would constitute a 'normal' environment for human development, apart from absence of obvious handicaps such as malnutrition and isolation. It is still more difficult to say what would be the ideal, and the numerous cases of exceptional achievement that have been mentioned strongly suggest that it may turn out to be unique to the individual.

Sternberg and Davidson (1985) distinguish between general theories of cognitive development, which can in principle be extended to deal with exceptional ability; and theories specifically proposed to account for such ability. The main general theories are stimulus-response, Piagetian, psychometric and cognitive. All these have some difficulty in dealing with exceptional ability. Stimulus-response theories account for behaviour essentially in terms of learning, and to say that the talented learn better than others does not get us very far. Psychometric theories are those which have produced the different versions of intelligence already mentioned. The congitive approach can be represented by Sternberg's own 'componential' theory, according to which there are three basic kinds of elementary information processes: metacomponents, which are higher order control processes that are used in executive planning and decision making in problem solving; performance components, which are lower order processes used in executing a problem-solving strategy; and knowledge-acquisition components, which are lower order processes used in acquiring, retaining and transferring new information. Intellectually gifted individuals are those who are particularly effective in their componential functioning and able to use the intercommunication between components to correct and improve task performance. Thus they are particularly able to recognize the nature of problems, to select appropriate strategies and to distinguish relevant from irrelevant information. While this may well be true, it again does not seem to explain how it is that they come to act thus. Indeed the behaviour does not seem so very distant from Binet's original definition of intelligence as 'judgment, otherwise called good sense, practical sense, initiative, the faculty of adapting oneself to circumstances'. 'To judge well, to comprehend well, to reason well, these are the essential activities of intelligence' (Binet and Simon, 1916).

The Piagetian approach might seem to be more hopeful, in that it seeks to show how intellect develops through the interaction of the individual and the environment. Piaget (1896–1980) himself was not particularly interested either in individual differences or in exceptional talent. His highest stage of cognitive development, that of 'formal operations', embraces the ability to reason logically and abstractly, but this seems inadequate as a description of what the most able thinkers do – the Russells and Einsteins, indeed the Piagets. Attempts have been made, for example by Commons, Richards and Kuhn (1982), to extend the theory into further stages, but as yet it seems unclear what causes an individual to reach these stages, or do so unusually early. Indeed, taking the point that few if any children have achieved at adult genius level, perhaps they do not reach such stages.

Specific theories of outstanding ability include those of Bamberger; Feldman; Gardner; and Gruber. Bamberger (1982) proposes an account of musical talent, which could in principle have wider application, and which involves two qualitatively distinct periods in the development of exceptionally gifted individuals, which she calls figural and formal. The precise specification of these is not altogether clear, but the general idea seems to be that the first is more tied to specific events (such as musical notes) and the ways in which they are grouped with other similar events. The formal mode of thinking involves higher order, more abstract categories of such elements. Bamberger argues that musical prodigies typically deal with information in a figural way; they may or may not make the transition to formal processes, and this step is often accompanied by a 'mid-life' crisis, so called although it usually occurs in adolescence. One might, of course, also describe such crises (as seen, for example, in Solomon and Nyireghàzi) in terms of the changing demands on the individual as he develops from a remarkable child to a professional adult.

Feldman (1980, 1986a) argues that most theories of development, and specifically that of Piaget, have been concerned with universal stages through which it is supposed all children pass. In fact, as pointed out in respect of intelligence, this has not actually been demonstrated. As mentioned before, Feldman's argument is that to explain exceptional performance, account must also be taken of non-universal factors. But it seems to be not so much that prodigies manifest different processes, rather that they go through them more rapidly and unevenly; and this in turn is probably due to exceptional circumstances which are largely a matter of chance, such as their talent being one which is valued and rewarded, and their being instructed and tutored particularly well. The question of universality versus individual patterns of development of cognitive processes is reviewed extensively by Fischer and Silvern (1985), who concluded that this is, in fact, a false dichotomy. There is evidence for distinct stages of development – at least eight from birth to the age of 18 in their view – but also for individual variation, and a complete account of development has to include a two-way interaction of people and environment: 'they work with it and affect it, and it works with them and affects them'.

Gardner's approach has already been described. Gruber (1986), like Feldman, stresses the social context in which extraordinariness appears and which gives it meaning. But he suggests, from the study of outstanding individuals, that the clue to their achievement lies in the pattern of their own activities and interests: an 'organized network of purposes' which make their lives more productive than average. Just how such patterns of behaviour develop, presumably through the interaction of individual and environment, is as yet only partially understood. Some indications come from attempts to raise levels of intelligence.

Improving intelligence

One of the continuing issues in intellectual development is the relative contributions of heredity and environment, and this is linked with the question of the limits of growth, since it has seemed that if the hereditary component is large, this must set a bound to what is possible. It has been fashionable to deny or belittle this component, but this will not do. There can be no doubt at all that inheritance is one factor, as one would suppose it to be in every aspect of living things. Vandenburg and Vogler (1985), reviewing what is now a vast and sophisticated literature, set the genetic contribution to phenotypic variability in intelligence at around 30 to 40 per cent. This, as they point out, makes it the largest single factor, but it also means that 60 to 70 per cent must be attributed to environmental factors (which of course include everything the organism undergoes from the moment of conception). DeFries, Plomin and LaBuda (1987) found in a longitudinal study of adopted children, the California Adoption Project, that genetic differences accounted for only 15 to 25 per cent of variability in intelligence on the Stanford–Binet test at age 3–4; however most of this variance co-varied with adult intelligence; in other words the genetic influence was small but persistent.

Earlier theories had attributed more to hereditary factors – Cyril Burt specified 80 per cent – and accordingly tended to regard intelligence as relatively fixed throughout life, and in any case as having an upper limit which the individual would never exceed. In fact heredity is not necessarily linked to stability. Lynn (1987) points out that genetic differences account for about 95 per cent of observed differences in height in a population. Yet between 1914 and 1982 the average height of men in England increased from 5ft 7½ins to 5ft 10ins. Of course one would not expect it to go on rising indefinitely; but behaviour may be another matter. Like many theories, that of fixed intelligence was under attack almost as soon as it became widely (though never universally) accepted. J.McV. Hunt in 1961 summarized much of the evidence then available on the other side, showing, for example, how test results varied both in the normal life of individuals, and, more dramatically, under changed circumstances such as institutionalization or adoption. He concluded optimistically that it should be possible 'to achieve a substantially faster rate of intellectual development, and a substantially higher adult level of intellectual capacity'.

As so often, however, subsequent research has not yet confirmed or refuted this, partly because there has been relatively little work with the specific aim of raising intelligence. Most investigators have been concerned either with naturally occurring changes in circumstances, such as adoption or social/educational factors, or with mainly remedial attempts to improve performance generally, such as the well-known 'Head Start' programmes. The latter have, in fact, been generally disappointing: gains made during pre-school programmes have typically been lost during the first year of formal schooling (Head Start Bureau, 1985). The most intensive such programme, sometimes known as the Milwaukee Miracle, appeared to do dramatically better, with children as late as fourteen still scoring, at an average IQ of 100, ten points above a control group. The programme lasted seven hours a day, five days a week, from 3 months old to the start of regular school at 5 or 6. Unfortunately, properly documented results have never been published and there has been no successful replication (Locurto, 1988). All such programmes are of course directed at children who, left to themselves, would on average score well below the population as a whole. Nevertheless it seems as though in the right circumstances performance can improve, even in terms of what is thought of as an underlying ability, that is intelligence.

It is methodologically and, even more, conceptually difficult to separate ability and performance. D.O. Hebb, in an influential book of 1949, made a distinction between 'intelligence A', an innate potential which cannot be measured directly, and 'intelligence B', or developed intelligence, which can. P.E. Vernon (1969) added the point that in fact only a sample can be taken, which he termed 'intelligence C'. The psychometric implication of this would be that several samples should be taken, under controlled conditions, to obtain a 'true' estimate of intelligence. This would be reasonable for something like temperature, but the athletics analogy already used may be a better one. A runner who on one occasion surpasses himself must be credited with his record even though he never afterwards equals it; it is just as much his 'true' performance as his slower times. And one would be inclined to conclude that if he could do it once he could do it again, if only the circumstances were right. This might be the case with the Head Start children.

If more permanent conditions hold the answer, it should appear in studies of adoption. Here we have a kind of natural experiment in which the environmental factors are neatly varied. In general, children from poorer conditions are adopted into better-favoured homes. Unfortunately, as Locurto (1988) points out, there are few areas of research that are more puzzling. This is largely because adoption is not, of course, done for experimental reasons, and all sort of crucial variables are not controlled, or even known about. Studies vary widely in nature and quality of information and so are difficult to compare. Nevertheless a number of studies give a fairly consistent picture of a rise of five to ten IQ points following adoption. But in these cases it is not clear how different were the original and the adoptive homes nor, more importantly, how close the adopted child was to what might be expected in the new home. Adoption agencies, in fact, try to match up children and homes, thus giving as it were less room for improvement. Where there is sufficient information to estimate what the children's intelligence would have been had they not been adopted – there are three such studies, according to Locurto – fairly consistent gains from about 94–95 to 106–107 have been found; in other words from somewhat below to somewhat above average.

This is far from the end of complexity. For one thing, when siblings are adopted into the same family, they seem oddly to become less alike the longer they remain, until at adolescence they are as unalike (in intelligence) as complete strangers, that is a correlation of zero (Locurto, *op. cit.*); whereas siblings in their natural families correlate about 0.3–0.4 (Bouchard and McGue, 1981). Furthermore, increases in IQ do not seem to be related in any simple way to such obvious variables as the educational status of the adoptive parents. It is rather, Locurto suggests, as if the effectiveness of adoptive parents is at least partly a matter of sensitivity to individual children's unique dispositions.

The notion of a general rise in intelligence has attracted at least one government, that of Venezuela, which in 1979 appointed Luis Alberto Machado Minister of National Intelligence. Salazar (1984) reported that fourteen projects had been begun with the aim of raising intelligence levels. Among them were one based on the well-known ideas of Edward de Bono on thinking, one similarly based on the 'instrumental enrichment' method of Reuven Feuerstein (e.g. Sharron, 1987), one using chess as a training technique and one concentrating on educating mothers in better child-rearing methods. These schemes, which are all in essence remedial, according to Salazar had been received by the participants with varying degrees of enthusiasm, and it was still too early to evaluate them.

The same thing applies to a more detailed effort in the same programme, reported by Herrnstein, Nickerson, de Sanchez and Swets (1986). This project comprised essentially a lesson, four days a week for a school year, in thinking skills, with the aim of enhancing performance 'on a wide variety of tasks that require careful observation and classification, deductive or inductive reasoning, critical use of language, hypothesis generation and testing, problem solving, inventiveness and decision making'. The students were over 400 13-year-olds, with a matched control group. The size and thoroughness of this project make it very unusual if not unique, and it is only briefly summarized here. It is clear that performance was significantly improved, to the greatest extent on the specific skills taught, but also on more general tests of mental ability. It was not clear, at the time of reporting, how long such effects would last, but the authors were optimistic.

Even more general effects have been reported in respect of apparent rises in national intelligence during the present century. Flynn (1987) reported rises of 2–12 IQ points per decade among fourteen economically advanced nations. Lynn, Hampson and Mullineaux (1987) in 1985 gave to a sample of over 1,000 English children aged 9–11 the same Cattell Non-Verbal test as had been given to a comparable sample in 1935. The average had risen from 100 to 112.42, equivalent to 2.8 points per decade over the fifty-year period. This test is held to be relatively 'culture-fair' since it consists of problems in picture and diagram form, though this is itself far from uncontroversial. Such results are the subject of unresolved argument, both as to how much they can be relied on and as to what they mean. In rather the same way, Torrance and Safter (1986) report that scores on tests of creative thinking were higher in 1976 than in 1967.

It might be that the cognitive skills acquired by children now are more closely related in some way to test items. The Cattell test is intended to assess 'fluid intelligence', and Lynn *et al.* accordingly conclude that there has been an increase in general mental capacity, which they attribute to environmental improvements such as better nutrition and health, smaller families, nursery education, more cognitively stimulating toys, books, television. Ray (1988) comments that improved methods of childbirth decrease the risk of oxygen deprivation to the brains of neonates.

It cannot be concluded from such findings alone how long

they may continue, nor that the numbers of exceptional individuals will increase. *How and How Much Can Intelligence be Increased?* is the hopeful title of a book edited by Detterman and Sternberg (1982). Unfortunately, as Brown and Campione point out in their final discussion, the query remains. Such answers as are offered seem to depend on what is meant by intelligence, and on how close are the tests of intelligence to whatever has been taught. At an absurd extreme, one can easily obtain perfect scores on a test by teaching the specific answers. Training on tests will produce some improvement on other tests. Cognitive skills can generally be improved, as in some of the Venezuelan projects, but it is still unclear how widespread or longlasting is the effect. Flynn (1987) argues that the tests which have yielded improved scores over the past few decades cannot be measuring intelligence in any real sense. If they were, there would be very noticeable effects such as greatly advanced educational standards, which have not been observed. Therefore, he argues, the tests must only be measuring some 'abstract problem solving ability', or abilities, relatively unrelated to the real world.

Haywood and Switzky (1986) conclude, after extensive reviews of the literature, first that adverse environmental conditions lower performance level (with the corollary that these can in principle be corrected); secondly that favourable circumstances do not of themselves create intelligence; and thirdly that intelligent behaviour probably requires both a component of 'naïve ability', largely genetic, and cognitive functions, largely learned. While all this may well be true, it remains to unravel the complexity.

Intelligence is not enough

It would be rash to conclude that a genetic factor sets a limit to development (as for example Colangelo, 1984 seems to do). As we have seen in the case of height, change is possible even with a very large genetic component. We do not know the ideal conditions for mental and psychological growth, so that its limits may well not yet have been reached. More fundamentally, cognitive performance, and thus inferred ability, is defined by the environment which it creates itself, in a way that is not true for height. While it is logically impossible to say for example, that Wittgenstein was more able than Aristotle, there is also a sense in which students today easily master problems once considered complex. It is common for parents to have difficulty with technology their children take for granted; one might say that they differ in 'crystallized' if not in 'fluid' intelligence.

Tested intelligence was fairly early on attacked as giving a poor account of creative thinking which, so it seemed, required novel responses rather than the standardized right answers of the tests. Guilford's multifactorial theory of intelligence, which came to the fore around 1950, included half a dozen components related to what came to be called 'divergent' as opposed to 'convergent' thinking. Tests of such thinking proliferated, though they never achieved the reliability and validity of what were by then conventional intelligence tests. In other words they gave less consistent results, and it was even less clear what they were measuring. On the other hand, many studies showed that the conventional tests correlated rather poorly with all sorts of talented accomplishments; for example Walberg (1971) found virtually no relationship between IQ and out-of-school achievements in creative writing, science, music, the visual arts, drama, dance, or group leadership. This is cited by Wallach (1985), who also quotes a number of failures to find any relationship between ability test scores and achievement in real life such as in professional work. He explains the apparent contradiction between this and the classical work of Terman (in particular) by the argument that the latter's sample was in effect selected for social class and thus for privilege and opportunity.

Accordingly, high scores on 'creativity' tests intended to measure such traits as ideational fluency (number of ideas produced) and novelty of ideas came for a time to replace intelligence as the mark of gifted children. But as Wallach points out, these tests too have been found wanting when compared with actual creative achievement in real life. More recently, stress has been laid on training and skills specific to particular domains of achievement. In the light of the long history of individuals in every field, from Mozart to Mill, from

Gauss to Graf, whose achievements followed intensive devotion to practice and study, this almost has an air of rediscovering the wheel.

There are other ways of considering the limits of intelligence, one of which is explored by Raaheim (1984). Among other experimental situations he has used a well-known laboratory war-horse, the Hat Rack problem. Subjects are presented with two poles and a clamp, and asked to make a hat rack. The solution is to use the clamp to fasten the poles together, making them of a length that can be wedged between floor and ceiling. The hat can then be hung on the clamp. The interesting thing about this odd little problem is that of the many hundreds of persons who have tried it, consistently about half get it; and there seems almost no way of determining which half it will be. None of the obvious variables such as intelligence, personality factors, school achievements, etc. consistently differentiate the successful from the unsuccessful. The significant difference that Raaheim has found is that the ultimately successful subjects make more unsuccessful attempts: 'if at first you don't succeed . . .' seems to receive experimental support. The persistence which occurs in accounts of so many prodigies – both the extremely able and the 'idiot savants' – comes to mind.

As regards intelligence, Raaheim's view is that, as usually considered (and measured), it is essentially concerned with the successful use of past experience and knowledge to solve problems. Although this may produce a novel solution, real creativity is only involved when the situation is such that the past is no longer applicable and it becomes necessary to step outside its constraints. A somewhat similar line is taken by Davidson and Sternberg (e.g. 1984) in suggesting the role of what they rather unfortunately term 'insight', a word which has caused almost as much trouble as 'intelligence'. They mean three separate but related processes: sifting out relevant information from irrelevant; synthesizing apparently unrelated information into a whole (which may or may not resemble the sum of its parts); and relating newly acquired information to what is already known. In terms of the Hat Rack, one has to leave the problem of making a certain piece of furniture, and tackle that of suspending a hat between floor and ceiling. It is interesting that (Raaheim reports) artists tend to be better than average at the problem. Picasso is said to have remarked, when he had made a sculpture of a bull's head from a bicycle saddle and handle-bars, that he hoped someone would say on seeing it: 'Ah, I think I could make a bicycle out of that'. It might not be unreasonable to suggest that child prodigies typically excel at what has been done before. To repeat, it is rare indeed for a very young person to produce creative work comparable with that of highly creative adults, and as Bamberger pointed out there may well be problems of transition from one stage to the other. Prodigies, however, would seem often to transcend intelligence in its more limited senses.

10 Exceptional Abilities

Inheritance of special abilities

Numerous well-known examples suggest that in some way talent runs in families. In music the Bach family is the most famous and the largest (Wolff, 1983). Nearly sixty members each appear in at least one musical reference work; some twenty might be described as eminent; and one, Johann Sebastian (1685–1750), was an outstanding genius. He was also precocious. It would be difficult to show that prodigies tend to be related, since they are too rare. It does seem that in music at least they often come from musical families (Judd, 1988), and it might be that some potential for specialized development is inherited, and in favourable circumstances appears early.

It was examples of related talent among his contemporaries that led Francis Galton to undertake his studies of *Hereditary Genius* (1869), which have had such a profound effect on the way we think about differences between people. As he pointed out in the edition of 1892, when the book was originally written 'the human mind was popularly thought to act independently of natural laws, and to be capable of almost any achievement, if compelled to exert itself by a will that had a power of initiation'. Galton's achievement was to bring at least some aspects of the human mind within the ambit of natural law; but it does not follow that his conclusions were necessarily true (or false). In the present case Galton applied, as far as he could, methods of objective measurement to human 'genius', which he considered as 'natural ability'. To this end he collated large amounts of biographical data on eminent individuals, and their relations, in different fields, including: the law, politics, military command, literature, science, poetry, music, painting, religious leadership, classical scholarship and athletics (rowing and wrestling). The total ran to 300 families and nearly 1,000 eminent men.

Galton's general conclusion, supported by novel and ingenious statistics, was that the more closely related an individual is to someone eminent, the more likely it is that he himself will be eminent. Among numerous other findings, he anticipated Terman by refuting the popular belief that men of genius were physically weak or sickly; on the contrary, as he put it: 'A collection of living magnates in various branches of intellectual achievement is always a feast to my eyes; being, as they are, such massive, vigorous, capable-looking animals'. As regards prodigies, Galton's tables of relationships demonstrated to him that sons of gifted men were more precocious than their parents. He believed, on less clear evidence, that such sons tended to be pushed forward to the serious detriment of their health.

Galton's work remains of interest in many ways. It has commonly been attacked on the grounds that he confused inheritance of ability with social opportunity. Thus it might be said that music was the Bach family occupation into which new members could enter with good prospects. It is worth noting that Galton specifically excluded from his data cases such as family engineering businesses where successive generations could relatively easily achieve results. A further argument is that genius is rare even among talented families; the Bachs produced only one Johann Sebastian.

Research to date has by no means solved all the questions raised by Galton. Hereditary factors in some kind of general potential are indicated by the evidence and by common sense; observation shows that babies differ markedly from birth in speed and variety of reaction, and thus in brain and nervous system. What is much less clear is how specific abilities come about. The general pattern of human development is one of gradual differentiation. Although specific abilities can be shown to exist in infancy (Plomin and DeFries, 1985), it is not certain how far they are inherited. This partly depends on the view that is taken of the structure of abilities. According to the hierarchical model of intelligence, two main sub-groups of abilities can be distinguished, labelled verbal and spatial, and these too show hereditary influence (Ambrose, 1978).

Spatial ability has been related to mathematical ability, and Benbow (1986, 1988) concludes that there is some evidence for a genetic component in the latter. Smith (1988) considers that there is no evidence that an ability for mental calculation is inherited, since it does not run in families. He does mention several related calculators, the most notable being Wim Klein and his brother Leo, and George Parker Bidder and his son, but he argues that in each case one was the original exponent, the other a less effective, and less motivated, emulator. Alexander Aitken reported that his daughter could equal some of his feats if she thought it worthwhile, but generally she did not. Chess, one of the main areas in which prodigies emerge, clearly involves an element of spatial intelligence. Some classic experiments by De Groot (1965), a psychologist who was also a chess master, showed that experts differed from novices in their ability to reconstruct from memory complex positions seen briefly. If the pieces were placed randomly there was no superiority. Subsequent experiments have shown that grandmasters possess vast repertoires of some 50,000 unique, non-random, configurations of pieces. Some of these occur very frequently in play, such as standard openings, and are well known to beginners; others very rarely. The grandmaster's knowledge is comparable to that of a native speaker of a language (Cranberg and Albert, 1988); and in the case of prodigies it develops with extraordinary speed–though not without intensive practice. It is reasonable to suppose that a potential for this involves hereditary factors, although chess does not seem to run in families.

Similarly, exceptional facility in language learning has been reported of many prodigies. Inherited verbal intelligence may well be one factor. If, on the other hand, intelligence is considered to involve a number of relatively independent modules, there seems no reason in principle why these should necessarily all be inherited to the same extent. Gardner's system would allow for both heredity and learning to play a part, but would also stress the importance of cultural factors which will influence which 'intelligence' is valued and thus likely to develop.

Waterhouse (1988) offers a new, although largely tentative, theory of special talents which attempts to accommodate the evidence both from normal development and from the unusual cases such as idiot savants. She argues that a wide range of special talents, including music, art, mathematics, poetry and exceptional memory:

all spring from the same global, preconscious, specific set of skills, namely the ability to generate accurate and elaborate mental representations of images and/or sounds, and to store, manipulate and recall these sounds, as well as– and more important–the ability to 'see' or 'hear' complex patterns in those mental sights and sounds.

Special talents, moreover, are essentially innate, although the genetic mechanism of this is not clear. Apart from identical twins, of course, no two human beings share the same genetic make-up; and neither can any two be said to have identical environments. Thus every individual is the result of a unique interaction of inheritance and circumstances. Special talents and precocity are simply unusual cases of general laws which have yet to be elucidated.

Inherited factors would seem not to be limited to the cognitive. It is abundantly clear that in the development of special talents traits of personality, such as motivation and emotionality, are also important, and the basis for these is likewise at least partly a matter of inheritance (Ambrose, 1978). The manager of Stephen Hendry, the snooker player, impressed by his protégé's calm temperament, is said once to have asked a doctor whether someone could be 'born without nerves'. As is common he confused 'nerves' with 'nervousness', but was perhaps correct in suspecting an inherited factor. In some fields, especially sport, relatively straightforward physical characteristics, largely inherited, are of importance. An extreme case would be height in basketball, but in many others it is difficult to excel with a physique too far outside a certain range– more especially too small, of course. Unusually rapid development, likewise largely under genetic control, is obviously a factor in sporting precocity.

Exceptional brains

It might seem obvious that an unusual ability implies an unusual brain. This is not necessarily so; brains might be something like motor cars, capable of different ranges of performance but often not used to the maximum. As yet, research is suggestive rather than conclusive. Take first the cases of 'idiot savants'. Charness, Clifton and MacDonald (1988) suggest the less controversial term 'mono-savants', indicating individuals who score very low on standard tests of intelligence, but nevertheless show exceptional ability in (usually) one particular activity; 'exceptional' meaning markedly greater than normal intelligent adults. As we have seen, this sometimes appears in children. (Some writers use the term 'savant' for those with one ability far above their others, but not necessarily exceptional by 'normal' standards.) The causes of low intelligence test scores are varied. Broadly they can be grouped as structural or functional. In some cases there is reason to suppose physical impairment of the brain; other cases are 'functional', but this term always covers the possibility of some as yet undiscovered structural factors.

Charness et al. report the case of 'JL', one of the lowest functioning musical mono-savants yet recorded. His general level of social behaviour – eating, washing, dressing, toileting, etc. – was roughly comparable to a 2-year-old's. His command of language was very limited, and in addition he was blind since shortly after birth, severely epileptic and paralysed on the right side. Tests showed clear damage to the left cerebral hemisphere. JL was studied in detail at the age of 36, but from about 3 had shown interest and ability in music, starting with the piano. There was a good deal of music of all sorts in the home, and JL spent a great amount of time playing or listening. JL's musical ability extended to playing the piano, organ, melodica, harmonica and guitar (all with one hand, and often with ingenious fingering to compensate); a considerable repertoire; absolute pitch; and good memory for tunes and chords. Experiments showed that, as in other cases, JL's ability was at least partly comparable in kind to that of normal musicians. It seems that this is a case of a severely handicapped person whose potential for music has been left at least partially intact, and then developed by extensive practice, it being almost the only field of activity in which any substantial satisfaction was possible. One might compare in this regard the several blind but otherwise normal traditional musicians–Willy Johnson, Lemon Jefferson, Doc Watson and others.

Hill (1977, 1978) estimated that the population of institutions for the mentally retarded in the USA contains one mono-savant in 2,000. Autistic children with special talents are more frequent. Some cases have already been mentioned, and Rimland and Fein (1988) suggest that as many as ten per cent may show such abilities; in order of frequency, music, memory, art, pseudoverbal ('reading' without understanding), mathematics, mechanical, direction (knowing routes in detail), co-ordination (e.g. swimming, balancing), calendar calculations and (rarely) apparent extra-sensory perception. The condition or conditions labelled autism are far from well understood, but are commonly marked by extreme withdrawal from social contact, which means in turn that estimates of ability are hard to interpret. Rimland and Fein make three suggestions as to possible neural mechanisms that might underlie savant abilities, either alone or in some combination.

The first is some deficiency in attentional systems. An early symptom of autism is abnormal orienting: young children do not show the usual tendencies to turn towards sights and sounds. This behaviour may well be the origin of later curiosity, exploration and interest in novelty. Autistic children do not develop these in the usual way but seem to be inward-looking and narrowly focused, engaging in repetitive, obsessive behaviour as though other, distracting stimuli were being kept out. In some cases the obsession is with a particular skill, such as playing music or calculating. The suggestion is that the neural mechanism of selective attention is in some way disordered. It is as yet unclear what that mechanism is: attention is a most complex phenomenon and probably involves brain systems at several different levels, though there is a suggestion that the hippocampus (a structure at the base of the brain with apparently complex and as yet only partly understood functions) is particularly concerned in orienting.

The second ideas is that areas of the cortex which would normally be concerned with abstract, conceptual thought become instead specialized to process information from one sense modality in a highly specific, image-bound form. Sacks (1985), among others, mentions savants who can produce astronomically large prime numbers almost instantly, and likewise instantly identify the numbers of objects in very large arrays – over 100. Whether this would involve any actual physical alteration of the cortex is again unclear. The third notion involves the hippocampus again. It seems to be involved not only in orienting but in the mapping of space, in place learning, and encoding memories contextually. Some autistic children are obsessed with spatial layouts and routes, and their memories often seem to be almost photographic. In contrast, patients with damage to the hippocampus may be able to recognize something as familiar but be unable to identify it or put it in context.

All this only serves to demonstrate how little the extraordinary complexity of the brain is yet understood; and of course it applies to individuals who, whatever their savant specialities, are incapable of functioning adequately in normal life. It would not be justified to infer the workings of the brain from handicapped to normal. On the other hand, the extreme dedication, amounting almost to obsession, of some child and adult geniuses has been noted. The 'absent-minded professor' lost in thought may not be entirely a popular fiction, and there are many anecdotes of artists ignoring food and sleep when engaged in creation. Their activities, however, would be considered to be at a much higher, more abstract level than those of the 'idiot' or 'mono-savant'.

When it comes to the properties of these presumably normal but special brains, matters are again rather unclear. Not many brains of geniuses, and still fewer of child prodigies, become available for post-mortem examination, though other techniques are of course in use. The greatest amount of speculation centres on what has become a rather over-popularized and over-simplified idea, that the two halves of the cortex have different functions. As is well known, broadly speaking the right cortex controls the left side of the body and vice versa, and at least some other functions seem generally to be localized, such as speech on the left and non-verbal, visuo-spatial processes on the right. Since most complex tasks involve both visuo-spatial and linguistic processes, the two hemispheres usually complement each other.

There is evidence to associate some forms of exceptional ability with brain organization. In particular, as mentioned in

Chapter 5, Benbow (1986, 1988) and others have demonstrated that among the mathematically talented (as studied in the SMPY programme) there is a tendency to be left-handed or ambidextrous, or to be right-handed but have family members tending to be left-handed. Benbow takes this to mean that the mathematically talented have more bilateral cognitive representation; and this would be consistent with research she quotes to the effect that computation and the ability to read and produce signs in mathematics are left-hemisphere functions, while the understanding of numerical relations and concepts is associated with the right hemisphere. Benbow's talented subjects also had a rate of 50 per cent proneness to immune disorders such as allergies, twice that of the general population. These two factors are consistent with a theory developed by the late Norman Geschwind, that in some male fetuses overproduction of the hormone testosterone slows development of the left hemisphere, leading to compensatory enhanced development of the right. This does not occur in female brains, and the mathematically talented are predominantly male. So, of course (with the extraordinary exception of Judit Polgar), have been the most notable chess players, and Cranberg and Albert (1988) argue similarly that chess involves the sort of spatial pattern recognition abilities associated with the right hemisphere. They report that left-handedness was twice as frequent, at 18.6 per cent, among the top 200 as it was among the bottom 200 rated players in the United States Chess Federation. This still leaves over 80 per cent right-handed, and one would have to suppose that they have right hemispheres that are well developed, but not sufficiently so to reverse the more usual handedness (which is also strongly socially reinforced). Judit Polgar is right-handed.

Women have not as yet excelled at pool, snooker or billiards, but perhaps these have too strong male connotations; there seems less difficulty with croquet. All are very similar in terms of spatial perception.

Conversely, Curtiss (1988) discusses the evidence relating language to the left hemisphere. Schneiderman and Desmarais (1988) consider the learning of non-native languages. After puberty it is rare to acquire native fluency, although anecdote suggests it is less so in women. The argument, briefly, is that while use of language, so to speak, is centred in the left hemisphere, this involves a loss of flexibility – neurocognitive and neuromuscular – which makes it more difficult to learn subsequent languages. Those who are good at this make use of the right hemisphere to develop unusual or innovative strategies; and there is some evidence to suggest that children and females tend to be less clearly left-lateralized for language than men. Nyborg (1987) pushes the idea of masculinization or feminization of the brain by fetal secretion of gonadal hormones even further, claiming that analysis of such biochemical factors will eventually provide the main explanation of individual differences, rather than the interaction of genes and environment; but this too remains speculation.

Mind and behaviour

Clearly there is a long way to go to establishing just what special features of the brain, if any, may underlie particular talents, still more so their very early appearance. Physical and mental factors interact in complex ways. It had long been assumed that the bespectacled 'swot' was a figment of old-fashioned comics. It turns out that there actually is a relationship between myopia (short sight) and some intellectual activities; Terman had noted something of the sort. Benbow (1986) observed that many of the SMPY subjects wore glasses. Systematic investigation showed that among extremely precocious mathematicians and verbal reasoners myopia was four times as frequent as in the general student population. It was more frequent in girls than in boys, and more frequent also in the verbally than in the mathematically talented. A very large-scale study by Teasdale, Fuchs and Goldschmidt (1988) of Danish 18-year old men drafted for military service compared 5,943 myopics with 9,891 nonmyopics. The former averaged seven IQ points more than the latter and were comparably superior on education scores. Myopia is unlikely to be caused by reading, since that would affect education more than IQ; but it might result, it is suggested, from habitual visual exploration of the near environment from an early age. Animal studies show that myopia often results from rearing in environments where distance vision is restricted. It is not clear, however, why this should have an effect on intelligence, nor that concentration on the near environment is not a result, rather than a cause, of myopia. One recalls Samuel Johnson, determined at the age of 4 to get home from school alone, going down on his knees to see his way across the street gutter.

Whatever the physical attributes, and the cognitive capacities, inherited or not, that may underlie exceptional ability, part of the explanation at least must be sought at the behavioural level. A strong case has been put by Ericsson (Ericsson and Chase, 1982; Ericsson and Faivre, 1988) that the principle factor in extraordinary performance is simply practice; the old adage that it 'makes perfect' is literally true. It is almost a return to a pre-Galtonian view, in a new guise. Three sorts of evidence are quoted. There are first the performances of savants such as have already been described. The argument here is that these performances are only exceptional in comparison with the rest of the retarded individual's behaviour (except for calendar calculations); they are well within the range attainable by normal persons; and the savants can be shown to devote great amounts of time to practice. Apparent exceptions may be mistakes, for example the very famous case (not mentioned by Ericsson) of Leslie Lemke (Monte, 1981). Born blind and severely crippled by cerebral palsy, he was reared by a devoted nurse, May Lemke. He did not speak his first sentence until he was 20, but at that age, it was reported, he suddenly began to play the piano with great skill. In fact, he had shown both interest and ability for a considerable time (Treffert, 1989, quoted pre-publication by Rimland and Fein, 1988).

Secondly, there is a lack of evidence that even in normal subjects exceptional performance ever occurs without practice (as Howe, 1988b also points out). In the mythology of pop music, Elvis Presley sprang forth as a teenage star from nothing; in fact he had won a talent contest as early as 8 at the Alabama – Mississippi State Fair, with 'Old Shep' (Carr and Farren, 1982). Ericsson argues that a good deal of practice may go unnoticed. Many mental skills can be practised alone. In any case the time needed is less than might be expected; many skills (such as basic competence in a foreign language) can be acquired with practice of the order of an hour a day over a year or so, far less than many people devote to sports or hobbies. (The politician Enoch Powell stated in an interview that as a young man he learned a language, and wrote a book, a year.) Ericsson's most remarkable evidence concerns the acquisition of exceptional skills by otherwise average subjects. For example, even memory for meaningless material such as digits, which has been thought to be more or less fixed within fairly narrow limits, can be enormously increased by practice – skilled subjects can memorize lists of 2,000 digits as fast as, or faster than, untrained subjects can memorize a text with a comparable number of words. (Ericsson might have compared the memories for extremely long epic poems and genealogies that are found in pre-literate cultures. The actor Alec McCowen, for his celebrated 'reading' of the Gospel of St Mark, actually learned the whole of it.) Practice can also be shown to affect what have been thought to be abilities that are possessed entirely or not at all such as 'absolute pitch'. In fact, pitch identification performance varies continuously from very poor to effectively perfect; and there is evidence that it can be developed by training.

In order for practice to result in exceptional performance, says Ericsson, three criteria must be satisfied. There must be sufficient time for practice. There must be some instruction and access to whatever tools are needed – for example in pitch identification one must hear the notes and have them named. Under 'instruction' Ericsson would presumably include feedback, without which any learning is difficult. Thirdly, the performance must count as exceptional. But as Ericsson points out, exceptionality is in the eye of the beholder. The ability to read would be almost magical in a non-literate society – just as memory for epics might seem to us.

It still has to be explained why only some individuals are prepared to undertake the extensive practice needed to excel, and Ericsson favours some possibly genetic factors underlying long-term motivation. However, it seems implausible to suggest that practice alone is sufficient for achievement. Many people work extremely hard at sport or at their job without great success. It is common for coaches and schoolteachers to bend every effort to producing champions or scholarship winners, yet succeed only rarely. Surely if practice were everything, Frank Richards (Charles Harold St John Hamilton, 1876–1961), the creator of Billy Bunter, would be the greatest writer in the world with his estimated 100 million words career record – about four or five times *War and Peace* each year (Beal, 1976). Perhaps instruction was lacking. Charness (1988) is surely right to hold that practice may be necessary but is not sufficient. In several fields, chess, music, telegraphy , reading, singing, playing soccer, juggling and becoming a professional psychologist for example, it is possible to estimate around 10,000 hours for mastery. One might compare Binet's cashiers who equalled Inaudi in calculating bills; or even perhaps the twelve years experience Nelson was able to gain before becoming a captain at 24. Clearly some attain at least consider-able mastery more quickly than this; others fail to complete the course, most obviously from lack of either ability or motivation.

There is also the question of why one particular activity should be chosen for practice. No doubt this is, as Johnson suggested, at least partly accidental, with initial and then increasing success reinforcing the choice. Waterhouse (1988) tentatively suggests that unique patterns of internal rewards might accompany the exercise of special talents. Piechowski and Colangelo (1984) describe five parallel dimensions of enhanced mental functioning or 'overexcitability' – what turns you on as it were – some pattern of which they think characterizes giftedness in different spheres. They are: psy-chomotor, sensual, intellectual, imaginational and emotional. Protocols suggest the way these are experienced by individuals. For example, 'intellectual overexcitability':

I can't resist maths puzzles, or brain teasers of any kind, and I go to ridiculous lengths to figure them out. When I'm being sensible I know they're a waste of time, but I can't see one without working it out. I guess I'm conceited – I don't like to think that there is anything I can't figure out.

This is an interesting start, though it does not in itself offer an explanation; and it remains to deal with individual obses-sions – of for example Matisse with colour and Henry Moore with three-dimensional form; of Nigel Short with chess and Bertrand Russell with mathematics. In a small group of thirteen artists Piechowski and Cunningham (1985) found several distinct patterns of overexcitability. In the case of values and interests, as in so many other ways in which human beings differ, scientific research has often resulted in identifying broad categories or dimensions. While this is in itself an advance, it necessarily leaves out the unique pattern which actually motivates an individual (see Kirby and Radford, 1976). Exceptional persons are by definition rare, prodigies especially so. It has long been argued that every man is in some respects like all other men, in some like some, and in some like none. But the pattern is not the same for all; a man of 6 feet 10 inches is like almost no one else, whereas he of 5 feet 10 inches is indistinguishable from the crowd. Each, however, has been produced by a unique concatenation of common processes – genetics, hormones, food, climate and so forth (some extremes may involve abnormalities of course). It remains to be established whether this is true of abilities. It may well be the case that even extreme gifts require the postulation of no special processes (Jackson and Butterfield, 1986); but the opposite is still a possibility.

Circumstances

The circumstances in which prodigious talent develops can be considered from the individual outwards. Numerous examples have been given of the role of mentors, who may well be parents. Parents are present from the start and more or less continuously; some parent substitutes such as a nanny or foster-parent may not be far behind, followed by successful coaches, who are frequently emotionally close to their charges, or teachers, or even managers. The entrepreneurial gurus who have stood behind, sometimes virtually created, so many young pop stars, have often been described (e.g. Rogan, 1988).

Many of the ways in which parents interact with the educational achievements of their children are summarized by Pandey (1984). In general, better-off, supportive homes with high expectations are associated with greater achievements, although it may be that some parental attitudes are elicited by the ability of the children. Most likely there is a complex interaction. Clearly in the cases of some individuals, such as

J.S. Mill and William Sidis, parental demands have outrun the reasonable; in others, such as John Adams and Ganesh Sittampalam, fathers seem to accept and support talent rather than exploit it. Wide differences in parental attitude are pointed up by cross-cultural studies. For example, Chen and Miyake (1984) show how in Japan mothers traditionally concentrate on keeping infants calm and happy and thus not a nuisance to others; see also Kojima (1986). I have not come across a study of Japanese prodigies. It has been suggested that the demanding nature of Japanese education is related to Japan's economic achievement (e.g. Lynn, 1988); but the education seems to be accompanied by an emphasis on conformity rather than individuality. Fowler (1981) concludes, consistently with much research already quoted, from case and other studies that in general exceptional early abilities flourish in highly intellectual families who early involve their children in rational communication with adults, and who intensively stimulate them cognitively during their early development. Two general strategies emerge from the case studies, though they overlap considerably; one involves more deliberate, systematic teaching, though often through play, the other is more a case of continuous interaction and stimulation. Both are highly flexible, interactive and child-oriented, with ever-increasing opportunities for the child to master more complex skills and bodies of knowledge. Fell, Dahlstrom and Winter (1984) found that fathers of gifted children tended to be more intelligent, independent, aloof, assertive and tense than average; mothers were likewise more intelligent and independent, but also more conscientious, persistent and controlled in their general approach to life.

Bloom (1985) argues (after forty years of educational research) that what any one person can learn, almost anyone can learn – given the right conditions. Again this looks like a pre-Galton view, with conditions substituted for will. The conditions are some combination of home, school and society. Bloom and colleagues studied intensively the backgrounds of twenty-five outstanding individuals, nearly all below the age of 35, in each of six fields of talent; pianists, sculptors, swimmers, tennis players, mathematicians and neurologists. They describe many of the differences between individuals and between the activities, but they were particularly interested in common features; and these appear to be most important with respect to home and parents, then teachers. Their general conclusions can be summarized thus. First, the development of talent begins as play, but this is followed by a long period of hard – though not necessarily unenjoyable – work with emphasis on high standards. Special learning experiences strengthen dedication to an avocation that combines features of work and play. Second, it is in the home that a habit of hard work and doing one's best is developed, at first generally, then in relation to the particular field. Third, parents strongly encouraged development in a particular activity in preference to others. Fourth, no talented individual reached their potential without great support, encouragement and training; parents and teachers were crucial. Lastly, the length of complex and difficult learning needed for the development of these very high level talents was never less than a decade. All these factors interact with an individual who must possess, or develop, a strong interest and emotional commitment to a particular talent field and is strongly motivated to put in the great amounts of time and effort needed for the highest achievement. Such a combination of qualities and resources is rare, and Bloom concludes that every society possesses vast untapped human potential. (One might compare the East German athletics successes; see Chapter 4).

Bloom also noted that it was extremely rare to find more than one outstanding child in a family. On the face of it this suggests (as with the Bachs and other families of talent) that there must be inborn differences, but it is also possible to suggest environmental factors. It might be that one child, showing some talent, or even being by chance a favourite, receives more positive encouragement which in turn leads to more rapid achievement, more encouragement, and so on. According to Rutter (1985), and consistently with what has already been said in Chapter 9, it is unlikely that favourable home environments have more than a modest effect on intelligence as such, so that it must rather be habits and practices that are in question: intellectual or other performance. Berbaum and Moreland (1985) discuss what is known as the confluence model of the relationship between family patterns and intellectual performance. A family's average intellectual ability is not necessarily stable over time but may alter with changing membership. The very fact that children get older and thus normally more capable changes the intellectual climate; older children may act as tutors for the younger, and may themselves benefit thereby.

Many researchers, from Cox (1926) onwards, have suggested the importance of birth order (Zajonc and Markus, 1975); for example, Runco and Bahlea (1987) reported higher divergent thinking scores for only children, followed by oldest, youngest and middle children, which rather neatly fits a pattern of likely parental involvement. More generally, Albert (1980a) points out that a 'special' position in the family may not be due to birth order as such; siblings may die, or be a long way apart, and so on. He gives data from Nobel prize winners showing that 10 per cent were only children, 26 per cent only sons and 76 per cent in some 'special' position – like the younger Pitt. Francis Galton, although the youngest, was so by six years, was the general pet, and the special charge of his sister Adèle, twelve years older. However, as already mentioned, Plomin and Daniels (1987) demonstrate that in any case the effective home environments of siblings are hardly any more similar than are those of strangers who grow up in different families. What parents do that is experienced similarly by their children has little or no effect on their behavioural development, that is on their personality, their psychopathology if any, and their IQ at least after childhood; the effects of parents on their children lie in the unique environment they provide for each child. Hence the Marx Brothers and the Polgar sisters.

Formal education, in which so much is invested, is likely to have less effect than home if only because it comes later and takes up less time; although Freeman (1988) shows the importance for gifted children of the learning environment in both home and school, in respect both of material provision and good communication. Education, besides, is normally a principal means by which an individual has access to particular areas of knowledge and expertise. These interact in complex ways with the development of thinking skills (Glaser, 1984). Moreover, without them it is difficult to excel in a particular domain. This was the case of the remarkable mathematician

Srinavasa Ramanujan (1887–1920). Relatively unschooled, he spent his early years working out for himself much of the mathematics that was generally known by others; by 16 he had verified 6,000 formulas in Carr's *Synopsis of Pure Mathematics*, which sounds impressive enough. He was eventually brought to Cambridge in 1914, was recognized as quite exceptional, but fell seriously ill in 1917 and died two years later (Andrews, 1988). Feldman (1988b) holds that giftedness, especially in the extreme form of prodigies, is relatively domain-specific. It is not just that individual abilities may be specialized; rather a domain or field of activity must exist that is a match for them as regards its own stage of development; it must be one in which it is possible for a young person to excel such as a new technology. One case might be computer software, in which (for example) David Bolton at 15 became one of Britain's youngest tax-paying self-made men (*The Times*, 2 November 1988). Against this it might be said that intellectual prodigies continue to be most frequent in mathematics and chess, which have both been available for centuries.

This reflects more general cultural factors, which, as Csikszentmihalyi and Robinson (1986) point out, are not necessarily stable even over one lifetime. Mistry and Rogoff (1985) mention evidence that the drawings of children in Bali, where artistic activity has high status, are superior to those of Americans, and that some African children are precocious in skills that are encouraged, such as sitting and walking, but not in others, such as crawling. Other broader cultural influences have already been discussed; see for instance the work of Berry; Cole et al.; and Simonton.

Patterns and peaks

Very many factors, of which some of the main groups are culture, education and training, family and peers, mentors, and innate endowment, interact to produce every individual. Whatever the precise weighting to be given to each, it is clear that they vary in their degree and range of flexibility. We still cannot add a cubit to our stature (it was about 20 inches) though improved conditions have certainly added something. In at least some activities it would be rash to put a limit to possible achievement. These extremely numerous factors, far from completely mapped, also vary in their relationships to each other. It is as though each were linked to many others by bands of varying strength and elasticity.

The result is a pattern of behaviour which may show almost any kind of variation, though not necessarily to any extent. There are no doubt those in whom every single factor is at average level throughout life (though the very concept of 'average' must be referred to a particular population). In others a more varied pattern is seen, so that (probably) most people are non-average in at least some respect. Some combinations of factors correspond to exceptional performance. What we may term superior exceptionality may take the form of one or a number of traits exceeding the norm either for the individual or for a reference group. (This is also true of inferior exceptionality, but for various reasons it would be misleading to think of the two as mirror images.) Wide discrepancies within the individual have been termed 'dyssynchrony' (Terrassier, 1985): for example reading may far outrun writing, and reasoning exceed command of language; intellectual precocity may conceal emotional immaturity.

To some extent the picture that appears of the pattern and development of talent depends on definitions. Albert (1980b, c), for example, restricts it to high IQ, and then concludes that children with a high IQ may or may not be creative; and that they excel not only in speed of development but in the range of abstract academic subjects they can master. Since IQ is an index of 'general intelligence' which by definition refers to what is common in such activities, the result is hardly more than tautologous. Webb and Meckstroth (1982) found that gifted children were judged to be more inquisitive, active and energetic; they were also perceived as obnoxious, unruly, strong-willed, mischievous, unmanageable and rebellious. On the face of it, these seem largely social judgements rather than statements telling us much about talent.

The individual pattern is variable to some uncertain extent over the life-span. Exceptionality appears, or at any rate peaks, at different times in different individuals. Smith and Carlsson

(1983, 1985), for example, trace the fluctuating pattern of 'creativity' – here defined as the inclination to transgress the confines of an established perceptual context – in children from 4 to 16. Bamberger's (1982) account of the 'mid-life crisis' of musicians has been mentioned, and Langer (1953) showed how the talents of prodigies in many arts are often those of technical mastery, which may or may not mature into adult genius; most often, she thought, the later career proved to be that of a good professional artist without special distinction.

The classic study of the ages of achievement is that of Lehman (1953), who from a vast mass of data in many areas concluded overall that superior creativity rises rapidly to a peak which occurs usually in the 30s, and then falls off slowly. Such a broad trend conceals many variations both in individuals and in activities. Lehman makes the familiar point that achievement in some fields, such as mathematics, may require less by way of external factors than does political or religious leadership, for example. His peak age for mathematical productivity nevertheless was 34 – 40. The lowest peak, 26 – 32, was for chemistry. Lehman also listed individual achievements but found those of the highest order to be very rare before the age of 17 or 18; they were mostly in poetry, as Sully had noted.

Simonton (1988) summarizes much further research. He distinguishes three sorts of eminence; creativity, leadership (in any field) and celebrity as in sport or entertainment, and he is concerned only with the first two. Generally the findings show a typical age curve as described by Lehman, rising fairly steeply to a peak and then slowly declining, though varying somewhat according to field of activity. And this pattern averages out individual variations. In particular, it conceals a positive relationship between precocity, longevity and productivity. That is, the more eminent start earlier in life, go on producing longer (if they live), and do so at a faster rate. These analyses do not deal with young children, since as has been seen they do not (with only the rarest of possible exceptions) produce work that would contribute to adult eminence. Extrapolating downwards, however, suggests that very gifted children are more likely to be potential adult geniuses than to fall by the wayside.

The distribution of achievement over age is thus a skewed,

non-symmetrical one; and the same thing applies to achievement within a population. Simonton (1987) quotes Price's law, which states that half of all scientific contributions (for example) will be made by the number that is the square root of the total of scientists contributing. Similarly, the usual classical music concert repertoire contains work by about 250 composers. Fifteen or sixteen account for half the music performed. It might look as though the most outstanding individuals possess abilities that are very far removed from the main body of those who are creative at all. But several other factors must be considered. One is that success breeds success; initial success, even if partly by chance, opens up opportunities which in turn result in further success; this has been called the Matthew effect – 'Unto every one that hath shall be given, and he shall have abundance; but from him that hath not shall be taken away even that which he hath' (Matthew 25:29). Other chance factors also may have a disproportionate effect. For example, it is relatively speaking a matter of chance for a talented person to meet with an appropriate mentor (both are rare), who may have a dramatic influence. Furthermore, if achievement depends on high scores on several factors, then even if all these factors were normally distributed in the population, the coincidence of high scores on all of them would not be so distributed. The productive genius is extremely rare, but is the result, not of some factors or processes which are unique to her or him but of a unique combination and interaction of normal processes.

Walberg, Strykowski, Rovai and Hung (1984) discuss the skewed distribution of many social phenomena more generally. If one were to assess performance of any particular athletic activity in the population as a whole, the relatively few who actually train would be sharply distinct from the rest. Within the active set there would be further distinctions; the bulk would be within a band of general competence while only a very small number would have both the potential and the extreme dedication to reach the highest standard. Walberg *et al.* contrast the hour or so a day over a period of years that seems to equate with performance in the top one per cent of the general population, with what is required for world-class standards, which may be of the order of seventy hours a week for a decade. Moreover, at that level instruction must also be of the best. This applies to such various activities as chess, swimming, mathematics and foreign languages.

Similar arguments can be applied to prodigies. Indeed this is more or less the line taken by Feldman (1986b). Feldman uses the term 'co-incidence' to refer to 'the fortuitous convergence of highly specific individual proclivities with specific environmental receptivity that allows a prodigy to emerge'. These factors operate, according to Feldman, in at least four different 'time frames'. One is the individual life-span; one the 'life-span' of the domain of knowledge, which must be at such a stage that it can be mastered by a child; the third is that of broader historical and cultural trends, within which activities are differentially encouraged or inhibited; and the last is the evolutionary context of the whole phenomenon of a prodigy emerging. This relates to Feldman's notion of the prodigy as 'nature's gambit' that is (if I follow it) a kind of try-out of extreme variation which may lead to the better fulfilment of potential, but which has a high risk of failure. The notion of 'co-incidence' would seem to accommodate the facts that on the one hand early talent in general tends to predict later achievement, while on the other hand that achievement may not be as exceptional, in comparison with others, as was the childhood performance. The specific combination of factors was at its best early on, and less favourable later.

Of course, random variation is intrinsic to the theory of evolution, which is generally accepted as providing the framework for understanding differences between species and between individuals. The evolution of species characteristically shows a decrease in specialization coupled with a tendency to retard growth rate so that the adult retains features of earlier periods of development (termed 'neoteny': see Ambrose, 1978). Thus man is the least specialized of animals, and has a uniquely long period of immaturity (Bruner, 1972). The brain of the child appears to be more flexible than that of the adult, but considerable flexibility is retained – sometimes exceptionally so. The 'childlike' quality of adult creativity, particularly in the arts, has often been described (e.g. Kris, 1953). In this regard child prodigies, sometimes very specialized and in some ways at least unchildlike, might appear to be steps back on the evolutionary path. Hence, perhaps, some of the popular fears and forebodings about them.

11 The Problem of the Prodigy

Investigating the unique

The general view taken here is that prodigies are not unique, except in the sense that every individual is unique. But they are by definition very rare. How rare depends on the definition. Statistically, a prodigy comes at the extreme end of a distribution of achievement in a particular activity (or activities). Following the argument of Walberg mentioned in the previous chapter, the rarity of individuals at that extreme end is influenced by the number of factors that have to combine to produce the performance. Many of these have already been mentioned. Tannenbaum (1986) gives another list of features that have to mesh for a child to become truly gifted; superior general intellect; distinctive special aptitudes; the right blending of nonintellective traits; a challenging environment; and 'the smile of good fortune at critical periods of life'. These, in varying proportions, would indeed fit almost any case one can think of. A bit more narrowly, Renzulli (1986) summarizes research in support of three clusters of factors; above average ability, task commitment and creativity. Giftedness lies in the interaction of all three. Feldhusen (1986) gives the slight variation; general ability, special talents, self-concept and motivation.

Taking a fifty-year retrospective view of psychological measurement, Anastasi (1985) notes a growing awareness of the modifiability of human behaviour, as shown particularly by cross-cultural comparisons as well as inter-generational changes within a single culture. Assessments of human abilities are much more considered with reference to the contexts in which they developed, and to those in which they function.

Norms established for measurements, such as intelligence tests, are taken as the performances of a particular population at a particular time and place, rather than as universal. As we have seen, some more recent views of intellectual abilities have either, like Gardner, emphasized a multiplicity of relatively independent components, or else, like Ericsson, the role of practice. Both imply modifiability. Both reflect changing fashions, which in some respects are returning to a period before the emergence of psychometrics.

Horowitz and O'Brien (1985b) join those who have pointed out that the upper end of the ability range has attracted far less in the way of research than the lower end. This is partly because it has received less funding, which is due largely to social and political factors too complex to analyse here. Major developmental theorists have not on the whole attempted to explain the extremes, but have concentrated on trying to account for the general process of normal growth – sometimes paying attention to particular factors which cause deficit, but seldom to the reasons why things might work exceptionally well. Horowitz and O'Brien (1985a) (at the end of a substantial volume of collected research) pick out three areas that need study. They are, perhaps obviously: understanding intellectual processes and functioning in the gifted and talented; determining social and personality characteristics that distinguish the gifted and creative from the competent; and assessing educational strategies. They argue elsewhere (1986) that information, particularly on how best to nurture talent, is at present insufficient to inform policy makers. This is perhaps too low a valuation; though one might cynically observe that policy makers seem remarkably resistant to information even when it is available.

Work on gifted children sheds some light on the very outstanding, though any group study may conceal important individual differences. The difficulty of extrapolation, and the rarity of subjects, have led some to urge the use of single-subject research. It is of course perfectly possible to do experiments on very small samples, even of one. The classic memory experiments of Ebbinghaus were done on himself, and those of Bartlett on few subjects. In the case of the extremely gifted it is usually rather a matter of case studies, such as those of Feldman which have been mentioned several times, or indeed those of Baumgarten or Révész. Foster (1986) argues that the individual case study has many advantages. It obviously allows a much more intensive study of the particular subject. It provides a holistic view of how an individual functions. It can inform theory and practice through insight based on observation. And it provides a framework for the generation of hypotheses based on data, which can be tested against other cases. Good case studies should, according to Foster, meet certain criteria. The subject should be selected not at random but as far as possible as representative of the type being investigated – not so easy in the case of prodigies. Hypotheses should be deferred until after data collection – in this regard a case study is the opposite of the model experiment. Both quantitative and qualitative data are important; as are both public and private (experiential) data. Wherever possible data should be gathered in natural and varied settings rather than in the laboratory, and over a period of time. Different data-gathering devices (such as tests, interviews, observation, diaries, etc.) can focus on the same point – known as triangulation. In addition, a flexible approach should be used as the study progresses – again different from the set procedure of experiment. It is one thing to specify desirable methods, however, and another to obtain subjects who are defined by their rarity.

It is of course quite unscientific to reject any source of information in principle, though one should be aware of the limitations in each case. Curtiss (1988), for example, in her discussion of the effects of language deprivation, includes the very famous case of Kaspar Hauser. Although he was discovered (in 1828, not 1882 as Curtiss has it) well before modern methods of investigation, the case was very thoroughly studied and recorded by highly regarded professionals. This study shows, according to Curtiss, that he retained, during the rest of his short life – he died in 1833 – a selective grammar deficit even though he mastered all other aspects of language and was noted for an 'astonishing intellect'. This account omits nearly all the circumstances which made Kaspar Hauser, known as 'The Child of Europe', the *cause célèbre* he undoubtedly was. Briefly, the young man, appearing to be about 16, appeared on 26 May 1828 in Nürnberg, with a story, supported by a letter, to the effect that he had been reared from an early age alone and imprisoned but had been taught to read and write. His vocabulary, however, is said to have been only some fifty words. Kaspar Hauser was indeed investigated and taught by a whole series of people, not always sympathetically. He also attracted the attention and erratic patronage of various eminent persons (including the godson and heir of the letter-writing Earl of Chesterfield). He became the subject of several complex theories, the most dramatic being that he was the rightful Crown Prince of Baden, snatched from his cradle in the best fairy-tale manner. The problem has never been resolved (Phillips, 1980). What we should note is that there is no independent evidence of the first sixteen years of his life, and that he drew the kind of impassioned partisanship that can readily confuse such facts as there are.

Data on exceptional individuals must come at least partly from biographical (including autobiographical) material. Howe (1982) discusses many of the positive aspects, particularly with regard to understanding early development. He points first to the wealth of detail available from these sources. They help to answer questions about the relationship of early to later achievement; and about the effects of family circumstances over long periods of time. Then there are effects of particular events during life, and their timing and sequence (such things as illness, patronage, or 'crystallizing experiences'). It seems from first-hand accounts that childhood may vary in intensity as well as variety of experience. This in turn relates to the origins of motivation, particularly the single-mindedness seen in so many artists and scientists. Finally there is the choice of specialization and interest in which motivation is manifest. This may sometimes be seen to be developing even when the child has not yet shown outstanding performance. Howe's argument is partly a plea for these matters to be considered, and data on them collected, more systematically than has yet been done.

Problems and prognosis

Freeman (1986a,b) points out what must by now be obvious, that 'giftedness' (to use the most popular term) is a relative description indicating outstanding ability, but most often taken to refer to intellectual ability. Narrowly, this means tested intelligence; more generally, school subjects. To this are added some sorts of 'special' ability such as art and music; more rarely, commercial, social, religious or indeed sporting skills. Given this, 'most gifted children can be expected to be as well balanced and happy as other children; the primary difference between gifted and other children is one of ability' (Freeman). The definition is in the tradition of Terman, but the view is now not so much of an all-round favoured group as of one that stands out in a particular respect. If the range of types of ability were widened, it might appear that the gifts of some children lie in exceptional maturity, social adjustment, or courage. As it is, research centres on the characteristics of the intellectually forward.

Much of this research is summarized by Janos and Robinson (1985a), although as they say, sixty years has barely scratched the surface so far as psychological and social development are concerned. It is fairly clear that moderately gifted children tend to be well adjusted, with greater than average energy, range of interests, self-sufficiency and various other favourable traits. The very highly talented are more vulnerable, as Hollingworth (1942) found. Most obviously, they are the most out of step with their contemporaries, and the most isolated from others with similar intellectual interests and levels. Janos and Robinson refer to research suggesting that a substantial minority of children of very superior intellectual ability suffer from psychosocial difficulties, including being bullied by older classmates, having play interests that agemates cannot share and being required to tolerate restrictions they find unreasonable. Figures quoted indicate up to a quarter of the very highly gifted having such problems, compared to just over 5 per cent of the moderately gifted and ten to fifteen per cent of average children.

Terrassier (1985) refers to the problems that may arise from dyssynchrony between intellectual and emotional or physical development. In the first case acute intelligence may provide the child with anxiety-provoking information which he or she is unable to process appropriately; in the second, parents may expect a child to behave in accordance with chronological rather than intellectual age. On the other hand, parents or teachers may expect too much. Freeman (1979) suggested that intellectually gifted children feel a moral obligation to society to fulfil their potential.

Almost by definition this is very difficult to achieve as children; and it might be a greater problem for the most gifted. An appeal by the writer to the members of British Mensa, entry to which depends on an intelligence test score in the top two per cent of the general population, brought a number of letters whose principal burden was a felt failure to fulfil potential, either in childhood or later. This was a self-selected sample of an already self-chosen population which, however, would qualify as 'highly gifted' on the sort of criteria commonly used. An interesting exception to the adult responses was that from the only respondent who would really approach the prodigy class: being then 7 (1988) she wrote a well-typed and well-informed letter full of information about her ambition to be a surgeon, the interests this led to, and successes in getting stories published. She reported talking at 6 months and walking at 8 months, and appeared quite satisfied with life apart from some boredom at school. Of course there are also many high-achieving adult Mensans.

Exceptionally gifted children are already in a very small minority, but problems are potentially greater when additional dimensions are taken into account, especially those associated with disadvantage. The obvious cases are sex and colour. It is of course well known that women and some ethnic groups are under-represented on almost every measure of success in our society. Historically they have accounted for fewer geniuses, and fewer prodigies. There are perhaps three main possibilities to explain this; they are in some important way endowed with less potential; they have a different pattern of potential, less well matched to a society geared to the more dominant groups; they have the same potential, but are prevented from developing it. It is likely that the last two are true in certain respects, and interact; the problem with the first is that it is almost impossible to avoid questions of values. This is so even with physical potential. There is no sign that women will be able to match male athletic feats. On the other hand, they consistently live longer.

Historical studies such as those of Galton and Cox had

relatively little to say about women. Terman's female subjects consistently achieved less in material terms than the men – even those women who entered professions and who remained single. Fifty years later, the Johns Hopkins (SMPY) study has found continuing differences. Boys show more frequent and more extreme giftedness in mathematics, whereas verbal precocity is more equally distributed. Girls, even from junior high school on, are less likely to take extra or accelerated courses or to enter college early. Eccles (1985) discusses the rather complex pattern of factors that appear to influence educational and vocational choices which, she thinks, in turn largely determine achievement. Most generally, two groups of factors emerge: the individual's expectations of success, and the importance or value the individual attaches to the various options perceived to be available. Achievement results from a long history of choices both small and large, conscious and unconscious, and the important question Eccles argues, is not why gifted women are not more like men, but why both sexes make the sequence of choices they do. Girls in particular may have poor information about career or educational choices, or doubt their own ability, or have negative views of some possibilities, and so on.

Some experimental work does hint at how such influences might work. Hudson (1968) showed that boys would respond in dramatically different ways to tests of 'creativity', such as giving as many uses as possible for some common object, when they were asked to do so in the role of two contrasting characters, 'Higgins' a conventional engineer, or 'McMice', a Bohemian artist. Some of 'McMice's' responses were too bizarre for Hudson to print. More recently, Hartley (1986) reports a small but intriguing experiment in which he was able to improve the performance of a group of disadvantaged children on a problem-solving test by asking them to pretend to be 'someone clever'.

Similar arguments are presented in respect of minority groups and/or nonwhites (a majority can be disadvantaged), for example by Baldwin (1985) and Gibson and Barrow (1986). Indeed they have perhaps come to be accepted uncritically. While gross disadvantages such as poor nutrition or exclusion from education are clear, a much closer analysis is needed to explain why, for example, children of different immigrant groups in the UK perform markedly differently in school (e.g. Verma and Pumfrey, 1988). The same thing applies to why sisters achieve less than their brothers, when both have talent and share a favourable background.

As has been implied more than once, many factors large and small probably contribute to performance. It is plausible to suggest that, rather as with sporting achievement, at the top levels very small differences may tip the balance. And there is no reason to suppose that the pattern must be the same in every case. Every teacher observes how greater talent in one pupil may be equalled by extra effort in another, and so on, and this is likely to apply throughout the whole range – prodigies included. This is partly why it is so difficult to predict the future of any exceptional individual. D.H. Feldman (1980) quotes Howard Gruber, putting it rather simply: 'Gifted children do not necessarily grow up to become creative adults, and creative adults were not necessarily gifted children'. Nevertheless there is a positive correlation. Gifted children are much more likely to be successful than nongifted, and outstanding adults are likely to have shown promise in childhood, even if, as Howe (1982) points out, it may not have been very obvious or in expected directions. We have also mentioned another class of reason for this, namely that the demands of each stage may differ. The behaviour that counts as prodigious for a child may not serve the adult (as, for example, Ruth Feldman (1982) pointed out in respect of the Quiz Kids). Hudson (1966) showed how often the most eminent persons had had much less distinguished early careers. Taking Cambridge research students, for example, there was no relationship between the class of their first degree and the probability, later on, of their becoming a Fellow of the Royal Society or being awarded a higher doctorate (D.Sc., D.Litt., etc.). Apart from any other factors, first degrees require quite different skills to research. And then too there is the difficulty of deriving general principles, and numerical values of variables, from samples that must always be small and often unavailable for systematic study.

Prodigies to order

Some parents – James Mill, Boris Sidis, Lazslo Polgar, for example – appear to have produced exceptional children by deliberate method. But we do not know how exceptional the children would have been without their unusual parents; nor how many parents have tried and failed. The existence of outstanding children with much more ordinary siblings may imply both that they varied in some sense in original potential, and that an educational method has to be fitted very exactly to an individual to bring about prodigious results. As has been suggested, almost certainly the limits of human achievement have yet to be reached, even in basic activities which have existed in more or less the same form throughout history (for example, running, or even memory); let alone those which will be the product of changes in society and technology (see for example Fowler, 1983; Druckman and Swets, 1988).

Many will perhaps regard the deliberate attempt to create a prodigy as verging on a forbidden experiment, much as we now find abhorrent the eighteenth-century taste for exploiting a particular characteristic of childhood in the creation of castrati singers. (The purpose was to fill female roles in opera, though as far as one can tell they sounded not much like either women or children; Heriot, 1956). Similarly, freaks are not currently exploited for gain, though at one remove the case of the 'Elephant Man' John Merrick, which had been available since it occurred (the writer quoted it thirty years ago), having presumably become safely historical provided profitable entertainment in our time – as Merrick himself once had done.

In a famous manifesto, J.B. Watson, the father of Behaviourism, proclaimed:

> Give me a dozen healthy infants, well-formed, and my own specified world to bring them up in and I'll guarantee to take any one at random and train him to become any type of specialist I might select – doctor, lawyer, artist, merchant-chief, and, yes, even beggarman and thief, regardless of his talents, penchants, tendencies, vocation and race of his ancestors. (Watson, 1926).

This went down well in a land where it has been an article of faith that any boy (though not as yet any woman, and excluding certain groups) can become President. It may be noted that Watson did not claim how good his experimental subject would be; and he did require total control – 'my own specified world'. It is comparable to the 'milieu control' fundamental to so-called thought reform programmes (Lifton, 1961). As we have seen, it has been achieved to an extent within some family settings.

The most reasonable hypothesis at the present time appears to be that, should one wish to do so, one could significantly increase the probability of a prodigy occurring in a given population. It is less plausible that every child could become one; of course in one sense this is impossible, since the concept of prodigy is defined by its rarity, and 'when everyone is somebodee, then no-one's anybody' (W.S. Gilbert, *The Gondoliers*). It is, however, likely that the performance of many, perhaps all or nearly all, children taken at random could be raised to some extent; and perhaps turned in a particular direction.

Apart from eugenics, the simplest method, given omnipotence, would be to structure society in such a way that there were rich rewards for precocity. A principal reason why prodigies are rare (one guesses) is that they yield relatively little compared with the money and status resulting from adult achievement. Individuals find their own ways, more or less efficient, of excelling, aided now in many cases by scientific knowledge of learning and training methods and so on. Training programmes are planned so as to peak at the point of greatest potential. If society as a whole could not be experimented with, then a small community such as a boarding school (preferably with no holidays) or a family would have to serve. Within that, a close one-to-one relationship between a mentor and a child would be created, and all the arrangements of daily life predicated on success at one, or a few closely related, activities. This would involve very large amounts of practice, motivated either intrinsically or extrinsically; rewards, in the latter case, being more effective than punishments. If this pattern were repeated in a number of cases, there is a fair probability that at least some prodigies would result. That probability would no doubt increase if steps were taken to match particular demands to natural inclinations – to make the most of any natural talents that might appear, spontaneously or through psychometric measures; and to adjust the regime to the child's personality.

It might be that we should get our prodigies most easily in the areas that have so often produced them in the past, such as music, mathematics, and chess, but one can hardly estimate the possibilities of a wider programme. Nor the possibilities of a programme that set out not just to produce exceptional if specialized performers, but more able all-round thinkers; somewhat as James Mill did with, it may be claimed, a more sophisticated psychology than his (see for example Glaser, 1984; Block, 1985). Within limits yet to be determined, children will do what they are asked to do. Precisely how this comes about (or does not), in each individual case, remains to be fully elucidated.

Chandos (1984) quotes the following translation of Horace's *Ode to Leuconoe* by one Thomas Palmer:

> Seek not ('tis wrong) to know Leuconoe
> What fate the Gods shall give to me and thee
> Nor to attempt the Babilonian strains
> To bear the times how better would it be
> Whether our age more circling years shall see
> Or this the last which now th'Etruscan sea
> Dashes against the foamy rock. (and so on)

The author was 9; and his father, a country clergyman, was preparing his three sons for entry to public school in the first decade of the nineteenth century. He thought Tom the least able of the three and none of them exceptional; and his regime of intensive classical study, which might seem oppressive to us, to them was only a natural part of an idyllic boyhood in unspoilt (as we say now) rural Oxfordshire. Some might think Tom's lines superior to those of Hollingworth's child H (Chapter 3). Returning to the present century, detailed reports (Pollins, 1983; Brody and Benbow, 1987) assert the generally beneficial effects of the SMPY programme of accelerated study for exceptionally gifted young mathematicians, in respect of social and emotional as well as intellectual development. As we have noted, there seems no reason to doubt that extraordinary achievements in (say) mathematics in GCE examinations can be part of an entirely happy and well-adjusted childhood. On the other hand, it is less clear that much is gained by precocity in itself.

There is at the time of writing already something of a backlash against indiscriminate 'hothousing' defined by Sigel (1987) as 'inducing infants to acquire knowledge typically acquired at a later developmental level'. (Although Zuckerman (1987) points out that American educators have been warning of 'overpressure' on children for more than a century.) Gallagher and Coché (1987) point to some demographic causes of the hothousing movement in the USA, including having a first child at younger ages, higher divorce rates and increased maternal employment. These have produced parents with less time to spend with children but more money, and higher achievement anxiety as regards both themselves and their children. Enrolments in early educational programmes rose from 4.1 million in 1970 to 6 million in 1986. Pressure to give children a good start in the academic race may be to the detriment of wider development – social, emotional, and even cognitive – which may have roots in more traditional explora-tory play and family experiences. Immaturity, as Bruner (1972) pointed out, has its uses. Sigel suggests that parents may risk giving their children the belief that they have value only when they are producing. The determinants of parental attitudes to their children are far from understood but must surely involve deeply rooted emotions. The behaviour noted by Sigel, and seen in at least some of the better-known prodigies' parents, is almost a mirror image of that described in cases of child abuse. To give just one example, Steele and Pollock (1978), from a five-year study of sixty families, reported the following as general characteristics of the parents:

they expect and demand a great deal from their infants and children. Not only is the demand for performance great, but it is premature, clearly beyond the ability of the infant to comprehend what is wanted and to respond appropriately. . . . It is not an isolated, rare phenomenon but rather a variant form, extreme in its intensity, of a pattern of child rearing pervasive in human civilization all over the world.

Less pathologically, Garamoni and Schwartz (1986) describe some types of obsessive personality marked by an urge to gain and maintain a sense of control, by aggressive achievement striving and emotional constriction, which are reminiscent of (for example) Boris Sidis. It has been suggested here that such personalities do not provide the only or best environment for a potential prodigy.

Provision for excellence

It is reasonable to assume that the greatest single influence on children is that of parents or parent substitutes. There is evidence that babies can imitate behaviour within the first hour of life (Reissland, 1988). There is a considerable, if inconclusive, literature on parenting gifted children (e.g. Chamrad and Robinson, 1986; Flohr, 1987; Shaughnessy and Neely, 1987), apart from the 'grow your own genius' prescriptions. Observation suggests that most of what parents do is the result of tradition and folklore, often replaced in western societies by fashionable gurus such as Truby King or Benjamin Spock. It can be argued that there are better ways. Without attempting to summarize the vast and heterogeneous evidence, it will be asserted here that one cardinal principle might be named, that of maximum reasonable autonomy: the child (or for that matter anyone) should be free to act unless harmful consequences can be clearly shown. Of course this is partly a matter of what is thought ethically desirable; and of course it is often quite difficult to work out in practice. But it would appear to be quite appropriate to the development of talent: it would appear, for example, to inform the practice of Dr Sittampalam, but not that of Boris Sidis, nor the parents studied by Steele and Pollock; and only partially that of the general run of parents of generally average children. Freedom within a context of support and encouragement in general works well; forcing and restriction do not. Freedom may be limited by lack of opportunity as well as by restriction, and while it is logically impossible to open up all conceivable opportunities, the range for most children is quite small even in 'advanced' societies. Sloboda (1988), for example, describes how in one area, that of music, negative reinforcements provided through the educational system can have a long-lasting inhibitory effect on the development of musical competence – and hence by implication excellence.

Formally, these societies seek to provide opportunity mainly through education. Connolly (1986) asserts: 'By and large, it is probably true that the most able and talented children in Europe and North America receive the poorest education'. So we return to an issue mentioned at the start. A television presenter in 1988 was able to introduce an item – it turned out to be on Adragon DeMello – with the words 'If child prodigies make you sick . . .' (BBC *Breakfast Time,* 17 June 1988). Try substituting 'blind children' or 'West Indians'. Without too much sociological speculation one may hypothesize a fashion for equality which legitimizes provision for the handicapped but denies it to the gifted. Howley (1986) writes of 'the spectre of elitism' besetting gifted education, at least in the USA. Although she sees this in somewhat political terms, as part of a struggle between intellectuals and those who possess power, she does provide evidence for persistent opposition to appropriate provision for the intellectually gifted.

Similar conflicts can be seen elsewhere. Equality is equally a tenet of Soviet society, and Dunstan (1978, 1987) describes the changing attempts, over the last thirty years, to reconcile this with the development of the special talents of individuals; in particular, as we have noted, by the provision of specialist schools. There have been schools for the arts, sports and circus, foreign languages, mathematics and physics. From 1962–3 there have been a tiny number of very high-powered boarding schools, mostly specializing in mathematics and physics, but (says Dunstan) marred by a one-sided academic approach. In practice, at least in some cases, specialist schools have tended to accumulate non-working-class pupils: partly through influence (Dunstan, 1988), and partly, no doubt, due to the sort of factors described so long ago by Terman. There is an analogy here with the English public schools which, it seems, were studied by Russian educationalists: intended by their founders (in many cases) to be open to all, they became restricted to the privileged. The great Dr Arnold deliberately ran down his lower school, making it impossible for poor local boys to gain the classical preparation through which alone they could enter the upper levels (Bamford, 1960). Another Soviet technique has been that of academic Olympiads, based on competitive examinations, which have been widely if not massively popular, and have been held particularly in mathematics and physical sciences, but also in biology, astronomy, geology and arts subjects. The function of these is to find and encourage the very highest talents. Dunstan (1988) sums up the Soviet compromise solution as follows: 'Individual abilities and needs are to be recognised as far as possible, but are subordinate to the needs of Society'.

Similarly in Japan, though for rather different reasons, there is some conflict of attitudes. Lynn (1988) reports that Japanese teenagers are on average educationally two years ahead of those in the West. His analysis indicates that there is no greater financial provision; but there are strong incentives for children, particularly in the form of examinations; there is a longer school year; and there are powerful incentives for teachers, with fierce competition for examination successes, and numerous private schools competing against those of the state. However Cummings (1980) shows that this is all in the context of both traditional and changing values which emphasize development of the whole person, over a long time-span, and equality as well as competition. He distinguishes six determinants of Japan's educational achievements; a general concern with education; an emphasis on cognitive and motivational equality; pressure to achieve; an egalitarian moral orientation; egalitarian social change; and equalization of educational and social opportunities. Many aspects of these interact. For example, there is a well-established national curriculum. This not only sets standards against which all can, indeed must, compete, but it sets them above the average. It also includes social and moral education as well as academic; and despite the emphasis on competition, children in schools work co-operatively to master the common task. Nevertheless, alongside the apparent successes, Stevenson, Azuma and Kenji (1986), for example, report discontent among students, and worry among academics about lack of individuality and creativity.

Such examples do no more than suggest the complexities of providing for the extremely wide range of individual needs, a few of which constitute exceptional gifts. Tannenbaum (1983) has presented a kind of manifesto of gifted children's rights, which includes the right to be identified at the earliest possible age, and before they can achieve renown; the right to differentiated, indeed superior, education, with teachers appropriately qualified for them; and the rights to be valued as individuals and as 'precious human resources out of proportion to their numbers'. Although it might well be said that every individual should be valued, the greater a talent the more isolated an individual possessing it is likely to be, and thus in practical terms there is need for tailored provision. Snow (1986) stresses the need, in general, to integrate psychological knowledge about the many kinds of individual differences and connect it directly to the design of adaptive educational systems, including teacher-training programmes and diagnostic assessment methods. He argues '. . . the most lasting contribution may be in the enriched conceptions of human diversity that psychology provides to educators'. Some of the ways this can work in practice are discussed in Pellegrini (1988); for example, Malkus, Feldman and Gardner describe a method of presenting children's capabilities, called a Spectrum Report, which is intended to be much wider than that normally used, and to show not only the whole range of activity in and out of school, but the individual pattern of aptitudes, proclivities and interests, and show how these may best be provided for. Again, Sulzby points to the value of children's spontaneous choices in fostering reading development: while Wolf and others urge a much broader than normal view of literacy, to embrace both breadth, that is different forms of record such as maps, texts, matrices and scores; and depth, to include a repertoire of skills such as selecting and coding information, grasping its structure and processing it.

While this approach is perhaps partly a matter of fashion, it is not unreasonable to see it also as an advance on more rigid and limited prescriptions. If a prodigy is taken to be an individual whose early achievement in any field is exceptional compared with other members of a group with which that individual may be classed, which is the approach taken here, then awareness of as wide a range of potential talents and opportunities as possible, makes the best sense. But this is also true in general. A skewed distribution is not necessarily a discontinuous one, and it is not to be supposed that the gap between the child who attracts the label 'prodigy' and the one who does not is necessarily empty. There exists in principle every grade of performance, however progressively rare the upper levels may be.

Little Peterkin

'But what good came of it at last?'
Quoth Little Peterkin.
'Why, that I cannot tell', said he . . .
(Robert Southey, 'The Battle of Blenheim')

A colleague takes me to task for not distinguishing between talent and the 'true prodigy', which he feels to be marked by 'some sort of destiny'. Apart from the fact that there have been at least some undoubted prodigies whose fate was undistinguished or unhappy, to my mind this is pure *post hoc* reasoning (high as is my general opinion of this colleague). Mozart appears to fulful his destiny because he did so. Even that is not quite correct, since we have no means of knowing whether he would have been even more prodigious as a chess player or a mathematician had his early circumstances set that pattern.

One reason that this seems unlikely is that there does seem to be a spontaneous, if not predestined, quality about exceptional – perhaps all – talent. There are numerous parents who appear not to force their children. There are also those who are wary of unusual gifts. Thomas Macaulay's mother feared that his precocity would lead to an early death (Cox, 1926). Pascal's father, while generally supportive, at first wished him to concentrate on the classics, and to that end forbade mathematics. The well-known story is that the boy worked out the principles for himself (as Ramunujan did later) up to the thirty-second proposition of Euclid: 'the sum of the angles of a triangle equals the sum of two right angles'. And there are cases in which rapid development is actively discouraged (Terrassier, 1985). One who made the headlines was Seriozha Grishin who, according to press reports (e.g. *The Sunday Times*, 28 September 1986), underwent five years of taunting and bullying, persecution and even psychiatric examinations as a result of his precocious brilliance and his mother's persistent efforts to obtain appropriate education for him, rather than that ordained for his age group. The story appears to have had a happy ending with the boy, now 12, attending first-year physics classes at Moscow University, with a view to taking examinations and entering as a regular student.

Such a child might appear to be 'out of the usual course of nature' (Feldman, 1986b) when he only was out of the usual course of bureaucratic administration. On the other hand it is perhaps likely (it requires investigation) that there are levels of exceptionality that would strike most people as in some way unnatural. One would hypothesize that this is more likely when there is a marked dyssynchrony between aspects of development, such as between intellectual and emotional. It might even be that exceptional intellect is more alarming than unusual sporting talent, for example, but this is speculation.

The view has been indicated here that any such alarm is ill-founded; that there is nothing in principle inexplicable about prodigies, although there is much to be explained. It is not more helpful to speak of a 'true prodigy' than of a truly strong or tall man. A 'true giant' (or dwarf) is an expression that might be used; it would probably imply something pathological. There is no reason to think this correct in the case of prodigies. We have, however, considered as in some sense 'prodigies' those whose general level of achievement is pathologically low, but who excel at some particular activity: the idiot or mono savants. This is because it is difficult to see how exceptional (and therefore prodigious) behaviour can be defined except by reference to some group. That group cannot be the whole human race, which is unknowable and unstable. It must be a subset, and that must be a set to which the individual might otherwise be thought to belong. It is not implied that the same processes are necessarily at work in producing all the individuals who are markedly exceptional compared with any particular group.

There are some points of comparison. For example, it seems that it is possible for a retarded individual to excel other retardates at calculation, but at nothing else, in a way which is at least analogous to passing A level mathematics, but nothing else, at a very early age. It would be going too far to suggest that the same processes underlie both feats, or that they have the same causes. Nevertheless one can point to some factors which often seem to accompany both, such as continued practice, encouragement, and so on.

The investigative approach taken here has been that of the ragbag, or to dignify it with a scientific name, the inductive method. There has been no attempt to formulate and test hypotheses, simply to collect what could be found that appeared to be relevant, and note some common features. This inevitably leaves many questions unanswered, partly because the material is fragmentary; in many cases it consists of no more than the record of an achievement, with no information as to circumstances or background.

There are perhaps three main groups of questions. One is concerned with explaining prodigies, whatever one likes to mean by 'explain'. This would include the circumstances under which they appear, the physiological, psychological and social factors that seem to be present and the experiental or mental processes that characterize them. A second is concerned with what can be learned from them about wider groups, or about psychological processes in general. And a third is concerned with the matter of prognosis, i.e. what happens to prodigies later on; and with the corollary, whether great talent manifests itself early. Something, at least, has been said about all of these.

These are what Peters (1953) termed questions of theory, or scientific questions. He pointed out that the study of behaviour involves three other sorts of question. One is questions of technology; how to bring about a given result, whether or not we can explain the processes – in this case, for example, produce prodigies. Another concerns policy, what ought to be done, how the very highly gifted should be treated. The last sort is philosophical and metaphysical, concerned with what sort of a being the human is, and how it may be investigated. All of these have been touched on, not so much deliberately as because they arise inevitably.

All of them have occupied psychologists, whether so titled or not, for many centuries, and continue to fill many volumes. This volume is almost full already. Perhaps it can be said that it subscribes to the view that human behaviour is a proper, indeed essential subject for the methods of science, and that this involves considering, though not uncritically, data from any source.

Ideally it involves experiment, failing that observation and compilation, in any case reason and reflection. These show, it is held, something of the extraordinary variety, and the still greater potential, of the human species. They show too some of the ways in which potential can be thwarted or perverted, though in this particular book we have been more concerned with achievement than failure. Moreover, something at least is understood of how these processes work and how they might be made better – very far from all, but still greatly more than even a generation ago.

In an age which often seems marked by a hatred of what is outstanding or even what is different, when the mass media seem sometimes to show us little world-wide but the destruction of our environment, cultural and physical, mobs shouting for death in the name of some bizarre ideology, leaders exploiting technology to enhance their power over others, and masses of uniformed men or women going about the business of repression, the existence of the few exceptionally gifted individuals of past and present may at least offer examples, for the most part, of some sanity and hope.

August 1988 – March 1989
sero sed serio

Bibliography

Abroms, K.J. (1986) 'Social giftedness and its relationship with intellectual giftedness'. In J. Freeman, *The Psychology of Gifted Children*, Chichester: Wiley

Adams, K. (1988) *Your Child Can Be A Genius - And Happy!* Wellingborough: Thorsons

Adamson, J. (1973) *Groucho, Harpo, Chico and Sometimes Zeppo*, London: W.H. Allen

Agassi, J. (1985) 'The myth of the young genius'. Interchange, *Special Issue: Creativity, education and thought*, 16 (1), 51–60

Albert, R.S. (1969) 'The concept of genius and its implication for the study of creativity and giftedness'. *American Psychologist*, 24, 743–753

Albert, R.S. (1975) 'Towards a behavioral definition of genius', *American Psychologist*, 30, 140–51.

Albert, R.S. (1980a) 'Family positions and the attainment of eminence', *Gifted Child Quarterly*, 24, 87–95

Albert, R.S. (1980b) 'Exceptionally gifted boys and their parents', *Gifted Child Quarterly*, 24, 174–9

Albert, R.S. (1980c) *Exceptional Creativity and Achievement*, San Francisco: Jossey-Bass

Albert, R.S. (ed.) (1983) *Genius and Eminence: The social psychology of creativity and exceptional achievement*. Elmsford, NY: Pergamon Press

Alexander, P.A. (1985) 'Gifted and nongifted students' perceptions of intelligence'. *Gifted Child Quarterly*, 29, 137–43

Allport, G.W. (1961) *Pattern and Growth in Personality*, NY: Holt, Rinehart and Winston

Ambrose, A. (1978) 'Human social development: An evolutionary-biological perspective'. In H. McGurk, *Issues in Childhood Social Development*. London, Methuen

Anastasi, A. (1985) 'Some emerging trends in psychological measurement: A fifty-year perspective'. *Applied Psychological Measurement*, 9, 121–38

Andrews, G.A. (1988) 'Introduction'. In S. Ramanujan, *The Lost Notebooks and Other Unpublished Papers.* New Delhi: Narosa Publishing House

Aram, D.M. and Healy, J.M. (1988) 'Hyperlexia: A review of extraordinary word recognition'. In L.K. Obler and D. Fein, *The Exceptional Brain,* NY: Guilford Press

Aries, P. (1960) *Centuries of Childhood,* Paris: Plon (trans. 1973, Harmondsworth: Penguin)

Armen, J.-C. (1971) *Gazelle-Boy: A child brought up by gazelles in the Sahara Desert.* London: The Bodley Head (trans. 1974)

Arnold, G. (1980) *Held Fast for England: G.A. Henty, imperialist boys' writer,* London: Hamish Hamilton

Ashby, W.R. and Walker, C.C. (1968) 'Genius'. In P. London and D. Rosenhahn (eds), *Foundations of Abnormal Psychology.* New York: Holt, Rinehart and Winston

Aspy, D.N. and Aspy, C.B. (1985) 'Intensity: the core of thinking'. *Education,* 105, 414–16

Aylward, E., Walker, E. and Bettes, B. (1984) 'Intelligence in schizophrenia: meta-analysis of the research'. *Schizophrenia Bulletin,* 10, 430–59

Baker, J. (1983) *Tolstoy's Bicycle,* London: Panther/Granada

Baldwin, A.Y. (1985) 'Programs for the gifted and talented: Issues concerning minority populations'. In F.D. Horowitz and M. O'Brien, *The Gifted and Talented: developmental perspectives.* Washington, DC: American Psychological Association

Bamberger, J. (1982) 'Growing up prodigies: the mid-life crisis', *New Directions for Child Development,* 17, 61–78

Bamford, T.W. (1960) *Thomas Arnold.* London: Cresset Press

Barlow, F. (1952) *Mental Prodigies.* NY: Greenwood Press (repr. London: Hutchinson, 1969)

Bates, E., Bretherton, I. and Snyder, L. (1988) *From First Words to Grammar: Individual differences and dissociable mechanisms.* Cambridge: Cambridge University Press

Baumgarten, F. (1930) *Wunderkinder Psychologische Unter- suchungen* Leipzig: Johan Ambrosius Barth

Baynham, H. (1969) *From the Lower Deck: The navy 1700–1840.* London: Hutchinson

Baynham, H. (1971) *Before the Mast: Naval ratings of the nineteenth century.* London: Hutchinson

Beal, G. (1976) *The Magnet Companion '77.* London: Howard Baker

Beck, F.A.G. (1964) *Greek Education 450–350 BC.* London: Methuen

Becker, G. (1978) *The Mad Genius Controversy.* Beverley Hills, CA: Sage

Bell, E.T. (1937) *Men of Mathematics*. NY: Simon and Schuster

Benbow, C.P. (1986) 'Physiological correlates of extreme intellectual precocity', *Neuropsychologia*, 24, 719–25

Benbow, C.P. (1988) 'Neuropsychological perspectives in mathematical talent'. In L.K. Obler and D. Fein, *The Exceptional Brain*. NY: Guilford Press

Benbow, C.P. and Stanley, J.C. (1983a) *Academic Precocity: Aspects of its development*. Baltimore: Johns Hopkins University Press

Benbow, C.P. and Stanley, J.C. (1983b) An eight-year evaluation of SMPY: What was learned? In C.P. Benbow and J.C. Stanley, *Academic Precocity: Aspects of its development*. Baltimore: Johns Hopkins University Press

Berbaum, M.L. and Moreland, R. (1985) 'Intellectual development within transracial adoptive families: Re-testing the confluence model'. *Child Development*, 56, 207–16

Bereiter, C. and Scardamalia, M. (1987) *The Psychology of Written Composition*. Hillsdale, NJ: Lawrence Erlbaum Associates

Berry, C. (1981) 'The Nobel scientists and the origins of scientific achievement'. *British Journal of Sociology*, 32, 381–91

Berry, C. (1988) 'Biographical databases as sources of information about exceptional achievements'. *Proceedings of the London Conference of the British Psychological Society*, 19–20 December

Berry, J.W. (1984) 'Towards a universal psychology of cognitive competence'. *International Journal of Psychology*, 19, 335–61

Binet, A. and Simon, T. (1916) *The Development of Intelligence in Children*. Baltimore: Williams and Wilkins

Bishop, P.J. (1974) *A Short History of the Royal Humane Society*, London: Royal Humane Society

Block, R.A. (1985) 'Education and thinking skills reconsidered'. *American Psychologist*, 40, 574–5

Bloom, B.S. (ed.) (1985) *Developing Talent in Young People*. NY: Ballantine Books

Bornstein, M. and Sigman, M.D. (1986) 'Continuity in mental development from infancy'. *Child Development*, 57, 251–74

Boswell, J. (1792) *The Life of Samuel Johnson LLD*. (repr. London: Dent, 1906)

Bouchard, T.J. and McGue, M. (1981) 'Familial studies of intelligence: A review'. *Science*, 212, 1055–8

Boyle, M. (in press) *Schizophrenia - A scientific delusion?* London: Routledge

Brandon, R. (1983) *The Spiritualists*. London: Weidenfeld and Nicolson

Breskvar, B. (1987) *Boris Becker's Tennis: The making of a champion*. London: Springfield Books

Brodribb, G. (1974) *The Croucher: A Life of Gilbert Jessop*. London: London Magazine Editions

Brody, L.E. and Benbow, C.P. (1987) 'Accelerative strategies: How effective are they for the gifted?' *Gifted Child Quarterly*, 31, 106–10

Bronfenbrenner, U., Kessel, F., Kessen, W. and White, S. (1986) 'Toward a critical social history of developmental psychology'. *American Psychologist*, 41, 1218–30

Brophy, J. (1986) 'Teacher influences on student achievement'. *American Psychologist*, 41, 1069–77

Brown, M. (1988) *Richard Branson: The inside story*. London: Michael Joseph

Brown, R. (1965) *Social Psychology*. NY: Collier/Macmillan

Brownell, C.A. and Strauss, M.S. (1984) 'Infant stimulation and development: Conceptual and empirical considerations'. *Journal of Children in Contemporary Society*, 17, 109–30

Bruner, J.S. (1972) 'Nature and uses of immaturity'. *American Psychologist*, 27, 687–708

Burroughs, E.R. (1912) *Tarzan of the Apes*. All Story magazine, October 1912 et sqq.

Burrow, J.A. (1986) *The Ages of Man: A study in medieval writing and thought*. Oxford: Clarendon Press

Burt, C. (1925) *The Young Delinquent*. London: University of London Press

Burt, C. (1975) *The Gifted Child*. London: Hodder and Stoughton

Campbell, R.N. and Grieve, R. (1982) 'Royal investigations of the origin of language'. *Historiographia Linguistica*, 9, 43–74

Carlsmith, L. (1964) 'Effects of early father absence on scholastic aptitude'. *Harvard Educational Review*, 34, 3–21

Caroll, J.B. (1988) 'Individual differences in cognitive function'. In R.C. Atkinson, R.J. Herrnstein, G. Lindzey and R.D. Luce (eds) *Stevens' Handbook of Experimental Psychology*, 2nd edn. Chichester: Wiley

Carpenter, H. (1982) 'Introduction'. In D. and A. Ashford, *Love and Marriage: Three stories*. Oxford: OUP

Carr, R. and Farren, M. (1982) *Elvis: The complete illustrated record*. London: Eel Pie Publishing

Caruso, D.A. (1984) 'Conceptualizing parent-child interaction: An historical review'. *Cornell Journal of Social Relations*, 18, 1–19

Cattell, J.McK. (1906) 'A statistical study of American men of science'. *Science*, 24, 732–42

Cattell, R.B. (1963) 'Theory of fluid and crystallised intelligence'.

Journal of Educational Psychology, 54, 1–22

Chamrad, D.L. and Robinson, N.M. (1986) 'Parenting the intellectually gifted preschool child'. *Topics in Early Childhood Special Education*, 6, 74–87

Chandos, J. (1984) *Boys Together: English public schools 1800–1864*. London: Hutchinson

Charness, N. (1988) 'Expertise in chess, music, and physics: A cognitive perspective'. In L.K. Obler and D. Fein, *The Exceptional Brain*. NY: Guilford Press

Charness, N., Clifton, J. and MacDonald, L. (1988) 'Case study of a musical "mono-savant": A cognitive-psychological focus'. In L.K. Obler and D. Fein (eds), *The Exceptional Brain*, New York: Guilford Press

Chen, S. and Miyake, K. (1984) 'Japanese vs United States comparison of mother-infant interaction and infant development: A review' *Research and Clinical Center for Development*, 82–83, 22–23

Chen, S.-J. and Miyake, K. (1986) 'Japanese studies of infant development'. In H. Stevenson, H. Azuma and H. Kenji *Child Development and Education in Japan*. NY: Freeman

Child, F.J. (1884–94) *The English and Scottish Popular Ballads*. NY: Houghton Mifflin (repr. Dover Publications, 1965)

Clark, E.F. (1983) *George Parker Bidder: The calculating boy*. Bedford: KSL Publications

Clarke, A.D. (1979) 'Predicting human development: Problems, evidence, implications'. *Annual Progress in Child Psychiatry and Child Development*, 105–25

Colangelo, N. (1984) 'A perspective on the future of gifted education'. *Roeper Review*, 7, 30–2

Cole, M., Gay, J., Glick, J.A. and Sharp, D.W. (1971) *The Cultural Context of Learning and Thinking*. London: Methuen

Collins, J. (1974) *My Seven Chess Prodigies*. New York: Simon and Schuster

Coltheart, M., Sartori, G. and Job, R. (1987) *The Cognitive Neuropsychology of Language*. London: Lawrence Erlbaum Associates

Commons, M.L., Richards, F.A. and Kuhn, D. (1982) 'Systematic and metasystematic reasoning: A case for levels of reasoning beyond Piaget's stage of formal operations'. *Child Development*, 53, 1058–1069

Connolly, K.J. (1986) 'Editorial Foreword'. In J. Freeman, *The Psychology of Gifted Children: Perspectives on development and education*. Chichester: Wiley

Coward, N. (1937) *Present Indicative*. London: Methuen

Cox, C.M. (1926) *Genetic Studies of Genius, Vol. II: The early mental traits of three hundred geniuses.* Stanford, CA: Stanford University Press

Cox, C.J. and Cooper, C.L. (1988) *High Flyers: An anatomy of management success.* Oxford: Blackwell

Cranberg, L.D. and Albert, M.L. (1988) 'The chess mind'. In L.K. Obler and D. Fein, *The Exceptional Brain.* NY: Guilford Press

Cravens, H. (1985) 'The wandering IQ: American culture and mental testing'. *Human Development,* 28, 113–30

Csikszentmihalyi, M. and Csikszentmihalyi, I.S. (1988) *Optimal Experience: Psychological studies of flow in consciousness.* Cambridge: Cambridge University Press

Csikszentmihalyi, M. and Robinson, R. (1986) 'Culture, time, and the development of talent'. In R.J. Sternberg and J. Davidson, *Conceptions of Giftedness.* Cambridge: Cambridge University Press

Cummings, W.K. (1980) *Education and Equality in Japan.* Princeton, NJ: Princeton University Press

Curtiss, S. (1977) *Genie: A psycholinguistic study of a modern-day 'wild child'.* NY: Academic Press

Curtiss, S. (1988) 'The special talent of grammar acquisition'. In L.K. Obler and D. Fein, *The Exceptional Brain.* NY: Guilford Press

Daix, P. (1965) *Picasso.* London: Thames and Hudson

Danziger, D. (1988) *Eton Voices.* London: Viking Books

Davidson, J.E. and Sternberg, R.J. (1984) 'The role of insight in intellectual giftedness'. *Gifted Child Quarterly,* 28, 58–64

Deakin, M. (1972) *The Children on the Hill: The story of an extraordinary family.* London: André Deutsch (repr. Quartet Books, 1973).

Deford, F. (1975) *Big Bill Tilden: The triumphs and the tragedy.* NY: Simon and Schuster

DeFries, J.C., Plomin, R.C. and LaBuda, M.C. (1987) 'Genetic stability of cognitive development from childhood to adulthood'. *Developmental Psychology,* 23, 4–12

De Groot, A.D. (1965) *Thought and Choice in Chess.* The Hague: Mouton

DeLeon, P.H. and Vandenbos, G.R. (1985) 'Public policy and advocacy on behalf of the gifted and talented'. In F.D. Horowitz and M. O'Brien, *The Gifted and Talented: Developmental perspectives.* Washington, DC: American Psychological Association

DeLong, G.R. and Aldershof, A.L. (1988) 'An association of special abilities with juvenile manic-depressive illness'. In L.K. Obler and D. Fein, *The Exceptional Brain.* NY: Guilford Press

De Mause, L. (1974) *The History of Childhood*. London: Souvenir Press

Dennis, W. and Dennis, M.W. (1976) *The Intellectually Gifted: An overview*. NY: Grune and Stratton

Detterman, D.K. and Sternberg, R.J. (1982) *How and How Much Can Intelligence Be Increased?* Norwood, NJ: Ablex

Doman, G. (1964) *Teach Your Baby to Read*. London: Cape

Druckman, D. and Swets, J. (1988) *Enhancing Human Performance: Issues, theories and techniques*. Chichester: Wiley

Dunstan, J. (1978) *Paths to Excellence and the Soviet School*. Windsor: NFER

Dunstan, J. (1983) 'Gifted Soviet children: Provision, problems and proposals'. *Gifted Education International*, 2, 28–31

Dunstan, J. (1987) 'Equalization and differentiation in the Soviet school 1958–1985. A curriculum approach'. In J. Dunstan, *Soviet Education Under Scrutiny*. Glasgow: Jordanhill College Publications

Dunstan, J. (1988) 'Gifted youngsters and special schools'. In J. Riordan, *Soviet Education: The gifted and the handicapped*. London: Routledge

Dweck, C.S. (1986) 'Motivational processes affecting learning'. *American Psychologist*, 41, 1040–8

Eccles, J.S. (1985) 'Why doesn't Jane run? Sex differences in educational and occupational patterns'. In F.D. Horowitz and M. O'Brien, *The Gifted and Talented: Developmental perspectives*. Washington, DC: American Psychological Association

Edwards, A. (1988) *Shirley Temple: American princess*. London: Collins

Ellis, C. (1984) *CB: The life of Charles Burgess Fry*. London: Dent

Ellis, H. (1904) *A Study of British Genius*. London: Hurst and Blackett

Elyot, S.T. (1531) *The Book Named the Governor*. (repr. London: Dent/Everyman)

Ericsson, K.A. and Chase, W.G. (1982) Exceptional memory, *American Scientist*, 70, 607–15

Ericsson, K.A. and Faivre, I.A. (1988) 'What's exceptional about exceptional abilities?' In L.K. Obler and D. Fein, *The Exceptional Brain*. NY: Guilford Press

Eyles, A. (1966) *The Marx Brothers: Their world of comedy*. London: Zwemmer

Eysenck, H.J. (1986) 'Toward a new model of intelligence'. *Personality and Individual Differences*, 7, 731–736

Feldhusen, J.F. (1983) 'Eclecticism: A comprehensive approach to education of the gifted'. In C.P. Benbow and J.C. Stanley, *Academic Precocity: Aspects of its development*. Baltimore: Johns Hopkins University Press

Feldhusen, J.F. (1986) 'A conception of giftedness'. In R.J. Sternberg and J. Davidson, *Conceptions of Giftedness*. Cambridge: Cambridge University Press

Feldman, D.H. (1980) *Beyond Universals in Cognitive Development*. Norwood, NJ: Ablex

Feldman, D.H. (1986a) 'Giftedness as a developmentalist sees it'. In R.J. Sternberg and J. Davidson, *Conceptions of Giftedness*. Cambridge: Cambridge University Press

Feldman, D.H. (1986b) *Nature's Gambit: Child prodigies and the development of human potential*. NY: Basic Books

Feldman, R.D. (1982) *Whatever Happened to the Quiz Kids?* Chicago: Chicago Review Press

Fell, L., Dahlstrom, M. and Winter, D.C. (1984) 'Personality traits of parents of gifted children'. *Psychological Reports*, 54, 383–7

Fischer, K.W. and Silvern, L. (1985) 'Stages and individual differences in cognitive development'. *Annual Review of Psychology*, 36, 613–48

Fisher, R. (1987) 'A question of excellence'. *British Journal of Physical Education*, 18, 66–8

Fitzgerald, J.M. and Mellor, S. (1988) 'How do people think about intelligence?' *Multivariate Behavioral Research*, 23, 143–57

Fitzgerald, P. (1977) *The Knox Brothers*. London: Macmillan

Flohr, J.W. (1987) 'Parenting the musically gifted'. *Creative Child and Adult Quarterly*, 12, 62–5

Flynn, J.R. (1987) 'Massive IQ gains in 14 nations: What IQ tests really measure'. *Psychological Bulletin*, 101, 171–91

Flynn, J.R. (1988) 'Japanese intelligence simply fades away'. *Bulletin of the British Psychological Society*, 9, 348–50

Fodor, J.A. (1987) *The Modularity of Mind*. Cambridge, Mass: MIT Press

Forrest, D.W. (1974) *Francis Galton: The life and work of a victorian genius*. London: Paul Elek

Foster, W. (1986) 'The application of single subject research methods to the study of exceptional ability and extraordinary achievement'. *Gifted Child Quarterly*, 30, 33–7.

Fowler, W. (1981) 'Case studies of cognitive precocity: The role of exogenous and endogenous stimulation in early mental development'. *Journal of Applied Developmental Psychology*, 2, 319–67

Fowler, W. (1983) *Potentials of Childhood*. Lexington, MA: Lexington Books

Fox, M. and James, R. (1981) *The Complete Chess Addict.* London: Faber and Faber

Fox, L.H. and Washington, J. (1985) 'Programs for the gifted and talented: Past, present and future'. In F.D. Horowitz and M. O'Brien, *The Gifted and Talented: Developmental perspectives.* Washington, DC: American Psychological Association.

Frazier, K. (1981) *Paranormal Borderlands of Science.* NY: Prometheus Books

Freeman, J. (1979) *Gifted Children: Their identification and development in a social context.* Lancaster: MTP Press

Freeman, J. (1983) 'Emotional problems of the gifted child'. *Journal of Child Psychology and Psychiatry,* 24, 481–5

Freeman, J. (1986a) 'Update on gifted children'. *Developmental Medicine and Child Neurology,* 28, 77–80

Freeman, J. (1986b) *The Psychology of Gifted Children: Perspectives on development and education.* Chichester: Wiley

Freeman, J. (1988) 'Highly successful learners in school'. *Proceedings of the London Conference of the British Psychological Society,* December

Freeman, N.H. and Cox, M.V. (1985) *Visual Order.* London: CUP

Fry, C.B. (1939) *Life Worth Living.* London: Michael Joseph (repr. London: Pavilion Books, 1986)

Fry, P.S. (1984) 'Changing conceptions of intelligence and intellectual functioning: Current theory and research'. *International Journal of Psychology,* 19, 301–326

Gabriel, C. and Shuter-Dyson, R. (1981) *The Psychology of Musical Ability.* London: Methuen

Gallagher, J.M. and Coché, J. (1987) 'Hothousing: The clinical and educational concerns over pressurizing young children'. *Early Childhood Research Quarterly,* 2, 203–10

Gallagher, J.M. and Sigel, I.E. (1987) 'Hothousing of Young Children'. *Early Childhood Research Quarterly,* Special Edition, 2, 201–300

Galton, F. (1869) *Hereditary Genius: An inquiry into its laws and consequences.* London: Macmillan (2nd edn. repr. 1982).

Galton, F. (1874) *English Men of Science.* London: Macmillan (2nd edn. repr. London: Frank Cass, 1970)

Galton, F. (1883) *Inquiries into Human Faculty and Its Development.* London: Macmillan

Garamoni, G.L. and Schwartz, R.M. (1986) 'Type A behavior pattern and compulsive personality: Towards a psychodynamic-behavioral integration'. *Clinical Psychology Review,* 6, 311–36

Gardner, H. (1983) *Frames of Mind: The theory of multiple intelligences.* London: Paladin

Garrison, C.G., Burke, A. and Hollingworth, L.S. (1917) 'The psychology of a prodigious child'. *Journal of Applied Psychology*, 1, 101–10

Gathorne-Hardy, J. (1972) *The Rise and Fall of the British Nanny*. London: Weidenfeld and Nicolson

Gauld, A. and Cornell, A.D. (1979) *Poltergeists*. London: Routledge and Kegan Paul

General Synod of the Church of England (1986) *The Nature of Christian Belief: A statement and exposition*. London: Church House Publications

Gibson, A. and Barrow, J (1986) *The Unequal Struggle*. London: Centre for Caribbean Studies

Glaser, R. (1984) 'Education and thinking: The role of knowledge'. *American Psychologist*, 39, 93–104

Goertzel, V. and Goertzel, M.G. (1962) *Cradles of Eminence*. Boston: Little, Brown and Co.

Goldstein, L. (1988) Sir Thomas Elyot and chess. (*Personal communication*)

Gombrich, H.E. (1977) *Art and Illusion*, 5th edn. London: Phaidon

Goodman, M.H. (1986) *The Last Dalai Lama: A biography*. London: Sidgwick and Jackson

Goodnow, J. (1984) 'On being judged intelligent'. *International Journal of Psychology*, 19, 391–406

Goodwin, J. (1988) *What a Go! The life of Alfred Munnings*. London: Collins

Gowan, J.C. (1977) 'Background and history of the gifted child movement'. In J.C. Stanley, W.C. George and C.H. Solano, *The Gifted and the Creative: A fifty-year perspective*. Baltimore: Johns Hopkins University Press.

Grace, W.G. (1899) *Cricketing Reminiscences and Personal Recollections*. Repr. London: Hambledon Books, 1980

Grinder, R.E. (1985) 'The gifted in our midst: By their divine deeds, neuroses, and mental test scores we have known them'. In F.D. Horowitz and M. O'Brien, *The Gifted and Talented: Developmental perspectives*. Washington, DC: American Psychological Association

Gruber, H.E. (1986) 'The self-construction of the extraordinary'. In R.J. Sternberg and J. Davidson, *Conceptions of Giftedness*. Cambridge: Cambridge University Press

Guilford, J.P. (1982) 'Cognitive psychology's ambiguities: Some suggested remedies'. *Psychological Review*, 89, 48–59

Guiness Conference of Sport (1981) *Towards Sporting Excellence*. A report of the conference held at Ulster Polytechnic, 18–20

September 1981. Belfast: Northern Ireland Institute of Coaching

Gutteridge, R. and Giller, N. (1987) *Mike Tyson: For whom the bell tolls*. London: W.H. Allen/Star

Haber, R.N., and Haber, L.R. (1988) 'The characteristics of eidetic imagery'. In L.K. Obler and D. Fein, *The Exceptional Brain*. NY: Guilford Press

Hareven, T. (1986) 'Historical changes in the family and the life course: Implications for child development'. *Monographs of the Society for Research in Child Development*, 50, 8–23

Harrod, R.F. (1951) *The Life of John Maynard Keynes*. London: Macmillan

Hartley, R. (1986) ' "Imagine you're clever" ' *Journal of Child Psychology and Psychiatry and Allied Disciplines*, 27, 383–98

Havelock, E. (1963) *Preface to Plato*. Cambridge, Mass: Harvard University Press

Havighurst, R. (1961) 'Conditions productive of superior children'. *Teachers College Record*, 62, 424–31

Haywood, H.C. and Switzky, H.N. (1986) 'The malleability of intelligence: Cognitive processes as a function of polygenic-experiential interaction'. *School Psychology Review*, 15, 245–55

Head Start Bureau (1985) *Final Report: The impact of Head Start on children, families, and communities* (DHSS Publications No. OHDS 85–311193). Washington, DC: US Government Printing Office

Hebb, D.O. (1949) *The Organization of Behavior*. NY: Wiley

Hemery, D. (1986) *Sporting Excellence: A study of sport's highest achievers*. London: Collins/Willow Books

Heriot, A. (1956) *The Castrati in Opera*. London: Secker and Warburg

Hermelin, B. and O'Connor, N. (1986a) 'Spatial representations in mathematically and artistically gifted children'. *British Journal of Educational Psychology*, 56, 150–7

Hermelin, B. and O'Connor, N. (1986b) 'Idiot savant calendrical calculators: Rules and regularities'. *Psychological Medicine*, 16, 885–93

Hermelin, B. O'Connor, N. and Lee, S. (1987) 'Musical inventiveness of five idiots savants'. *Psychological Medicine*, 17, 685–94

Herrnstein, R.J., Nickerson, R.S., de Sanchez, M. and Swets, J.A. (1986) 'Teaching thinking skills'. *American Psychologist*, 41, 1279–89

Hibbert, C. (1971) *The Personal History of Samuel Johnson*. London: Longmans

Hill, A.L. (1977) 'Idiots savants: Rate of incidence'. *Perceptual and Motor Skills*, 44, 161–2

Hill, A.L. (1978) 'Savants: Mentally retarded individuals with special skills'. In N.R. Ellis, *International Review of Research in Mental Retardation*, Vol. 9. NY: Academic Press

Hitchfield, E.M. (1973) *In Search of Promise: A long-term, national study of able children and their families*. London: Longmans/ National Children's Bureau

Hoc, J.-M. (1988) *Cognitive Psychology of Planning*. London: Academic Press

Hoghughi, M. (1983) *The Delinquent*. London: Hutchinson

Holding, D. (1989) *Human Skills* (2nd edn). Chichester: Wiley

Hollingworth, L.S. (1942) *Children above 180 IQ*. NY: World Book Co. (repr. Arno Press, 1975)

Hope, J.A. (1987) 'A case study of a highly skilled mental calculator'. *Journal for Research in Mathematics and Education*, 18, 331–42

Horne, J.A. (1988) *Why We Sleep*. Oxford: OUP

Horowitz, F.D. and O'Brien, M. (1985a) *The Gifted and Talented: Developmental perspectives*. Washington, DC: American Psychological Association

Horowitz, F.D. and O'Brien, M. (1985b) 'Perspectives on research and development'. In F.D. Horowitz and M. O'Brien, *The Gifted and Talented: Developmental perspectives*. Washington, DC: American Psychological Association

Horowitz, F.D. and O'Brien, M. (1986) 'Gifted and talented children: State of knowledge and directions for research'. *American Psychologist*, 41, 1147–52

Horowitz, R. and Samuels, S.J. (1987) *Comprehending Oral and Written Language*. London: Academic Press

Howe, M.J.A. (1982) 'Biographical evidence and the development of outstanding individuals'. *American Psychologist*, 37, 1071–81

Howe, M.J.A. (1987) 'Memory in mentally retarded "idiots savants"'. *Proceedings of the Second International Conference on Practical Aspects of Memory, Welsh Branch of the British Psychological Society*, 2–8 August

Howe, M.J.A. (1988a) 'Intelligence as an explanation'. *British Journal of Psychology*, 79, 349–60

Howe, M.J.A. (1988b) 'Is it true that everyone's child can be a genius?' *The Psychologist*, 1, 356–8

Howe, M.J.A. (1988c) 'Parents' questions about accelerating early learning'. *Proceedings of the London Conference of the British Psychological Society*, December

Howe, M.J.A. (forthcoming) *The Making of Genius and Talents: The causes of exceptional ability.*

Howe, M.J.A. and Smith, J. (1988) 'Calendar calculating in "idiot savants": How do they do it?' *British Journal of Psychology,* 79, 371–86

Howley, A. (1986) 'Gifted education and the spectre of elitism'. *Journal of Education,* Boston, 168, 117–25

Hoyt, E.P. (1974) *Horatio's Boys: The life and work of Horatio Alger, Jr..* NY: Clifton

Hudson, L. (1966) *Contrary Imaginations.* London: Methuen

Hudson, L. (1968) *Frames of Mind: Ability, perception and self-perception in the arts and sciences.* London: Methuen

Hughes, A.O. and Drew, J.S. (1984) 'A state creative?' *Papers in the Social Sciences,* 4, 1–15

Humphreys, L.G. (1985) 'A conceptualization of intellectual gifted-ness'. In F.D. Horowitz and M. O'Brien, *The Gifted and Talented: Developmental perspectives.* Washington, DC: American Psychological Association

Hunt, J.McV. (1961) *Intelligence and Experience.* NY: Ronald Press

Hunter, I.M.L. (1962) 'An exceptional talent for calculative thinking'. *British Journal of Psychology,* 53, 243–58

Hunter, I.M.L. (1977) 'An exceptional memory'. *British Journal of Psychology,* 68, 155–64

Illick, J.E. (1985) 'Does the history of childhood have a future?' *Journal of Psychohistory,* 13, 159–72

Inglis, B. (1986) *The Hidden Power.* London: Cape

Ingram, J.H. (1883) *Oliver Madox Brown: A biographical sketch.* London: Elliot Stock

Jackson, N.E. and Butterfield, E.C. (1986) 'A conception of giftedness to promote research'. In R.J. Sternberg and J. Davidson, *Conceptions of Giftedness.* Cambridge: Cambridge University Press

Jackson, N.E., Donaldson, G.W. and Cleland, C.N. (1988) 'The structure of precocious reading skills'. *Journal of Educational Psychology,* 80, 234–43

Jacquard, A. (1985) 'La tentation eugénique'. *Génitif,* 6, 61–76

Janos, P.M. (1987) 'A fifty-year follow-up of Terman's youngest college students and IQ-matched agemates'. *Gifted Child Quarterly,* 31, 55–8

Janos, P.M. and Robinson, N.M. (1985a) 'Psychosocial development in intellectually gifted children'. In F.D. Horowitz and M. O'Brien, *The Gifted and Talented: Developmental perspectives.* Washington, DC: American Psychological Association

Janos, P.M. and Robinson, N.M. (1985b) 'The performance of students in a program of radical acceleration at university level'. *Gifted Child Quarterly,* 29, 175–9

Jarman, A.O.H. (1976) *The Legend of Merlin*. Cardiff: University of Wales Press

Johnson, S. (1777) *The Lives of the English Poets*. Repr. London: Dent, 1925

Judd, T. (1988) 'The varieties of musical talent'. In L.K. Obler and D. Fein, *The Exceptional Brain*. NY: Guilford Press

Jung, C.G. (1923) *Psychological Types: Or the psychology of individuation*. London: Kegan Paul, Trench, Trubner

Kane, J.E. and Fisher, R.J. (1979) 'Giftedness in Sport: A desk study for the Sports Council'. London: The Sports Council (unpublished)

Keith, T.Z., Pottebaum, S.M. and Eberhardt, S. (1986) 'Effects of self-concept and locus of control on academic achievement: A large-sample path analysis'. *Journal of Psychoeducational Assessment*, 4, 61–72

Kelly, M.P. (1985) 'Unique educational acceleration: The dilemma of John Stuart Mill and contemporary gifted youths'. *Gifted Child Quarterly*, 29, 87–9

Kessel, F.S. and Siegel, A.W. (1983) *The Child and Other Cultural Inventions*. New York: Praeger

Kipling, R. (1907) *The Jungle Book*. London: Macmillan

Kirby, R. and Radford, J. (1976) *Individual Differences*. London: Methuen

Kline, P. and Cooper, C. (1986) 'Psychoticism and creativity'. *Journal of Genetic Psychology*, 147, 183–5

Kojima, H. (1986) 'Japanese concepts of child development from the mid seventeenth to mid nineteenth century'. *International Journal of Behavioural Development*, 9, 315–29

Kris, E. (1953) *Psychoanalytic Explorations in Art*. London: Allen and Unwin

Kroll, J. and Bachrach, B. (1984) 'Sin and mental illness in the Middle Ages'. *Psychological Medicine*, 14, 507–14

Kunkel, J.H. (1985) 'Vivaldi in Venice: An historical test of psychological propositions'. *Psychological Record*, 35, 445–57

Lane, H. (1977) *The Wild Boy of Aveyron*. London: Allen and Unwin

Langer, S. (1953) *Feeling and Form: A theory of art*. NY: Scribner

Lave, J. (1988) *Cognition in Practice: Mind, mathematics and culture in everyday life*. Cambridge: Cambridge University Press

Lebrun, Y., Van Endert, C. and Szliwowski, H. (1988) 'Trilingual hyperlexia'. In L.K. Obler and D. Fein, *The Exceptional Brain*. NY: Guilford Press

Lees-Haley, P.R. (1980) 'The city of the gifted: Akademgorodok'. *G/C/T*, No. 13

234   *Child Prodigies and Exceptional Early Achievers*

Lehman, H.C. (1953) *Age and Achievement.* Princeton, NJ: Princeton University Press
Lenneberg, H. (1980) 'The myth of the unappreciated genius'. *The Music Quarterly*, 54, 219–31
Lewis, D. (1981) *You Can Teach Your Child Intelligence.* London: Souvenir Press
Lewis, D. (1987) *Mind Skills.* London: Souvenir Press
Lifton, R.J. (1961) *Thought Reform and the Psychology of Totalism: A study of 'Brainwashing'.* London: Gollancz
Liggett, J. (1974) *The Human Face.* London: Constable
Livingstone, M.C. (1984) *The Child as Poet: Myth or reality?* Boston, Mass: The Horn Book, Inc.
Locurto, C. (1988) 'On the malleability of the IQ'. *The Psychologist*, 1, 431–5
Lombroso, C. (1891) *The Man of Genius.* London: Walter Scott
Lucci, D., Fein, D., Holevas, A. and Kaplan, E. (1988) 'Paul: A musically gifted autistic boy'. In L.K. Obler and D. Fein (eds), *The Exceptional Brain.* NY: Guilford Press
Lutyens, M. (1975) *Krishnamurti: The years of awakening.* London: John Murray
Lynn, R. (1987) 'Japan: Land of the rising IQ'. *Bulletin* of the British Psychological Society, 40, 464–8
Lynn, R. (1988) *Education and Achievement in Japan: Lessons for the West.* London: Macmillan
Lynn, R., Hampson, S.L. and Mullineaux, J.C. (1987) 'A long-term increase in the fluid intelligence of English children'. *Nature*, 328, 797
Mackenzie, V. (1988) *Reincarnation: The Boy Lama.* London: Bloomsbury
Maclean, C. (1977) *The Wolf Children.* London: Allen Lane
Macnab, R. (1988) *For Honour Alone: The cadets of Saumur in the defence of the Cavalry School, France, June 1940.* London: Hale
Macnab, T. (1981) 'Talent screening and performance prediction. The British approach. In Guinness Conference on Sport: *Towards Sporting Excellence.* Ulster: Northern Ireland Institute of Coaching
McCurdy, H.G. (1957) 'The childhood pattern of genius'. *Journal of the Eleanor Mitchell Society*, 73, 448–62
Madsen, K.B. (1988) *A History of Psychology in Metascientific Perspective.* Amsterdam: Elsevier
Marjoram, T. (1988) *Teaching Able Children.* London: Kogan Page
Marjoram, T. and Nelson, R.D. (1986) Mathematical Gifts. In

J. Freeman, *The Psychology of Gifted Children*. Chichester: Wiley

Marx, H. (1976) *Harpo Speaks!* London: Hodder and Stoughton

Maslach, C., Stapp, J. and Santee, R.T. (1985) 'Individuation: Conceptual analysis and assessment'. *Journal of Personality and Social Psychology*, 49, 729–38

Midgley, M. (1978) *Beast and Man: The roots of human nature*. Ithaca: Cornell University Press

Mill, J.S. (1873) *Autobiography*. Repr. Oxford: OUP, 1924

Mistry, J. and Rogoff, B. (1985) 'A cultural perspective on the development of talent'. In F.D. Horowitz and M. O'Brien, *The Gifted and Talented: Developmental perspectives*. Washington, DC: American Psychological Association

Mitchell, F.D. (1907) 'Mathematical prodigies'. *American Journal of Psychology*, 18, 61–143

Monte, S. (1981) *May's Boy*. Nashville: Thomas Nelson

Montour, K. (1976) 'Three precocious boys: What happened to them?' *Gifted Child Quarterly*, 20, 173–9

Montour, K. (1977) 'William James Sidis, the broken twig'. *American Psychologist*, 32, 265–79

Morris, D. (1967) *The Naked Ape*. London: Cape

Morris, D. (1983) *The Book of Ages*. Harmondsworth: Penguin

Murphy, D., Jenkins-Friedman, R. and Tollefson, N. (1984) 'A new criterion for the "ideal" child?' *Gifted Child Quarterly*, 28, 31–6

Needham, J. (1969) *The Grand Titration*. London: Allen and Unwin

Nelson, K. (1981) 'Individual differences in language development: Implications for development and language'. *Developmental Psychology*, 17, 170–87

Novoa, L., Fein, D. and Obler, L.K. (1988) 'Talent in foreign languages: A case study'. In L.K. Obler and D. Fein, *The Exceptional Brain*. NY: Guilford Press

Nyborg, H. (1987) 'Individual differences or different individuals? That is the question.' *Behavioral and Brain Sciences*, 10, 34–5

Obler, L.K. and Fein, D. (1988) *The Exceptional Brain: Neuropsychology of talents and special abilities*. NY: Guilford Press

O'Connor, N. and Hermelin, B. (1984) 'Idiot savant calendrical calculators: maths or memory?' *Psychological Medicine*, 14, 801–6

O'Connor, N. and Hermelin, B. (1987a) 'Visual memory and motor programmes: Their use by idiot savant artists and controls'. *British Journal of Psychology*, 78, 307–23

O'Connor, N. and Hermelin, B. (1987b) 'Visual and graphic abilities of the idiot savant artist'. *Psychological Medicine*, 17, 79–90

O'Connor, N. and Hermelin, B. (1987c) 'Low intelligence and special abilities'. *Journal of Child Psychology and Psychiatry*, 29, 391–6

Oden, M.H. (1968) 'The fulfilment of promise: 40-year follow-up of the Terman gifted group'. *Genetic Psychology Monographs*, 77, 3–93

Olson, D.R. (1986) 'The cognitive consequences of literacy'. *Canadian Psychology*, 27, 109–21

Opie, I. and Opie, P. (1959) *The Lore and Language of Schoolchildren*. Oxford: OUP

Pandey, K. (1984) 'Parent-child relationship and achievement: A review'. *Child Psychiatry Quarterly*, 17, 139–48

Pariser, D. (1985) 'The juvenilia of Klee, Toulouse-Lautrec and Picasso'. *The History of Art Education*, Proceedings of the Pennsylvania State Conference.

Pariser, D. (1987) 'The juvenile drawings of Klee, Toulouse-Lautrec and Picasso'. *Visual Arts Research*, 13, 53–67

Pellegrini, A.D. (ed.) (1988) *Psychological Bases for Early Education*. Chichester: Wiley

Percival, J. (1985) *For Valour: The Victoria Cross: courage in action*. London: Thames Methuen

Peters, R.S. (1953) *Brett's History of Psychology*. London: Allen and Unwin

Peterson, J.W. (1987) *The Secret Life of Kids*. Wheaton, Ill.: Theosophical Publishing House/Quest Books

Phillips, J. (1980) 'Kaspar Hauser'. *The Times*, 16 August

Piechowski, M.M. and Colangelo, N. (1984) 'Developmental potential of the gifted'. *Gifted Child Quarterly*, 28, 80–8

Piechowski, M.M. and Cunningham, K. (1985) 'Problems of overexcitability in a group of artists'. *The Journal of Creative Behaviour*, 19, 153–74

Plato (*c.* 427–347 BC) *The Republic*. Trans. H.D.P. Lee. Harmondsworth: Penguin, 1955

Plomin, R. and Daniels, D. (1987) 'Why are children in the same family so different from one another?' *Behavioral and Brain Science*, 10, 1–16

Plomin, R. and DeFries, J.C. (1985) *Origins of Individual Differences in Infancy: The Colorado Adoption Project*. NY: Academic Press

Polit, D. and Falbo, T. (1987) 'Only children and personality development: A quantitative review'. *Journal of Marriage and the Family*, 49, 309–25

Pollins, C.D. (1983) 'The effects of acceleration on the social and emotional development of gifted students'. In C.P. Benbow and

J. Stanley (eds), *Academic Precocity: Aspects of its development.* Baltimore: The Johns Hopkins University

Popper, K. (1963) *Conjectures and Refutations.* London: Routledge and Kegan Paul

Porges, I. (1975) *Edgar Rice Burroughs: The man who created Tarzan.* Salt Lake City: Brigham Young University Press

Pottebaum, S.M., Keith, T.Z. and Ehly, S.W. (1986) 'Is there a causal relationship between self-concept and academic achievement?' *Journal of Educational Research,* 79, 140–4

Pressey, S.L. (1955) 'Concerning the nature and nurture of genius'. *Scientific Monthly,* 81, 123–9

Raaheim, K. (1984) *Why Intelligence Is Not Enough.* London: Sigma Forlag

Raaheim, K. and Radford, J. (1984) *Your Introduction to Psychology.* Oslo: Cappelen

Radford, J. (1985) 'Is the customer right? Views and expectations of psychology'. *Psychology Teaching,* Special Edition, April, 15–27

Ray, J.T. (1988) 'IQ gain as an outcome of improved obstetric practice'. *The Psychologist,* 1, 498

Reissland, N. (1988) 'Neonatal imitation in the first hour of life: Observations in rural Nepal'. *Developmental Psychology,* 24, 464–9

Renzulli, J.S. (1986) 'The three-ring conception of giftedness: A developmental model for creative productivity'. In R.J. Sternberg and J. Davidson, *Conceptions of Giftedness.* Cambridge: Cambridge University Press

Reuben, S. (1989) 'The Polgar sisters'. *British Chess Magazine,* January, 12–13. And personal communications, 1988

Révész, G. (1925) *The Psychology of a Musical Prodigy.* Repr. Freeport, NY: Books for Libraries Press, 1970

Richards, J. (1988) *Happiest Days: The public schools in English fiction.* Manchester: Manchester University Press

Rimland, B. and Fein, D. (1988) 'Special talents of autistic savants'. In L.K. Obler and D. Fein, *Exceptional Brains.* NY: Guilford Press

Rodger, N.A.M. (1986) *The Wooden World: An anatomy of the Georgian Navy.* London: Collins/Fontana

Roe, A. (1952) 'A psychologist examines 64 eminent scientists'. *Scientific American,* 187, 21–5

Roe, A. (1953) *The Making of a Scientist.* NY: Dodd Mead

Rogan, J. (1988) *Starmakers and Svengalis.* London: Macdonald/ Futura

Rolfe, L.M. (1978) *The Menuhins: A family odyssey.* San Francisco: Panjandrum/Aris Books

Rosenblatt, E. and Winner, E. (1988) 'Is superior memory a component of superior drawing ability?' In L.K. Obler and D. Fein (eds) *The Exceptional Brain*. NY: Guilford Press

Rosenthal, R. and Jacobson, L. (1968) *Pygmalion in the Classroom.* NY: Holt, Rinehart and Winston

Ross, A. (1983) *Ranji.* London: Michael Joseph

Rowley, S. (1986) *The Effect of Intensive Training on Young Athletes*. London: The Sports Council

Rowley, S. (1987) 'Psychological effects of intensive training in young athletes'. *Journal of Child Psychology and Psychiatry*, 28, 371-7

Rubinstein, A. (1973) *My Young Years*. London: Cape

Runco, M.A. and Bahlea, M.A. (1987) 'Birth order and divergent thinking'. *Journal of Genetic Psychology*, 148, 119–25

Russell, B. (1967) *Autobiography*. London: Allen and Unwin

Rutter, M. (1985) 'Family and school influences on cognitive development'. *Journal of Child Psychology and Psychiatry and Allied Disciplines*, 26, 683–704

Ryle, G. (1949) *The Concept of Mind*. London: Hutchinson

Sacks, O. (1985) *The Man Who Mistook His Wife For A Hat*. NY: Summit Books

Salazar, J.M. (1984) 'The use and impact of psychology in Venezuela: Two examples'. *International Journal of Psychology*, 19, 113–22

Sattler, J.M. (1982) *Assessment of Children's Intelligence and Special Abilities*, 2nd edn. Boston, Mass.: Allyn and Bacon

Scarr, S. and McCartney, K. (1983) 'How people make their own environments: A theory of genotype-environmental effects'. *Child Development*, 54, 424–35

Schneiderman, E.I. and Desmarais, C. (1988) 'A neuropsychological substrate for talent in second-language acquisition'. In L.K. Obler and D. Fein, *The Exceptional Brain*. NY: Guilford Press

Seagoe, M.V. (1975) *Terman and the Gifted*. Los Altos, CA: William Kaufman

Selfe, L. (1977) *Nadia: A case of extraordinary drawing ability in an autistic child*. London: Academic Press

Selfe, L. (1983) *Normal and Anomalous Representational Drawing Ability in Children*. London: Academic Press

Sharron, H. (1987) *Changing Children's Minds: Feuerstein's revolution in the teaching of intelligence*. London: Souvenir Press.

Shaughnessy, M.F. and Neely, R. (1987) 'Parenting the prodigies: What if your child is highly verbal or mathematically precocious?' *Creative Child and Adult Quarterly*, 12, 7–20

Shaw, J.A. (1982) 'The postadolescent crisis of John Stuart Mill'. *Adolescent Psychiatry*, 10, 85–98

Short, D. (1981) *Nigel Short: Chess Prodigy*. London: Faber
Shuter-Dyson, R. (1986) 'Musical giftedness'. In J. Freeman, *The Psychology of Gifted Children*. Chichester: Wiley
Sigel, I.E. (1987) 'Does hothousing rob children of their childhood?' *Early Childhood Research Quarterly*, 2, 211–55
Simonton, D.K. (1978) 'History and the eminent person'. *Gifted Child Quarterly*, 22, 187–95
Simonton, D.K. (1984) *Genius, Creativity and Leadership: Historiometric enquiries*. Cambridge, Mass.: Harvard University Press
Simonton, D.K. (1987) 'Developmental antecedents of achieved eminence'. *Annals of Child Development*, 4, 131–69
Simonton, D.K. (1988) 'Age and outstanding achievement: What do we know after a century of research?' *Psychological Bulletin*, 104, 215–67
Sinclair, M. (1988) *Hollywood Lolita*. London: Plexus
Sitwell, E. (1933) *English Eccentrics*. London: Faber and Faber
Sitwell, E. (1966) *Taken Care Of*. London: Hutchinson
Sloboda, J.A. (1988) 'Musical excellence: How does it develop?' *Proceedings of the London conference of the British Psychological Society*, December
Sloboda, J.A., Hermelin, B. and O'Connor, N. (1985) 'An exceptional musical memory'. *Music Perception*, 3, 155–70
Smith, M.D. (1978) 'Hockey violence: Interring some myths'. In W.B. Straub (ed), *Sport Psychology: An analysis of athlete behaviour*. NY: Mouvement
Smith, S.B. (1983) *The Great Mental Calculators*. NY: Columbia University Press
Smith, S.B. (1988) 'Calculating prodigies'. In L.K. Obler and D. Fein, *The Exceptional Brain*. NY: Guilford Press
Smith, G. and Carlsson, I. (1983) 'Creativity in the early and middle school years'. *International Journal of Behavioral Development*, 6, 167–95
Smith, G. and Carlsson, I. (1985) 'Creativity in middle and late school years'. *International Journal of Behavioral Development*, 8, 329–43
Smith, P.K. and Cowie, H. (1988) *Understanding Children's Development*. Oxford: Blackwell
Snow, R.E. (1986) 'Individual differences and the design of educational programs'. *American Psychologist*, 41, 1029–39
Spearman, C. (1904) '"General Intelligence": objectively determined and measured'. *American Journal of Psychology*, 15, 201–292
Stanley, J.C. (1977) 'Rationale of the study of mathematically precocious youth (SMPY) during its first five years of promoting

educational acceleration'. In J.C. Stanley, W.C. George and C.H. Solano, *The Gifted and the Creative: A fifty-year perspective*. Baltimore: Johns Hopkins University Press

Stapledon, O. (1935) *Odd John*. London: Methuen

Steele, B.F. and Pollock, C.B. (1978) 'General characteristics of abusing parents'. In C.M. Lee, *Child Abuse: A reader and source book*. Milton Keynes: Open University Press

Stephen, L. and Lee, S. (1885) *et sqq. Dictionary of National Biography*. Oxford: OUP

Sternberg, R.J. and Davidson, J.E. (1985) 'Cognitive development in the gifted and talented'. In F.D. Horowitz and M. O'Brien, *The Gifted and Talented: Developmental perspectives*. Washington, DC: American Psychological Association

Stevenson, H., Azuma, H. and Kenji, H. (1986) *Child Development and Education in Japan*. NY: Freeman

Suetonius (Gaius Suetonius Tranquillus, born *c.* AD 69) *The Twelve Caesars*. Trans. R. Graves. Harmondsworth: Penguin, 1957

Sully, J. (1886) 'Genius and precocity'. *Nineteenth Century*, 19, 827–48

Sully, J. (1891) 'The education of genius'. *English Illustrated Magazine*, January

Tacitus (Cornelius Tacitus, born *c.* AD 65) *The Annals of Imperial Rome*. Trans. M. Grant. Harmondsworth: Penguin, 1956

Tannenbaum, A.J. (1983) *Gifted Children: Psychological and educational perspectives*. NY: Macmillan

Tannenbaum, A.J. (1986) 'Giftedness: A psychosocial approach'. In R.J. Sternberg and J. Davidson, *Conceptions of Giftedness*. Cambridge: Cambridge University Press

Taylor, J. (1977) *Superminds*. London: Warner Books

Taylor, R.L. (1949) *W.C. Fields: His follies and fortunes*. NY: New American Library

Teasdale, T.W., Fuchs, J. and Goldschmidt, E. (1988) 'Degree of myopia in relation to intelligence and educational level.' *The Lancet*, No. 8264, 1351–3

Terman, L.M. (1906) [published 1975] *Genius and Stupidity*. NY: Arno Press

Terman, L.M. (1918) 'An experiment in infant education'. *Journal of Applied Psychology*, 2, 219–28

Terman, L.M. (1925) *Genetic Studies of Genius, Vol. 1. Mental and physical traits of a thousand gifted children*. Stanford, CA: Stanford University Press

Terman, L.M., and Oden, M.H. (1947) *Genetic Studies of Genius, Vol. 4. The gifted group grows up: Twenty-five years' follow-up of a superior group.* Stanford, CA: Stanford University Press

Terman, L.M. and Oden, M.H. (1959) *Genetic Studies of Genius, Vol. 5. The gifted group at mid-life: Thirty-five years' follow-up of the superior child.* Stanford, CA: Stanford University Press

Terrassier, J.-C. (1985) 'Dyssynchrony–uneven development'. In J. Freeman, *The Psychology of Gifted Children.* Chichester: Wiley

Thompson, C.J.S. (1968) *The Mystery and Lore of Monsters.* NY and London: University Books Inc.

Thomson, A.A. (1957) *The Great Cricketer: A biography of W.G. Grace.* London: Hutchinson

Thomson, R.W. and Beavis, N. (1985) *Talent and Identification in Sport.* Report on behalf of the Otago University and Community Sports Trust for the New Zealand Sports Foundation Inc. and the Ministry of Recreation and Sport. Dunedin, NZ: Faculty of Physical Education, University of Otago

Thurstone, L.L. (1938) *Primary Mental Abilities.* Chicago: Chicago University Press

Tillett, G. (1982) *The Elder Brother: A biography of Charles Webster Leadbeater.* London: Routledge and Kegan Paul

Todd, A.L. (1983) *Mendelssohn's Musical Education.* Cambridge: Cambridge University Press

Torrance, E.P. (1983) 'Role of mentors in creative achievement'. *The Creative Child and Adult Quarterly*, 8, 8–16

Torrance, E.P. and Safter, H.T. (1986) 'Are children becoming more creative?' *Journal of Creative Behaviour*, 20, 1–13

Treadwell, P. (1987) 'Giftedness and sport in schools–a comparative perspective'. *British Journal of Physical Education*, 18, 63–5

Treffert, D.A. (1989) *Extraordinary People: An exploration of the savant syndrome.* London: Bantam Press

Tropp, M. (1977) *Mary Shelley's Monster : The story of Frankenstein.* Boston: Houghton Mifflin

Vandenberg, S.G. and Vogler, G.P. (1985) 'Genetic determinants of intelligence'. In B.B. Wolman, *Handbook of Intelligence: Theories, measurements and applications.* Chichester: Wiley

Verma, G. and Pumfrey, P. (1988) *Educational Attainments: Issues and outcomes in multicultural education.* London: Falmer Press

Vernant, J.-P. (1962) *The Origins of Greek Thought.* Trans. 1982. London: Methuen

Vernon, P.E. (1969) *Intelligence and Cultural Environment.* London: Methuen

Walberg, H.J., Strykowski, B.F., Rovai, E. and Hung, S.S. (1984) 'Exceptional performance'. *Review of Educational Research*, 54,

87–112

Wallace, A. (1986) *The Prodigy: A biography of William James Sidis, the world's greatest child prodigy.* London: Macmillan

Wallach, M.A. (1985) 'Creativity testing and giftedness'. In F.D. Horowitz and M. O'Brien, *The Gifted and Talented.* Washington, DC: American Psychological Association

Walmsley, J. and Margolis, J. (1978) *Hothouse People.* London: Pan Books

Walters, J. and Gardner, H. (1986) 'The crystallizing experience: Discovering an intellectual gift'. In R.J. Sternberg and J. Davidson, *Conceptions of Giftedness.* Cambridge: Cambridge University Press

Wansell, G. (1988) *Tycoon.* London: Grafton

Waterhouse, L. (1988) 'Speculations on the neuroanatomical substrate of special talents.' In L.K. Obler and D. Fein, *The Exceptional Brain.* NY: Guilford Press

Watson, J.B. (1926) 'Experimental studies on the growth of emotions'. In J. Murchison, *Psychologies of 1925.* Worcester, MA: Clarke University Press

Webb, J.T. and Meckstroth, B. (1982) *Guiding the Gifted Child.* Columbus, Ohio: Ohio Psychology Publishing Co

Weeks, D.J. and Ward, K. (1988) *Eccentrics: The scientific investigation.* Stirling: Stirling University Press

Werner, E. (1984) 'Resilient children'. *Young Children*, 40, 68–72

Wertsch, J.V. (1986) *Vygotsky and the Social Formation of Mind.* Cambridge, Mass.: Harvard University Press

Whitehurst, G.J., Falco, F.L., Lonigan, C.J., Fischel, J.E., Debaryshe, B.D., Valdez-Menchaca, M.C. and Caulfield, M. (1988) 'Accelerating language development through picture book reading.' *Developmental Psychology*, 24, 552–9

Wiener, N. (1953) *The Autobiography of an Ex-prodigy.* Extract in W. and M.W. Dennis, *The Intellectually Gifted: An overview.* NY: Grune and Stratton

Wiener, N. (1976) 'The autobiography of an ex-prodigy'. In W. Dennis and M.G. Dennis (eds) *The Intellectually Gifted: An overview.* NY: Grune and Stratton

Willats, J. (1985) 'Drawing systems re-visited: The role of denoting systems in children's figure drawing.' In N.H. Freeman and M.V. Cox (eds), *Visual Order.* London: Cambridge University Press

Wilson, E.O. (1975) *Sociobiology: The new synthesis.* Cambridge, Mass: Harvard University Press

Winkler, A. (1988) 'From second rate to White House'. *The Times*

Higher Educational Supplement, 7 October

Winter, E.G. (1981) *World Chess Champions*. London: Pergamon

Wolff, C. (1983) 'The Bach Family'. In S. Sadie, *New Grove Diction-ary of Music and Musicians*. London: Macmillan

Wolman, B.B. (1985) *Handbook of Intelligence: Theories, measure-ments and applications*. Chichester: Wiley

Wortham, H.E. (1927) *Oscar Browning*. London: Constable

Wyndham, J. (1957) *The Midwich Cuckoos*. London: Michael Joseph

Yorkshire and Humberside Council for Sport and Recreation (1980) *The Needs of the Gifted in Sport*. Unpublished

Zajonc, R.B. and Markus, G.B. (1975) 'Birth order and intellectual development.' *Psychological Review*, 82, 74–88

Zigler, E. and Farber, E.A. (1985) 'Commonalities between the intellectual extremes: Giftedness and mental retardation'. In F.D. Horowitz and M. O'Brien, *The Gifted and Talented*. Washington, DC: American Psychological Association

Zuckerman, M. (1987) 'Plus ça change: The High-Tech child in historical perspective'. *Early Childhood Research Quarterly*, 2, 255–64

Index

248   *Index*